W9-BLE-497

WHEN WE WERE
YOUNG IN THE WEST

WHEN WE WERE YOUNG IN THE WEST

True Stories of Childhood

Edited with an Introduction and Conclusion by
RICHARD MELZER, Ph.D

SUNSTONE
PRESS

SANTA FE

© 2003 by Richard Melzer. All rights reserved.

No part of this book may be reproduced in any form or by any electronic or mechanical means including information storage and retrieval systems without permission in writing from the publisher, except by a reviewer who may quote brief passages in a review.

Sunstone books may be purchased for educational, business, or sales promotional use.
For information please write: Special Markets Department, Sunstone Press, P.O. Box 2321, Santa Fe, New Mexico 87504-2321.

Library of Congress Cataloging-in-Publication Data:

When we were young in the West: true stories of childhood in the 19th & 20th centuries/edited with an introduction and conclusion by Richard Melzer.
    p. cm.
    Summary: Presents biographical sketches of New Mexican children from different cultures, races, and classes who represent the strength and diversity of this state's heritage.
    Includes bibliographical references and index.
    ISBN: 0-86534-338-1 (pbk.)
    1. New Mexico—Social life and customs—19th century—Anecdotes. 2. New Mexico—Social life and customs—20th century—Anecdotes. 3. Children—New Mexico—Social life and customs—19th century—Anecdotes. 4. Children—New Mexico—Social life and customs—20th century—Anecdotes. 5. Children—New Mexico—Biography—Anecdotes. 6. New Mexico—Biography—Anecdotes. [1. New Mexico—Biography. 2. New Mexico—Social life and customes.] I. Melzer, Richard

F796.6. W43 2003
978.9'04'083—dc21   2003042572

Published in

SUNSTONE PRESS
Post Office Box 2321
Santa Fe, NM 87504-2321 / USA
(505) 988-4418 / *orders only* (800) 243-5644
FAX (505) 988-1025
www.sunstonepress.com

To Rena,

who personifies all that is
good and beautiful in New Mexico

New Mexico

© 2001, Jill Chapman

CONTENTS

PREFACE

This is a book for and about the children of New Mexico. Although it may well appeal to readers of all ages, it is primarily written for the youth of today who will, hopefully, enjoy reading about their peers of the past and might even gain some insight into what it means to successfully grow to adulthood and become a New Mexican.

When We Were Young In the West is the fruit of more than two decades of pleasurable labor in gathering some of the best oral histories, memoirs, and autobiographies ever written about childhood in New Mexico. There were many sources to choose from—from the best known to the most obscure—but each selection was made to serve a specific purpose in perspective or meaning or just plain human interest and fun. As with every anthology, the most difficult task was not deciding what to include as much as somehow deciding what had to be left behind on the cutting room floor.

Many friends and colleagues have patiently helped in this collecting, sorting, and writing process. As always, none of my historical work would have been possible without the assistance of Kris Warmoth and her tireless, efficient library staff—Kris White and Judy Marquez—at my home institution, the University of New Mexico's Valencia Campus in Tomé. Tomás Jaehn and Arthur L. Olivas of the Fray Angelico Chavez History Library at the Museum of New Mexico, Nancy M. Brown at the Center for Southwest Research at the University of New Mexico, Austin Hoover and Dennis Daily of the Rio Grande Historical Collections at New Mexico State University, José L. Villegas, Sr., of the New Mexico State Record Center and Archives, Joan Trujillo of the Museum of Fine Arts,

Mo Palmer at the Albuquerque Museum, Kathleen L. Gavey of the Menaul Historical Library of the Southwest, and Cameron L. Saffell of the New Mexico Farm and Ranch Heritage Museum in Las Cruces could not have been more helpful and generous with their time. Historians Nelson Van Valen, William Collins, Jenna Newell, and Margaret Espinosa McDonald read all or parts of the manuscript, kindly adding their always astute comments and suggestions. Child development expert Edwina Weathersby contributed remarkable insight as well. Microbiologist Miriam Chavez helped with the discussion of childhood diseases. Diana V. Cole provided valuable technical support.

Finally, my wife, Rena Chavez, contributed the most insightful perspective of all: the view of a proud New Mexican, born and raised happily in the state. It is fitting that this book about New Mexicans is dedicated to Rena, the most important New Mexican in my life.

INTRODUCTION

I f we are all products of our childhood surroundings, then adults who were fortunate enough to grow up in New Mexico are products of an incredible array of physical, social, and cultural influences. Few states in the nation can boast the range of physical characteristics (from river valleys to high mesas and rugged mountains), social classes (from the very rich to the very poor), and varied cultures (from ancient traditional to so-called modern). Not every child in New Mexico was exposed to this entire range of influences, but most experienced or appreciated enough of them to have felt their powerful impact. As a result, most were formed into distinctive, proud individuals called New Mexicans. If New Mexico is a richly woven tapestry of bright and subtle hues, New Mexicans are the human threads that share certain characteristics and hold the colorful, intricate, textured tapestry together for all to admire, enjoy, and, ideally, preserve.

The purpose of *When We Were Young In the West* is two-fold. First, the book offers its readers the sometimes happy, sometimes sad, but always compelling stories of more than three dozen children raised in New Mexico and generally exposed to the state's great diversity. Children from many cultures, many races, many social classes, many communities, many historical periods, and both genders are included. Their true stories are organized in twelve categorical chapters, ranging from childhoods spent in military forts and top secret towns to childhoods spent on valley farms and frontier ranches.

But what were the characteristics that New Mexicans shared in their youth that made them strong and durable enough to help hold the tapestry of their state together as adults? There are at least ten discernible characteristics held in common by most, if not all, the children who describe their earliest memories in this anthology. Identifying these cross-cultural characteristics over several generations is a challenging task, yet strong similarities can be found in the nineteenth and much of the twentieth centuries. Enumerating these themes is the second main purpose of *When We Were Young In the West*, a task best left for our conclusion.

1

TRAIL CHILDHOODS

MARION RUSSELL
ADVENTURE ON THE SANTA FE TRAIL, 1852[1]

Marion Sloan Russell was born on June 26, 1845, in Peoria, Illinois, the youngest of three children in her family. Her father, William Sloan, was killed while serving as an army surgeon in the U.S.-Mexican War, less than two years after Marion's birth. Her mother, Eliza Sloan, remarried, but Eliza's second husband was also killed in military action, in this instance in war against the Indians. Twice widowed (and having lost her first child in infancy), Eliza and her two surviving children, Marion and Will, planned to start a new life in California, where the great gold rush had begun in 1848.[2]

Rather than take the more usual pioneer trails to California, Eliza and her small family traveled down the Santa Fe Trail with Eliza's friend and "ardent admirer," Francis X. Aubry, as the captain of their wagon train. Marion and her mother thus became some of the first females on the male-dominated Santa Fe Trail, following in the footsteps of Mary Donoho and Susan Magoffin on the west-bound route to New Mexico and Dolores Perea and Carmel Benavides on the east-bound journey to Missouri.[3]

When school closed in the spring of 1852, mother decided that [it was time to go to California]. So we left Kansas City and moved to Fort Leavenworth where immigrant trains were wont to assemble in preparation for the trip westward. Fort Leavenworth was a little city of tents. . . . Wagons from the east and west were arriving daily.

Mother's friend and ardent admirer was Francis Xavier Aubry, a famous wagon master.[4] He was a young man somewhere in his late twenties. I remember his young piercing eyes and his boundless energy. . . . Mother had planned that we were to take passage in Captain Aubry's train, for the Indians were bad along the Santa Fe Trail and she had great confidence in him. . . .

[A]t Fort Leavenworth, Will and I had become acquainted with Captain Aubry. He was our very good friend. We took our childish woes to him for solace, visiting him in his great covered wagon. . . .

The dread cholera was raging in Fort Leavenworth the day our white-hooded wagons set sail on the western prairies. Our little city of tents dissolved like snow in a summer sun. Captain Aubry broke camp first; his great wagon swayed out onto the trail. We heard his powerful voice calling orders to follow. Wagon after wagon rolled onward. . . . The timid were always frightened, but most of the people felt safe for the train now numbered more than five hundred wagons. . . .

I remember so clearly the beauty of the earth, and how, as we bore westward, the deer and the antelope bounded away from us. There were miles and miles of buffalo grass, blue lagoons and blood-red sunsets. . . . Our trail often led among herds of buffalo so numerous that at times we were half afraid. . . .

Frightening thunder storms came up suddenly. They would sweep over us, and away they would go as suddenly as they had come. When the sky would darken and the forked lightning sent the thunder rolling, the drivers would wheel the wagons so that the mules' backs were to the storm. The men who had been walking would seek shelter with the women and children inside the wagons. The prairies would darken and then would come a mighty clap of thunder and a sheet of drenching water would fall from the skies upon us. . . .

There was the desert mirage, a will-o'-the-wisp that beckoned and taunted. Sometimes it would look like a party of mounted Indians and the women would cry and begin counting their children. Sometimes it would look like a tall castle set among the trees, or a blue lake with waves lapping white sand. It danced ever before us through the hot hours and only disappeared at sunset.

There were also the rainbows.... The rainbows I love to remember are the ones that spanned the old trail. One evening a great rainbow flashed through the sun-lit rain. It was so big and so lovely! I called out to mother. . . . Turning and facing the red splendor, she cried out in delight. Will . . . said with some eloquence, "There is always a pot of gold at the end of each rainbow."

"Mother, is it really true about the pot of gold?" I asked, awed by Will's knowledge. . . . "They say so, child," was her only answer.

"Why the end of the rainbow is just beyond the little green hill before us. If Will will come with me, we will bring the pot of gold to you." I was delighted.

Mother's eyes came to rest on her small daughter. She smiled as she answered, "The end of the rainbow is always much farther away than it seems, dear. If you climb the green hill the rainbow will still be before you. I think perhaps, that it rests in California. . . . We can only follow the rainbow and hope that it leads to fame and fortune."

For years I thought that the end of the rainbow was in California. . . .

Our wagon was packed with boxes and bales of merchandise for Fort Union. Only the high spring seat was left for mother, Will, and me. Back of the freight and on top of the packed merchandise was our bedding and camp equipment. . . .

Mules draw a wagon a bit more gently than horses, but oxen are best of all. 'Tis true that they walk slowly, but there is a rhythm in their walking that sways the great wagons gently. . . .

Mother usually sat erect on the spring seat, her face rosy in the depth of her bonnet; she burned easily. Frequently she knitted as the wagon bumped along, and often as meal and camp time drew near she sat there and peeled potatoes.

Will usually walked . . . , and as the days passed he. . . . tanned in the prairie sun and there seemed boundless energy in his slender body. It was his chore to build the little cooking fires for mother; but as soon as he was free he would disappear to be with Captain Aubry.

I was seven on this trip in 1852 across the prairies, and I could not keep up with Will [walking] by the wagon. Often, when I got tired of sitting on the hard spring seat by mother, I would crawl back among the blankets where I would play with my doll or fall asleep.

Each noon we would halt for a brief hour's rest. The lunch that we ate was a cold one. The mules fed on the crisp buffalo grass while the drivers rested. After the noon rest, we would go on again until the sun was low in the West. Then the outriders would locate the night resting place and we would stop. . . .

Each night there were two great circles of wagons. . . . Inside the corral were the cooking fires, one for each wagon. After the evening meal we would gather around the little fires. The men would tell stories of the strange new land before us, tales of gold and of Indians. The women would sit with their long skirts drawn up over a sleeping child on their laps. Overhead brooded the night sky, the little camp fires flickered, and behind us loomed the dark hulks of the covered wagons. . . .

Between the two night circles formed by the wagons was a bit of no-man's land which the children used as a playground. The ball games that went on there! The games of leap-frog and dare base. One night I lingered long alone in little no-man's land to gather a species of white poppy that bloomed only at night. To me those prairie poppies were a fascination, blooming only when the evening shadows fell. . . . While most of the drivers slept under the wagons, the women and children slept inside the wagons or in tents. Each night we pitched the tent close to the wagon and it spread its dark wings over the three of us. . . . Our bed on the matted grass was comfortable, but sometimes in the night I would awaken to hear the coyote's eerie cry in the darkness. I would creep close to mother and shiver. . . .

Sometimes far away we heard the war whoop of the Indians. Two men stood on guard each night, rifles in hand. They circled and recircled the big corral never slackening vigilance. Every precaution was taken so that we would not be surprised by the Indians. . . .

Each morning we awoke rested, and the camp was astir at daybreak. Men began rolling out from under the wagons. . . . Soon breakfast fires were burning and the men were catching and harnessing the mules. . . . Children cried at being forced out from under warm covers. I found it hard to button all the buttons that ran up and down the back of my dress. Why couldn't they have been put in front where I could get at them?

Packing was done swiftly and the mules hitched to the wagons. Then the children were counted and loaded. A swift glance about to see that nothing was left behind and we were off for another day on the trail. Drivers were calling, "Get up there! Come along, boys!" Bull whips were cracking and all about the heavy wagons began groaning. . . .

The camp at Fort Mackey lingers as a pleasant memory. Mother had given Will and me a small piece of money that we might spend as we liked at the commissary at Fort Mackey. It was with vision of red and white candy in our minds that we arose early and went to the commissary. It must have been early for I remember it was not quite light when we crept from our tent. The commissary was not open so we decided to go and visit Captain Aubry. He was up and sitting on the tongue of his wagon. . . .

The Captain seemed uneasy about us and said that we must never leave the train alone to go even a little way. . . . There were too many Indians and all seemed sullen, treacherous, and ready to go on the war path. We promised the Captain we would not wander. He went with us to the commissary, added licorice to the red and white candy, and walked with us back to where mother waited breakfast for us. . . .

Soon we were on the Cimarron Cut-off and were building our cooking fires with buffalo chips. My chore was to gather the buffalo chips. I would stand back and kick them, then reach down and gather them carefully, for under them lived big spiders and centipedes. Sometimes scorpions ran from beneath them. I would fill my long full dress skirt with the evening's fuel and take it back to mother.

It was on this trip that I made my first acquaintance with the big hairy spider called a tarantula. . . . Sometimes little jeweled lizards would dart across our path, to stop, panting, in the shade of a scanty bush. Birds with long tails would walk the trail before us; walk upright and faster then our mules could walk. The drivers called them roadrunners.

We left the beautiful grassland behind us and struck in a southwesterly direction for the Arkansas River. There was less and less forage for our mules and horses. We found rattlesnakes and a variety of cactus that resembled trees. . . .

Captain Aubry told us how the muddy water in the buffalo wallows had often saved human lives. "One dying of thirst," he said, "does not stop for gnats or impurities." Once we traveled two whole days without water and, thirsty child that I was, I felt sorrier for the straining mules than for myself. . . . Mother, Will, and I had to wash our face and hands in the same basin of water. Will washed last, for mother said he was dirtier.

After we had traveled for what seemed like an eternity across the hot, dry land, we awoke one morning to find the air filled with a cool, misty rain. Although the cool, drizzling rain fell all day long, it was a happy band that followed the Cimarron Cut-off. . . .

That evening when Captain Aubry came to sit at our fireside, he told us we were now in New Mexico Territory. "This is the land," said Captain Aubry,. . . . "that has brought healing to the hearts of many. Many an invalid I have had in my caravans, but before they reached Santa Fe they were eating buffalo meat raw and sleeping soundly under their blankets. There is something in the air of New Mexico that makes the blood red, the heart to beat high and the eyes to look upward. Folks don't come here to die—they come to live and they get what they came for."

At Fort Union our great cavalcade rested. . . .

After a time when the mules were rested, we struck the westward trail again. . . . How our hearts waited for a sight of the Santa Fe of our dreams. We thought it would be a city, and waited breathlessly for the first sight of towers and tall turrets. We were in Santa Fe before we knew it. We crossed a water ditch where half-naked children stood unashamed and unfrozen to watch us. Then we passed through a great wooden gateway that arched high above us. We moved along narrow alley-like streets past iron-barred windows. We were among a scattering of low, square-cornered adobe houses. We saw a church with two cupolas. Mexicans, Indians, and half-breeds shouldered by us. We saw strings of red peppers drying, and brown babies asleep by old adobe walls.

Our caravan wriggled through donkeys, goats, and Mexican chickens. . . . Dogs barked at us. Big-eyed children stared at us. Black-shawled women smiled shyly at us. . . .

As darkness deepened, Santa Fe threw off her lassitude. Lights glowed in saloons and pool-halls and in the Fonda, a great mud-walled inn. . . . From a dance hall came the tinkle of guitar and mandolin, a *baile* was forming. . . . We slept in the wagon, or tried to, but the noise and confusion kept us awake. . . .

We were in Santa Fe [at last].

Marion Sloan's 1852 journey down the Santa Fe Trail was not her last. After several other trips on the trail, she met twenty-five-year-old Lieutenant Richard D. Russell at Fort Union, New Mexico, in 1864. Deeply in love, they were married six months later at Fort Union's small military chapel. Their marriage was a happy one until tragedy struck twice, first when their first born child died in infancy and in 1888 when Richard was killed in a shoot-out over the old Maxwell land grant. Marion never remarried. Although advanced in age, she dictated her now-famous memoirs to her daughter-in-law. She died in a car accident not far from the old Santa Fe Trail at the age of ninety-one.

Will Sloan grew up to serve in the Union Army during the Civil War and as a Protestant missionary until his retirement in 1911. He died in 1917.

Eliza Sloan lived much of the rest of her life in California, her original destination on the Santa Fe Trail.

The gallant Francis X. Aubry set the record for the fastest trip over the Santa Fe Trail: 850 miles in five days, sixteen hours. But, as with so many of the men in Marion's life, he died a violent death when he was killed by Colonel Richard H. Weighman during an argument in Santa Fe in 1854. He was only twenty-nine years old.

JOSÉ LIBRADO GURULÉ
WORKING ON THE SANTA TRAIL [1]

José Librado Gurulé was eighty-eight years old when Mrs. Lou Sage Batchen interviewed him in his native village of Las Placitas in 1940. José was the direct descendent of one of the first families to settle Las Placitas when the village was founded on a Spanish land grant in the mid-eighteenth century. By 1867, José's family, like most in his area, was poverty-stricken and in debt to the fabulously rich José Leander Perea of Bernalillo. To help pay off their debts to Perea, many villagers worked on the patrón's *trading caravans destined for Missouri on the Santa Fe Trail. José was one of hundreds of Hispanic males who labored on the trail, but his boyhood story of adventure—and misadventure—is the only one that survives to this day.[2]*

It was in February 1867 that José Gurulé, then a lad of sixteen, went adventuring to Los Estados [The States], which was the common name for Kansas City.

Esquipulo Romero, El Capitán of the José Leander Perea freighting outfit, came to Las Placitas to look over Perea's men for the purpose of selecting the most able-bodied to make the annual trek over the Santa Fe Trail to Kansas City with the many thousands of pounds of wool, and then to bring back the golden returns to Perea and Nesario Gonzales, who combined their freighting but under the direction of Perea's men. These two men were among the wealthy of New Mexico in their day. Perea was not only wealthy but powerful and an outstanding politician of Bernalillo County. At that time most of the men in Las Placitas were

Perea's men and at his command, and all because the Perea ledger showed nearly all of them to be in his debt.

Esquipulo could tell at a glance a trail-worthy man, a man who could keep going. Youth offered possibilities for those endurance trips. . . . Juan Baptiste had proven his mettle on a previous trip as had Nicolás Gurulé, so both were chosen. José Gurulé, son of Nicolás, had grit and wit and was tough as a pine knot. He wanted to go and was taken. . . .

For the journey the men needed clothing which would stay on their backs for at least three months, and shoes and *tewas* [leather Indian moccasins], whichever they could afford. Each man must take his own bedroll. These were usually made up of *serapes* [men's shawls] woven on the village looms, or home-woven Mexican blankets. The men's suits were *mantas* (drawers and shirt of coarse white cotton cloth) and underwear made of goat hair woven into cloth on the household looms. . . .

But the greatest preparations for the trip went on in the cook-house of the José Leander Perea place in Bernalillo. There *tortillas* were made by the hundreds and packed away. Bushels of dried peas were finely ground between stones to make "coffee." Huge quantities of mutton and goat meat, onions, *frijoles*, black eyed peas, . . . and *chile* were amassed. All meat was dried. These supplies were put away in the rolling commissary from which Esquipulo dispensed meals daily. Besides each man was allotted a limited quantity of cube sugar and some tobacco, which he carried with him. . . .

At the appointed time some ten wagons which would form a part of the Perea-Gonzales train rumbled through Placitas. Heavy wagons loaded with wool, each of them drawn by five spans of oxen; for the roads were heavy with mud, especially on the *plana* (level ground). In February or early spring, when the wagons left for Los Estados, the road through the village and on toward Tejón was a popular route. The men at Las Placitas joined the procession as it passed through. . . .

When the wagons rattled through the gate of the town of Tejón the villagers swarmed about them, saying farewells and wishing their friends a safe journey. Some accompanied the expedition as far as Golden, the next village. . . .

Las Vegas was the starting point of the big adventure as well as the meeting place for those who wished to add their wagons and *carretas* to the train. . . . There were about four hundred carriers in all besides the herds of mules and oxen being driven along to take the place of the animals that happened to fall by the way.

In organizing for the trip each outfit held its own place in the caravan. The Perea-Gonzales layout was well in the lead with its fifty wagons or more of various sizes. Wagons piled high with wool, feed for the mules and oxen, the commissary, wagons loaded with firewood and small barrels filled with water to be used where such necessities were not to be found. The barrels were refilled wherever water was found. No man in the outfit was without his *guaje* (long-neck gourd) which he carried with him as he went along and drank sparingly from it frequently or moistened his lips. These were refilled from every watering place they came upon. In taking wood and water with them much time was saved. On these trips to the wool market time was important.

About the middle of February the caravan started. . . . [I]n every home from which these men had come to venture upon the long and dangerous voyage, simple but impressive ceremonies were held. In every home candles were lit before favorite saints and prayers were offered. Then the wives or mothers to the departed men wrapped a cloth about the saints supplicated and put them in captivity to hold them there as hostages for the safe return of their men. . . .

Lemita was the last settlement in New Mexico they passed before going into Kansas, José said. They went along the Cimarron Route to the Arkansas River. . . . From the beginning of the march both men and animals were pushed to the limit. A schedule was set and every effort made to maintain it. The drive was kept as near a continuous eighteen hours as was possible. The halt came at ten in the morning or as near that time as could be managed. There was a rush and bustle to get the animals unhooked from the wagons, to feed the men and the beasts and get in some sleep in the allotted time. Before the last lap of the Cimarron Trail was reached the animals were so exhausted that they almost dropped when released from the wagons.

Within six hours of the halting moment the train was again in motion. This order was not relaxed until after the Cimarron was crossed. Then there was much less danger of attacks by the Indians. In traveling all night they could not break camp in the mornings and find themselves surrounded by the enemy. Maintaining the eighteen hour travel schedule and not the driving through the nights was to blame for weakened condition of both men and beasts. That was an unjustifiable hardship.

In making the one stop in the twenty-four hours the scouts looked for camping grounds where there were no signs of prairie dogs. That meant that the area would be absolutely barren of vegetation and no fires could menace them; which was another safeguard against the raiding Indians. Often the whole caravan was raced in order to reach such a place. The men who guided the oxen with their long goads must run to keep the pace.

There was but one full meal during each twenty-four hours. It was supplemented by two light snacks; the first consisting of a *tortilla* and an onion in the hand to be eaten on the run; the second, an onion and a *tortilla* eaten likewise. The men were drawing heavily upon previously stored up energy. The army of hirelings was traveling on its feet with very little assistance from its stomach. . . .

And as for rest or recreation, there was none. The stops made on the entire trip were too short to permit such indulgences. The stops made on the entire trip where too short to permit such indulgences. The halts were purely business matters made for the purpose of feeding and getting snatches of sleep. José said when they slept at mid-day their sleep was broken each day at 12:00 by the braying of the mules in the train. The men referred to them as clocks.

One afternoon a near panic was created in the Perea-Gonzales section of the caravan. Frightened oxen brought a heavily loaded wagon to a tipsy angle. The wagons and animals following were brought to an abrupt stop. An exhausted man who had stretched himself upon the tongue of the wagon preceding the one tip-tilted by the frightened ox, had fallen into a deep sleep and rolled off to the ground. He was trampled to death before he could be rescued. A solemn pause was made while the victim was buried. This tragedy happened in other outfits on that journey. Under the strain of eighteen hour marches the men were giving way. "Too much awake. Too little water to drink, too little *frijoles*; men go to sleep anywhere," was the comment of the narrator.

One morning when they halted to make ready to cross El Arroyo Grande (the Big Arroyo) and which they later learned was the Arkansas River, they sighted on the plains coming toward them a band of Indians. . . . There was a hasty conference among the captains of the caravan.

There was excited talk and anxiety among all the others in the train. On came the Indian band, looming large and ominous in the distance. Nearer they came. The order went out from the captains not to fire or make a move until word came from the proper authority.

But as the band bore down upon them the ordeal of waiting proved too much for a few near the point of approach. They fired. At once the fire was returned and one man near the Perea-Gonzales outfit went down. For a moment it looked as if the situation was out of hand. But Esquipulo and a few other courageous ones stepped forward and made signs of friendship to the Indians. At that all appearances of hostility vanished and the band advanced.

Some were on foot, a few rode mules, some drove mules hitched to queer looking conveyances built exactly like ladders; two stout poles with strong cross pieces. One end of the ladder was harnessed to the mule, the other dragged the ground. Bundles, pots, small articles of wearing apparel, and a lot of little things (José said he never saw anything like them before and what he dubbed *junco* [junk]) were tied to the poles and dangled down. Women and children sat on the cross pieces of the ladders as if on seats in a wagon. Many of the Indians rode horses, the prizes for which they would murder or plunder. Luckily, the caravan boasted no horses, and there was a reason. It made trips less hazardous in cases like the one they were experiencing. The train contained little to tempt the Indians on the east bound trip.

One old woman drove her mule and ladder close to the spot where José Gurulé was standing. She dismounted and approached him, her eyes upon the cube of sugar he held untasted in his hand. He sensed her desire and at once took another cube from the scanty hoard in his pocket and gave the two to her. She thanked him, or he supposed that was what she said, for he had no understanding of her language. Then she went to the ladder and untied a bundle. From it she took a pat of ground meat and came back and gave it to him. He thanked her in his own language. She smiled, returned to her seat on the top cross piece of the ladder, and took up her lines.

In time the band passed peacefully on its way. . . .

At last the caravan rolled into the appointed grounds in Kansas City and on time, that is, they made it in three months. Then more work for the men; unloading and carting wool to storage and conditioning the mules, oxen, and wagons for the homeward trip.

On the first day of their arrival some of the men[, including José,] wandered idly from the camping grounds. They walked along hoping to see wonderful sights. The very first thing which met their eyes was a huge, bright-colored picture of an Indian on the front of a wooden building. He was wearing a war bonnet. The words under the Indian read, TOMASITO THE FAMOUS WARRIOR OF THE FAMED VILLAGE OF TAOS. "We all laughed," José said, "to find Tomasito [a leader of the Revolt of 1847 against New Mexico governor Charles Bent and other Americans] in Los Estados."

After enjoying the colorful likeness of the Taos warrior, they wandered on. They heard a welcome sound. It was music, and they hurried on to find it. It was the first sound of music they had heard since they left Las Placitas. They almost danced along, José said. . . . But never had they heard such music as this. It was a Negro band and they were all dressed up in white coat and pants and tall black hats. They played outside a place where there was a minstrel show. The men had no money with which to buy tickets to go in, so they just stood around and listened. José carried money enough to pay for a worsted suit out of a store and nothing could tempt him to part with one penny of it. He had boasted around Las Placitas that he would bring back a suit of clothes from Kansas City and he had sold some of his goats to get the money.

The stay in Kansas City was short. . . . Once again the train was on the march, but westward now. Wagons were loaded with merchandise of every description. There were copper kettles and there were pans and pots and dishes of china and plated and steel wear for table use and many bolts and bundles of cloth and there were hats for women and men and shoes; all these to be put into the Perea store in Bernalillo. . . .

It was on the return trip that they sighted scarcely any buffalo. A scattered few and only one was within rifle range. Someone who owned a gun fired at the lone animal and he fell. [The shooter] was José Montaño. The animal no sooner dropped than José was on top of him. To the surprise of José and all those who saw it, the buffalo leaped up and bolted forward. The man on his back could do nothing but grab the animal's long hair and cling to his back for dear life. It was nearly twenty minutes before some sign of weakness was seen in the buffalo. He was staggering;

the lead José Montaño had sent into his body bringing him down. José was saved. The buffalo had galloped about a thousand yards. He was butchered and taken along as the caravan marched on.

That was the only excitement on the return trip. The remainder of the trip was a nightmare. The men became weak and ill, the animals dropped. But when they fell by the way there were mules and oxen enough in the herd to replace them.

And then what José Gurulé called a "plague" broke out among them. It was called cholera. At first those who went down with it were laid in the wagons, [and] those who stayed on foot kept the caravan moving. They just crept along. Then so many of them were down that the train was halted at a cold spring, José Gurulé said. There they were doctored. The men were given water with plenty of whiskey and *chile* in it. The whiskey came from the stock being brought from Kansas City to Perea. It was Penguin. (Good corn whiskey, José said.) But somehow it did not cure the cholera, and the New Mexico *chile* failed them.

After a halt of twelve days they moved on with hardly men enough on foot to keep the caravan moving. they made frequent short stops just to rest. There were other stops made, and always after those they left one of their number behind under a mound of earth. Many died of the plague, José said.

It was December before what was left of the Perea-Gonzales outfit dragged into Las Vegas. "A dejected looking outfit," said the story teller, "with maybe a third of it left somewhere on the way." In another week they were back in Bernalillo.

The entire trip had consumed almost eleven months. Each man who survived it was paid eight dollars in cash. . . . It was not known whether the families of the men who died on the way received any part of the eight dollars. None of the Las Placitas men was stricken by the plague it seemed, and each one of them received the eight dollars. . . . But the rejoicing at home, the resurrection of the saints from the bottoms of chests, the feasts and the *bailes* (dances)—not to mention the wine made in their absence and saved for the occasion—was a rich compensation in itself for the hardships that were now in the dead past.

José Gurulé was a man of seventeen when he reached home. And he made good his boast. He brought home a suit of worsted from Los

Estados and donned it for the admiration of the whole village. It was the first suit of clothes ever worn in Las Placitas.

We know little about José Librado Gurulé's life after his eleven-month journey up the Santa Fe Trail and back home. We are simply fortunate that, thanks to the New Mexico Federal Writers Project, he was able to share his still-vivid memories of life on the trail as an impressionable, hard-working young man.

2

MILITARY CHILDHOODS

DOUGLAS MACARTHUR
THE FUTURE GENERAL'S YOUTH AT FORT SELDEN, 1884-86[1]

Douglas MacArthur was one of our nation's most famous and successful army generals. As supreme commander of Allied forces in the Southwest Pacific during World War II, he was given much of the credit for the United States' ultimate victory over Japan in 1945. But few New Mexicans realize that MacArthur spent most of the first six years of his life (1880-86) in New Mexico while his father served as a company commander at both Fort Wingate and Fort Selden. In fact, as Douglas reveals in the following excerpt from his autobiography, his first memories of life were of his family's trip accompanying "K" Company from Fort Wingate in western New Mexico to Fort Selden far to the south.

Officers Quarters, Fort Seldon, New Mexico, ca. 1870s. Henry Berroteran Collection, Neg. No. A74-12/14. Courtesy of the Rio Grande Historical Collections, New Mexico State University Library, New Mexico State University, Las Cruces, New Mexico.

[Captain Arthur MacArthur married Mary Pinkney "Pinky" Hardy] at [the Hardy family's Norfolk, Virginia, mansion called] "Riveredge" on May 19, 1875. Their first child, Arthur, was born on August 1, 1876, and then Malcolm in October of 1878. Each time "Pinky" came home to Norfolk for the big event, Captain MacArthur's [Army] station was changed, first to Baton Rouge, Louisiana, then to Little Rock, Arkansas. A third child was on the way and, as usual, arrangements were made to bring him into the world at "Riveredge," but something went awry and the birth took place in 1880 at the Arsenal Barracks of Little Rock. But Virginians are nothing if not loyal, and the Norfolk papers covered me beautifully with headlines reading, "Douglas MacArthur was born on January 26, while his parents were away."

Five months later, Captain MacArthur, in command of "K" Company of the 13th Infantry, was on the way to distant Fort Wingate in New Mexico. In 1883 tragedy struck and Malcolm died. They brought him back to Virginia soil and buried him in the old Hardy plot in Norfolk. His loss was a terrible blow to my mother, but it seemed only to increase her devotion to Arthur and myself. This tie was to become one of the dominant factors of my life.

We numbered but four in our little family when orders came in 1884 for "K" Company to march overland three hundred miles from Fort Wingate to tiny Fort Selden, some sixty miles from El Paso, to guard the forts of the Rio Grande from the ever-present danger of Geronimo's marauding Indians. My first memories are of that march.

How well I recall veteran First Sergeant Peter Ripley as I trudged with him at the head of the column. At each halt a big Irish recruit named Moriarity would come complaining of sore feet and ask to ride in the ambulance. Each time the sergeant would refuse. At last the Irishman insisted on speaking to the captain, and Ripley brought him to my father. The recruit was a glib talker with his Irish wit and blarney, and seemed to me to have a good case until my father closed the matter decisively. "Moriarity," he said, "growl you may, but march you must."

And there was the native rancher of whom we asked, "How far to the next water hole?" "About ten miles," he replied. On we labored for nearly three long, hot, dusty hours when we met another homesteader. "How far," asked Ripley again, "to the next water hole?" And again the reply, "About ten miles." And Ripley, turning to the sweating men listening anxiously on the rough trail, said, "It's all right, boys. Thank God, we're holding our own."

The little outpost of Fort Selden became our home for the next three years. Company "K," with its two officers, its assistant surgeon, and forty-six enlisted men comprised the lonely garrison, sheltered in single-story, flat-roofed adobe buildings. It was here I learned to ride and shoot even before I could read or write—indeed, almost before I could walk and talk. My mother, with some help from my father, began the education of her two boys. Our teaching included not only the simple rudiments, but above all else, a sense of obligation. We were to do what was right no matter what the personal sacrifice might be. Our country was always to come first. Two things we must never do: never lie, never tattle.

Life was vivid and exciting for me. In addition to my brother, there was William Hughes, the son of the first lieutenant of the company. We were inseparable comrades then, but little did we dream that years later we would be comrades-in-arms on the far fields of France. He was my operations officer . . . and later my chief of staff . . . during the First World War.

We found much to divert us. There were the visiting officers and mounted details from the cavalry post at Fort Stanton to the east guarding the nearby Mescalero Reservation. There were the bumpy rides on the mule-drawn water wagons that would make the daily trip to the Rio Grande several miles west of the post. And toward twilight each evening, the stirring ceremony of retreat, when we would stand at attention as the bugle sounded the lowering of the flag.

One day, while on herd the horses and mules panicked at the sight and smell of a strange new animal moving along the sandy wastes like some shaggy ghost out of the pages of wonderland. It was a camel, lonesome survivor of a herd that in 1855 Jefferson Davis, then Secretary of War, had brought from Egypt to serve as pack animals to supply the chain of isolated forts in this vast desert country.

An educational system for officers was being introduced into the Army, and the Cavalry and Infantry School had been established at Fort Leavenworth, Kansas. Selected companies from the various regiments were concentrated there for the purpose of training the officers. "K" Company was one of that chosen group, and late in 1886 we moved eastward.

For the first time, I attended a regular school and was exposed to the regimen of studies, to the competition between classmates. It opened new vistas for me.

It was a never-ending thrill for me to watch the mounted troops drill and the artillery fire on the practice range. . . . There was extra excitement when my father commanded the afternoon parade, with the cavalry on their splendid mounts, the artillery with their long-barreled guns and caissons, and the infantry with its blaze of glittering bayonets.

The "blaze of glittering bayonets" and other aspects of military life appealed to Douglas so much that he followed in his father's footsteps and trained for a military career. He graduated from the U.S. Military Academy at West Point in 1903 and, in the course of a long, illustrious— and sometimes controversial—career, rose to the rank of five-star general of the army.

AUBREY LIPPINCOTT
THE POST SURGEON'S SON AT FORT UNION, 1887-1891[1]

The Indian wars ended in New Mexico with Geronimo's surren-
der in 1886. By the end of the nineteenth century, each of the remaining
forts in the New Mexico Territory was closed, military anachronisms that
had served their deadly purpose on the closing frontier. Fort Union, along
the old Santa Fe Trail, was one of the last to close, abandoned in May
1891. Dr. Henry Lippincott was the last army surgeon to serve at Fort
Union, living there in officers quarters with his wife and two sons from
1887 to 1891. Aubrey, the doctor's youngest son, shared his distinct child-
hood memories of life in the fort's declining years in a 1968 interview with
military historian Dale Giese.

I was born at West Point, New York. My father[, Dr. Henry Lippincott,]
was an Army Surgeon. We went to Fort Union [, New Mexico, when
I was a boy, ten years of age. Some of my] boyhood recollections . . .
are rather keen. The post I remember very distinctly: the layout, buildings, ceremonies. I remember all of that, and I remember certain incidents that are not [always] historic, but are funny.

Here's one of them. There was one other Army boy on the Officers'
Line besides myself, about my own age, and we played together. [He was
George Douglass, the son of the fort's commanding officer, Colonel Henry
Douglass.] There was a custom that [several times a week] there'd be a
military band concert. [The fort's band] would play from the bandstand
in the center of the parade ground and the officers and ladies on the
Officers' Line would sit on their front porches [facing the parade ground]
and listen to the music.

As I say, this one boy of my own age was the only playmate I had, and we got into all kinds of deviltry. Among other things, we rounded up a bunch of burros that were unbranded and . . . we'd go out and ride and try to race them. You couldn't make a burro go beyond a walk much, you know. But we discovered that if we tied a tin can on a rope and hauled the can in towards us, that would speed him up.

So one dark night the band was playing and George and I thought we'd have a [burro] race on the parade ground during the concert. At each end of the parade ground was a chain draped on posts, [an] ornamental sort of thing, two or three feet high. So we started that night on our race. Each of us had a five-gallon empty tin can on a long rope and we began to haul in on the rope, and the more we'd haul, the faster these burros would go until . . . we made a hell of a noise going down the parade ground. [In the dark the] burros didn't see the chain at the end of the [field] and we both hit it and there was a mix-up of two kids, two burros, and two tin cans. . . .

My father always had a pony for me to ride, [but when I was young] he never allowed me to have a saddle, afraid I'd be hung up on the stirrups. So I rode with a blanket and a surcingle [or strap to hold a blanket or saddle]. But I couldn't get on the pony because I was too small. [To solve this problem] I used to carry gingersnaps or some sugar in my pockets. . . . The pony was a gentle little soul, and I'd put a gingersnap or the sugar on the ground and he'd reach down to get it and I'd put my leg over his head and he'd lift his head and I'd go back and turn around. And that's how I'd mount the horse. It got to be such a joke around the fort that if I rode by the store the people would always get me to ride into the [post trader's] store to pull this stunt. Somebody'd put the sugar on the floor, [the little horse] would reach for it, I'd get on his neck, slide back, turn around, and ride out. . . .

One night [in December 1889 the post trader's] store run by a man named [Edward P.] Woodbury caught fire and burned and most every man in the command with their fire axes and fire buckets . . . had to pass right by our house running to the fire. That was the fire equipment we had—axes and buckets, that's all. And [the fort's trumpeter, an Englishman named] Cary, came running down the street, . . . running and blowing fire call. And it was the most vivid thing I have ever heard because of the exquisite tone this man got out of [his horn]. And he could blow it on the run. The building was totally destroyed, of course. . . .

We had no games, just riding ponies most of the time. My recollection is living on a pony.

[George and I rode to the fort's arsenal] all the time. They had some [Apache] Indians sent there for safe-keeping. They used to tent there, and we could hear [the music of] their dances from the post—it would carry that far in the clear air. [We'd] walk over there and watch their dances at night.

[I admired my father greatly.] His magnificent character really showed during a diphtheria epidemic at the fort [in 1889]. After treating so many people with the disease] he wouldn't come into our house and bring it to me. I was a little boy and my brother was away at school. [So my father] had a tent pitched in our backyard and there he slept in that tent in the wintertime for I guess two months and the meals would be taken out to him and he'd eat them cold out in that tent. Incredible. . . .

When you think of those long rides he'd make in his buckboard to treat an Indian or . . . anybody else and he didn't get a nickel for it. He was the only medical man to save them. Never got a nickel for it. When I think of the nobility of this father of mine. I can remember his driving to the Rosebud Agency, sixty or so miles [away], and he had to wear a mask to keep his face from freezing. . . .

[The fort had quite a good] baseball team. I remember there was a [particularly good] young lieutenant named [Robert C.] Van Vliet who was the catcher [and the fort's adjutant]. Officers played with enlisted men. . . . They'd put four sacks [filled with sawdust or something] out there [on the parade ground] and play ball. . . . [It wasn't a] well laid-out thing—just improvised. Put home plate here, pace off for first base and pace around. That was the extent of the surveying they did. . . .

School consisted of one room in one vacant set of quarters. One front room. There were no married enlisted men so it became a school for the officers' children. They [included ten to fifteen kids of] all ages, all taking the same course. They had a regular bugle call for school. . . . [The schoolmaster] was a private, an old-timer getting ready for retirement . . . . His name was [Alonzo] Plumb. Smoked a big pipe all the time. What we learned there, I don't know. Probably nothing. . . .[2]

They had a telegraph station [at Fort Union whose telegraph line connected to a little railroad town called Watrous, nine miles away.] As the troops were withdrawn [from Fort Union when the fort began to close] one of the first things they pulled out was the telegraph station. [Actually,] they left the station there, but sent the telegraph operator away. They knew that as a little boy I'd tinkered [with Morse code] and could send and receive [telegraph messages] a little bit. . . . [O]n one occasion they had an urgent message and there was no telegraph operator. . . . [T]hey sent for me and I told them I could send it all right, but wasn't sure I could receive it, they were so fast. . . . [W]e went over there and I knew the letter call. So I called and called and called. Well, the line was disconnected in Watrous so the message never did get through. . . .

[At other times I could be more useful, as when some soldiers put on a play and] required a little kid in the play and I was it. I was a distinguished actor in [at least that show]. Just the [residents of the] post came to see [such plays]. The surrounding country was pretty void [of people who otherwise might have attended].

I can remember the day my mother's piano came. Mother was quite a musician and played very well. It was shipped overland from the railroad in Watrous. I can remember the room it was [put] in and the couch in the room. I'd lie on this couch as long as they'd let me while she was playing, and I'd go to sleep there. There was only one other piano at the post. [People came in and sang; my] father was a very hospitable person. . . .

One night [George and I] knew our mothers and fathers had gone out to dinner. So I went to George's house. There was a big fire in the fireplace and there was a box of good cigars. Now we were pretty small. We sat down and we each lit one of those cigars and the first puff or two was rather nice, even to a child. But the third puff didn't taste so good so we threw [them] in the fireplace and took another one out and lit that up. After having done that two or three times, we were both so sick we couldn't stand up. I finally went home. And it was the only time in my life my father whipped me.

We had a Chinese cook from Omaha. [She was the] only Chinese cook I remember. They were good cooks and boss of their domain. I've had our cook run me out of the kitchen—scared me to death. If I was ill, I'd rather have a Mexican woman take care of me than any other. They're motherly, gentle, patient, everything a boy would need [for a speedy recovery]. . . .

[Life at western forts could be monotonous.] But you become accustomed to anything. If you have to do it, you do it. Finally, it becomes second nature. Like I said, it was rough, but rough was the normal thing. [We] didn't know anything else.[3]

On leaving Fort Union and New Mexico, the Lippincott family traveled far to the east for Dr. Lippincott's next assignment at Fort Adams, Rhode Island. Like Douglas MacArthur, Aubrey followed his father by joining the army and leading a long and productive military career. Rising to the rank of colonel, he retired and lived into his nineties. He was clearly articulate, and still a bit mischievous, when he granted this valuable interview at the age of ninety-one.

3

VILLAGE CHILDHOODS

ABE PEÑA
CÍBOLA MEMORIES FILLED WITH TRADITION[1]

Abelicio (Abe) M. Peña was the second of seven children born to Pabloand Pablita Peña of San Mateo, New Mexico. Abe grew up in a very traditional, religious Hispanic home while working on his family's sheep ranch from an early age. Proud of his culture and with an excellent memory for details, he was asked to write a series of articles about his boyhood for his local newspaper, the Grants Daily Beacon. *That was in 1987. His book,* Memories of Cíbola, *is largely a compilation of Abe's wonderful articles, parts of which are included here.*

Village Home

[Our] village was built at the mouth of San Mateo Canyon . . . in the shadow of Mount Taylor. . . . An abundant spring provided water to the settlers for home use, livestock, and irrigation.

The settlers chose the name San Mateo for the church, after St. Matthew. . . . In the Hispanic period, villages generally adopted the name given the church. . . . I was born and raised in San Mateo, and the village still draws me, as it does the others who grew up there. Our roots go deep. . . .

Parents

[My mother] Pablita was very religious and followed the tenets and commandments of the Catholic Church with fervent determination. We all bathed religiously on Saturdays, in *cajetes en la casa vieja* [tubs] and never missed Mass on Sundays. Our Franciscan priest came from Grants, and all my brothers and I served as altar boys at one time or another, as did the other boys in the village. We all got a chance to pull the rope and ring the bell and recite the responses in Latin. . . .

[And my mother always prayed.] "Prayer," she used to say, "is very important in our lives." She frequently reminded us, *"Resen, hijitos. Dios nos ama mucho."* ("Pray, my children. God loves us very much.") Our whole village was generally oriented toward prayer. . . .

[My mother's relatives] and neighbors, especially Tía Sostena Trujillo and Tía Sostia Baca, helped Pablita raise her seven children. I recall Tía Sostena telling us stories of *brujas* [witches]. . . . She told us the story of the "mad dog" that came barking to the door of a house in San Mateo one night. The man of the house, after repeated attempts to chase the "mad dog" away, finally took his gun and shot the menacing creature. The next day came news from San Fidel, twenty-five miles across the mountain, that a certain lady reputed to be a *bruja*, had died during the night of gunshot wounds!

Mother instructed us not to fight. . . . I recall being in a fistfight only once. I was being beaten up on the way back from school and I fought back. Policarpio Montaño was the constable, and he locked the three of us in a chicken coop! When word got to mother that I was in Flavio Montaño's coop for fighting, she told the messenger, "Just leave him there. It will teach him a good lesson!" It was one of the most important lessons I learned in my youth. . . .

Los Comanches

As a youngster in the village of San Mateo, I recall excitedly painting my face red with *almagre*, putting on a feathered headdress, and dancing Los Comanches for Christmas. According to this custom, the image of the Christ Child would be kidnapped at a *velorio* [evening party] from his crib and taken by Comanche Indians to their distant lands. Preparations and rehearsals started about the second week in December. The producers were older and generally very talented singers and composers. . . . About fifteen Comanches, both boys and girls and some older villagers, learned the steps, verses, and chants. . . .

On Christmas Eve there was a *velorio* at someone's home. The living room was arranged with an altar, generally a small table covered with a finely embroidered white linen cloth, with the image of the Christ Child in a crib resting in the center and a candle on each side. The *padrinos* [guardians] were generally a married couple and sat at each end of the altar, representing Mary and Joseph keeping watch over the Child. People sat in chairs around the room and prayers were constantly recited as they kept their vigil over Christ the King.

Around 8:00 p.m. a band of Comanches arrived silently at the door. After some clearing of throats, our chief gave a sign and lead us a cappella into the first song:

En el marco de esta puerta,	At the threshold of this door,
El pie derecho pondré,	My right foot I'll place,
A los dueños del velorio,	Of the sponsors of this vigil,
La venia les pediré.	Permission to enter I will ask.

After about a dozen or more verses telling about the long and arduous journey from the plains, the door opened and we'd glide into the room, singing at the top of our lungs. At this point the *padrinos* would double their hold on the crib, as the spirited Comanches danced past the altar singing and chanting with their eyes glued on the Child. . . .

We sang to [the Child's] beauty, we sang to his sanctity. We told him we would take care of him if he came with us across the miles to our faraway lands. After lulling the *padrinos* to relax their hold on the crib, a darting Comanche grabbed the Child in a flash and held him up in the air as we withdrew in triumph, singing

Se retiran los Comanches,	The Comanches are withdrawing,
Ya cumplen su devoción,	With satisfied devotion,
Con tu mano poderosa,	With your all-powerful hand,
Échanos tu bendición.	Give us your benediction.

In those days I never thought to ask how and where this custom originated, but in recent years I've started asking. . . . The Comanche Indians, coming out of the Great Plains . . . , raided the Hispanic villages, kidnapping our children, both boys and girls, and taking them to serve as warriors or as servants to augment their declining tribal numbers. . . . Hispanic villages began the custom of Los Comanches to keep alive the memory of their captured Christ-like children, kidnapped by Comanches in war paint and feathers and taken to the distant plains.

La Matanza

Mantanza. Photograph by Russell Lee. LC-USF 33, Neg. No. 1284-M5. Courtesy of the Library of Congress, Washington, D.C.

"Go invite Don Desiderio to *la matanza*," said my mother. Pig killing was not only an important source of villagers' food supply, it was much more—a social event, a working feast, and a ritual in San Mateo and other villages. . . . Don Desiderio García, an old widower, was considered an expert in bleeding the swine to produce tender and flavorful pork and properly rendered lard.

Almost all the villagers had pigs, fed the leftovers from our tables, but most importantly, corn. . . . Pigs were butchered at various times during the year for meat, but *la matanza*, for lard, was the big one in the late fall or early winter, in preparation for Christmas. It yielded as much as 150 pounds of lard, enough to serve the cooking needs of a family for several months.

Pigs selected to be fattened were generally two years old or older. The heavy corn feeding started with the corn harvest in September. A couple of pounds in the morning and a couple in the evening was increased gradually to as much as the animal could eat. By November or December, they were sometimes so heavy they couldn't rear up on their hind legs. It was time for *la matanza*.

The day before we would hand carry water in two-gallon buckets from *la acequia* and fill two fifty-gallon drums, which rested either on a stand or on large rocks. Then we would arrange firewood under the barrels. Even before daybreak the firewood would be lit and the water heated to a boil, before Don Desiderio and the other invitees arrived. At sunrise the pig would be walked or hauled in a wheelbarrow to the butchering platform constructed nearby of planking elevated about a foot off the ground.

With the blunt heel of an ax, the pig would be struck hard between the eyes and knocked out. Then Don Desiderio would take his special sharp, long-bladed kitchen knife, saying, "Jesus y Cruz," and pierce through the breast to the heart. A bucket or large pan would be held to catch the gushing blood, which would be made into *morcilla*, a fine food rich in proteins and minerals. The pig would then be rolled onto the platform and after boiling water was poured over the animal, it would be covered with gunny sacks. In a few minutes the hair would loosen and could be pulled off easily with razor-sharp knives. The naked pig shone like a freshly shaved face.

The animal would then be carefully cut open and the internal organs removed one at a time. In a very fat pig this would be quite a task, because the fat layers would keep covering the organs. . . .

The blood and some meat would be sent to the kitchen crew, and [with] the cooking of red *chile* with the fresh meat, the central activity of the *matanza* feast, would begin. . . .

When all the innards had been carefully removed and sent to the kitchen, the *lonjas* would be removed and hung on a clothesline. *Lonjas* are two-inch strips of skin with about a three-inch thick layer of fat, cut lengthwise; the pig butchers would literally skin the pig in strips. While the *lonjas* hardened, the crews feasted, joked, and visited. Most of the talk would be about the fine pig, and the guessing game would be on. How much lard would it render? Stories of legendary pigs that rendered up to two hundred pounds and the men who raised them were told and retold. Some would even boast of having heard of one that rendered three hundred pounds!

In about an hour the *lonjas* would harden and the stripping of the fat from the skins would begin. The crew would sit around the planking and dice the fat into about one inch cubes. Large cast-iron or brass *ollas* [pots] would be filled with diced fat and stirred and stirred for about two hours over the fire, to render the precious lard.

Then distribution of the food would start. Children would be sent in all directions throughout the village to deliver food. . . . By the end of the day most of the pig would be distributed and shared by the village. . . .

Others in the village would also have *matanzas*, so there would be a constant sharing with each other in the fall and winter. In this way the meaningful custom of sharing was not only carried out at Christmas time but all year long.

El Corrido del Gallo (The Rooster Pull)

The *gallo*, a live rooster, was buried to his neck in the middle of the street [of our village]. Horsemen, one at a time, made passes at him from about thirty yards, attempting to grab his head and pull him out while running at full speed. The feisty rooster nervously kept jerking and bobbing his head. It was a tough target to grab.

Eventually someone grabbed him and while on the run, tried to turn him and grasp him by the legs, to use the bird like a club when other riders came at him, trying to take it away. If the rider didn't turn him and instead swung it with the head, he'd yank the head off and someone else would grab the body and use it in turn to protect himself form the onslaught, while trying to reach a designated area. I never saw a rider reach the designated area before the rooster was torn apart. When it was over every rider was bloody, messy, and feathered. . . .

In the village of San Mateo, preparations for the Rooster Pull on June 24, St. John's Feast Day, started in late May. The men would feed their horses a little extra grain and practice short bursts of speed with quick starts. The feasts of Santa Ana, on July 26, and San Mateo, on September 19, were also occasions on which the *Corrido del Gallo* was generally run. An experienced rooster puller lengthened his left or right stirrup, depending on his preferred side, in order to reach the small, moving rooster head while on the run. The very good ones could sweep the ground with the palm of their hand while holding on to the saddle horn, *látigos* (leather strings holding the saddle together), or mane with the other hand. The best ones were usually tall and lanky, with long arms and legs.

About 1942 we ran the last of the *Corridas del Gallo* in San Mateo. As far as I can recall, some of the last riders were my age. . . . [As one resident of San Mateo] says, "It was a dangerous sport. You could fall off your horse on the run or get trampled by horsemen fighting for the rooster." . . . In some of the Indian pueblos, the custom, learned from the Spanish, continues to this day.

As an adult, Abe Peña ran his family's sheep ranch for many years. After a trip to Australia as a Fulbright scholar, he returned to New Mexico to serve as the foreman on one of the state's largest sheep ranches. In the 1970s he served as the director of several Peace Corps and USAID (U.S. Agency for International Development) programs in Latin America. He is currently retired in Grants, but still collects stories and still writes for the Daily Beacon, *which has been wise enough to have published every story Abe has ever submitted.*

CLEOFAS MARTÍNEZ
A LIFE OF HARMONY AND RESPECT[1]

Cleofas Martínez Jaramillo was born in Arroyo Hondo, New Mexico, on December 6, 1878. Although Cleofas was born and raised in this tiny village of northern New Mexico, her family was neither poor nor powerless. On the contrary, her ancestors were owners of considerable land grants and her father, Don Julián, raised sheep and cattle, farmed, and ran a profitable mercantile store. One of seven children, Cleofas lived a privileged childhood, steeped in relative wealth and Hispanic culture. Equally proud of her family and her culture, she wrote extensively of both in an autobiography she completed at the age of seventy-seven in 1955. Now in its second edition, Romance of a Little Village Girl *is considered a classic work of Southwest literature.*

The country had adjusted itself to the new changes, and prosperity had helped my father's business. His chief industries were sheep raising, farming, and mercantile. But being so energetic, he touched on almost every kind of work.

Occasionally on Sundays father [Julián Antonio Martínez] and mother [Marina Lucero Martínez] sought relaxation from their heavy responsibilities and took the family out on . . . long rides and picnics. It was sheer delight to roll along in our horse-drawn buggy, gradually winding up fragrant, timbered hills, past remote villages silently drowsing on green carpet valleys. Or we rode across wide plains to the foot of high mountains and through Taos' scenic canyon.

I can still see myself, like a wild bird set free of a cage, running from one berry bush to another, filling my little play bucket, my heart beating with delight at the sight of beautiful mariposa lilies, blue bells, yellow daisies, feathery ferns—plucking some to trim the pretty sunbonnets mother made for me.

My brothers found these places a fisherman's and hunter's paradise. They caught long strings of speckled mountain trout in the streams. In lakes they found wild ducks, and on prairies they hunted wild rabbits, hen, quail, and other game.

Even on these outing days, pleasure was combined with usefulness. Lupe, our cook, and Nieves, the nurse, filled flour sacks with wild hop blossoms, to be dried and kept for winter use. These were steeped in hot water and the water used to make the bread yeast. They picked berries and chock cherries for preserves.

Refreshed by the invigorating pine-fragrant air, my parents returned with renewed energy to take up their numerous tasks. Both were equally energetic. They had time for everything—work, hospitality, religion, and even politics. While my father lived at Arroyo Hondo, his political party never lost their election in that precinct. He ran his combined dry goods and grocery store without help. He directed the work on his farms, and his lands produced all kinds of grain, vegetables, [and] fruit. He raised beef, sheep, pork, and race horses. These were his chief industries, but there was no limit to his ambitions. He branched out into many others. He read his Bible and kept in it a record of the births and deaths of members of his family. . . .

During my early childhood, an epidemic of diphtheria swept through the village and took little brother Tomasito. He was dressed in a long lace-trimmed dress and laid on the black round table that stood in the corner of the living room. A wreath of white artificial flowers crown[ed] his fair forehead and a smaller one held his little clasped hands together. José Manuel, the carpenter, made the small board casket; and my aunts covered it with pink muslin, trimming it with white lace inside and outside. The family and relatives gathered in the *sala* early in the evening to sing the rosary and hymns. Even the "Our Father," "Hail Mary," and "Glory Patri" were transposed into hymns and song, for no sad *alabados* were sung at *angelitos* (little angels') wakes.

The next morning, Tiodora, our nurse, gathered the children in the play room. I recall her putting me up in the window, so that I could see the silent line of carriages forming the funeral procession. Then she let us out into the sun-filled patio to play.

I was then the baby of the family. So Tiodora, feeling her arms empty that night, picked me up and rocked me to sleep, singing softly the sweet lullaby that she was accustomed to singing to little brother:

Señora Santa Ana,	Blessed Saint Ann,
Señor San Jauquin,	Blessed Saint Jauquin,
Arulla este niño	Rock this baby,
Sé quiere dormir. . . .	He wants to go to sleep. . . .

At nine years old, when I attended my Uncle Tobias' school, my father had José Manuel, the carpenter, make a little desk for me exactly like my teachers', but painted the brightest red. He also ordered him to make a pew to be put in the old church, where there were no seats, for our family.

My mother did her share of the work, raising her family of five boys and two girls. She kept three, and sometimes more, servants busy. If my father was out busy with the peons and someone came who wanted something at the store, mother dropped her work and went and waited on the customer. Our store supplied the simple needs of the people, from dry goods and groceries to patent medicines, which mother would tell the people how to use.

Change of work was their relaxation. My father found it in cool evenings directing Erineo in planting the vegetable garden, and mother in bringing the children out to pick currants and gooseberries for jellies, and for the pies we were so fond of. Lupe and Nieves found relaxation in going out to the green bean or green pea beds to pick large dishpans full. Then fat Lupe would sit on the kitchen porch, with her legs stretched out to rest her tired feet, and called us children to help her shell the peas.

The compensation for an everyday full day's work was not material, but rather the kind that is felt in the soul. The satisfaction of having accomplished something, of doing even the small things right. For the servants it was satisfaction of doing their duty well.

Harvest time was the busiest and the happiest. I loved the loud "gid-up" and the loud cracking of the long whip that kept the herd of wild horses running around the golden wheat and oat stacks until the stacks were trampled to the ground. Then came the rumble of heavy wagons loaded with the riches of the fields to fill granaries to the ceiling. On moonlit, Indian summer evenings, it was fun to sit around the corn pile, helping to husk the corn, while listening to the witty jokes and stories of our house servants or of neighbors who came to help. Then, later, sitting in front of a warm fireplace to watch the shelling. The corn was roasted in the large adobe oven, or boiled in lime until it peeled, then spread to dry in the sun and sent down to our log, water-run mill, to be ground into meal, and brought back to the house to be sifted and sacked.

The beeves and porks were then butchered. Hundred-pound cans were filled with the rendered pork lard. From the residue, large kettles of hard soap were made. The fruit from the big orchard that father planted across the river was picked and brought in. . . .

Our home was so abundantly supplied, it was always ready to receive unexpected, uninvited guests, some just passing through. Even traveling men who came to take papa's orders for the store found some excuse for stopping overnight. With that old hospitality, they were always cheerfully received. After the harvesting was over came the general house cleaning. Mattresses, blankets, and carpets were washed with amole root soap suds in a long trough by the river. The walls were whitewashed inside and on the porches. Floors were smoothly plastered.

The *capilla* was treated in the same way. Religious Grandpa Vicente had built this family private chapel by the house. After the whitewash on the walls dried, the many holy pictures were hung back in their places. There were two especially beautiful ones, one of the Holy Family painted by Manuel Maceda in 1852 at Guadalajara, Mexico, and the other, also an original, of the Madonna. In it, the Virgin's face was so beautiful that I used to climb up on the altar to get a closer view at it. I loved this picture, which looked to me like a very good copy of Raphael's "Madonna."

In those days the stores did not carry children's ready made clothes. All items of clothing, from under vests to . . . ruffled dresses, were made at home. Mother made her babies' layettes by hand from the sheerest nainsook. She never dressed her boys in overalls, and short pants were hard on long-stocking knees; her mending basket was never empty.

She cured all our ills, from measles to tonsillitis, without aid of a doctor. Herbs have medicinal virtue, and our mountains and fields are full of them. That was all she needed. My father brought vaccine from the doctor in Taos and vaccinated all the family and some of the village children. It took so well that we never had to have it done again. . . .

Everyone was happy in those days. . . . These good people made use of God's gifts and relaxed in their beauties, while living from the good earth's natural resources.

Children fed with simple food raised on their lands, and housed in neat little whitewashed houses with large sunny yards, were healthy and happy, too. But they were quiet and respectful, not spoiled by too much liberty. . . . Juvenile delinquency? No one knew what it meant. People's lives radiated between church and home. Mothers stayed home taking care of their children, satisfied to live on their husbands' earnings. . . . No one was ever late for church, although some of them lived two and three miles distant and rode in slow wagons or even walked. . . .

My parents were scrupulously strict in the performance of their duties, but always gentle and patient. I never heard them raise their voice to correct anyone. They lived with spiritual dignity and respect. Although never demonstrative in their affection toward their family, there was no need of display. We felt their love in everything they did for us. Mother was so refined. Once on the way to Church she noticed my gloveless hands, saying: "Bare hands?" This was enough for me not to forget my gloves again.

She often quoted from her book of *Urbanidad y Buenas Maneras.* Her favorite proverb was *Nada quita al valiente lo cortez*, which meant that to be courteous even to the most humble never lowered anyone. She practiced what she preached by being kind to all. A friend said once to me: "You don't make enough distinction between yourselves and your servants." My parents were not the haughty kind of Dons; they never made their servants feel that they were inferior. There was no need, for our servants knew their places and kept [them].

I loved to watch them at work. *"Comadrita,"* they called me, so kindly. I answered with a silent smile. Only with my mother or someone of my own age did my tongue ever loosen. It was that reverent respect we were taught to have for our elders, more by example than by word, that made us so quiet and restrained in our outer feelings, even among brothers and sisters. *"Hermanita"*—"Little Sister"—all my brothers and my sisters call me even to this day.

Harmony existed always. If father or mother had a different idea about something, they talked it over in a nice way. If mother could not convince my father as to how a thing should be done, she dropped the subject without arguing. When father built the new store extending into the courtyard, she said it would ruin the looks of the house, and it did. It shut out the light from the inside windows. We lost the east inside porch on the court, and with it went my swing that I enjoyed so much, the locust tree, and elevated adobe garden around it where mother grew her old-fashioned marigolds and larkspurs. Around it we had played *mónita siega,* blind man's bluff. The porch posts we had used for bases in playing at *"las iglesias."*

The outside porch on the east side was also torn down and a new parlor and two bedrooms were built. The family was growing up and we must have more room, and father must have the store where it would be more handy, and not away between the house and the chapel, where my mother wanted it. She saw the attractive side rather than the convenient one. Although the change would save her all the work of having those long porches whitewashed and plastered every year, still she wanted it left in its lovely old style. [But once father had decided, mother accepted his decision and said no more.] . . .

[When resting, my mother] told us beautiful stories. Twenty-five of these stories I translated into English and had them published in my book *Spanish Fairy Tales.* Tiodora, our nurse, told us some creepy, ghost and witch stories and when we children were not very good she would call *orejas de burro* or the *vieja ganchos* to her aid. The *burro* would stick his long donkey ears through a crack in the door, and the *vieja* would appear crouching at the door, showing us her long hook. My cry would suddenly catch in my throat. . . . But oh! those awful dreams, in which I saw myself being carried out to the mountains hanging from the *vieja ganchos'* hook. I would wake up stiff with fright. I believe now that these awful stories, the fear of the *abuelos,* and the sore example put before us of bad children like the *mal hijo,* made our lives exceedingly repressed. . . .

[At the end of our summer days,] in very warm weather, mother allowed our maids to take our beds to the inside porch. What fun it was to find our beds by moonlight and to lay there looking up at the starlit

49

heaven! We did not gaze long. After a full day of active work or play, there was no need of sleeping powders for anyone in the family. By nine o'clock every one was ready to drop into dreamland [ready to face good and bad dreams alike].

Cleofas was educated at the Loretto Convent School in Taos and at theLoretto Academy in Santa Fe. She grew to marry adulthood and married Venceslao Jaramillo in 1898. The couple had three children before Ven died at a young age. Left a widow, Cleofas learned to care for herself and her children by becoming a wise businesswoman. Lamenting that New Mexico was becoming a "land of haste and hurry,"[2] she became interested in preserving Hispanic culture by writing four books, culminating with Romance of a Little Village Girl, *and founding La Sociedad Foklórica. She died a year after the first edition of her now-famous autobiography appeared in print.*

4

CITY CHILDHOODS

JOHN WATTS
A HEALTHSEEKER'S DIARY, SANTA FE, 1859[1]

New Mexico has long served as a destination for ailing Easterners determined to regain their failing health in the dry climate and clean air of the Southwest. While thousands who arrived on such personal missions were adults, many others were youths like John Watts of Bloomington, Indiana. John was a student in Bloomington when be began to suffer from chills and a high fever. His father, a well-known land grant lawyer in New Mexico, decided that the Southwest was the ideal place for John's recovery. After traveling down the Santa Fe Trail, John spent most of 1859 in Santa Fe, rooming with his older brother, Joshua Howe Watts, and keeping a journal to practice his penmanship and to foster good habits. John gives us a unique view of the territorial capital and its residents on the eve of the Civil War. John tells us what it was like to be an Anglo youth eager to improve himself and grow, but also quite willing to be distracted by the people and events in this early period of New Mexico territorial history.

Friday, March 4, 1859

Here I am again another day having swiftly flown. I rose about my usual time and went up with [my older brother] Howe to breakfast. I have not played any pool to day. I and Howe went up at 11, O'clock and recited our lesson to the Governor with the rest of

51

the class. I played one game of billiards to night at the Fonda [hotel] with Willie Rencher and he beat me of which he made a great fuss—it was on the upper table. I have not paid my billiard [bill?] for the month yet. Howe and Willie and myself all went out by the capitol where there were plenty of boys (grown) playing town ball [a form of baseball] and the[y] asked us to play—which of course we were glad to do. We had a pleasant time—they catch one fellow out three time [hard?] running it puts all out. It was fine exercise and I enjoyed [it]. I have read some little today in "Ralph Rattlin" but I am not getting along as fast as I would like. I practiced on the guitar some to day. . . . To day has been a very pretty day—the sun shone out warm all day. I helped snow ball some boys [and girls] with [my friend] Jesus—he and I against three or four. . . . I hit one of the women in the belly and knocked her down so they tell me.

Saturday, March 5, 1859

To day has been a very blustery cold day. It has snowed hard all afternoon or rather drifted about. It has been quite a snow storm. . . . I had such a nice dream last night—I dreamed that I was at home up stairs in Bettie [Ruter's] room sitting in the old rocking chair and that Bettie was sitting by me—I dreamed [of her] "snugged down" in my arms I gave her three sweet kisses which has made me feel better all day to day when I thought about it. . . .

Sunday, March 6, 1859

Well we have been treated very well to day and could not complain. . . . I did not put on a clean shirt this morning. I thought the one I had on was clean enough. I . . . went to church and listened to a sermon preached by Mr. [Samuel] Gorman. . . . . This afternoon I wrote a long letter to Bettie although I have not received a line from her for two months and I think it is time she was answering some of my letters. Howe wrote four or five letters to day [but] I only two.

Tuesday, March 8, 1859 (8:00 p.m.)

This is rather early to write in my Journal but as I may go to a *baile* [dance] at Tom Valentia's to night I thought I would post up quick and on time. Howe and I went to a *baile* at Tom's last night and to night is the last one there will be for a long time because "Lent" commences soon and there are no *bailes* I believe until it is over which is forty day[s] I think. I recited French to day. Samuel [Ellison] being away we cannot recite in Spanish. There was a horse race this morning but I had no way to go down to the track so I staid at home. [Finis E.] Kavanaugh's horse and Jones pony I believe were the ones that run—Pointer and Jones bet—$300 I believe. Pointer gave Jones twenty feet I believe and beat him twenty. Howe bought some marbles and a ball this afternoon and he Willie R. and I all played marbles. I beat Colorado this evening [in] two games of billiards. I got another book of Hovey—"Percival Keene"—which I have commenced—I am wearing a ring of Sallie Rencher's. I played town ball this morning.

Thursday, March 10, 1859

Well to day has been exciting and full of adventure. . . . There was a fight this morning up at the Fonda between Col Menes [Thomas Means] and Leo Smith. The Col sneaked up on Leo with a cane and lit into him and whipped him before he had any chance to retaliate. And again this afternoon there was a big fight down at Kavanaugh's Office between Drue and Menes chiefly but Leo Smith helped Drue. There was considerable shooting of pistols and some how or other Rogers was in the scrape—all four were shooting. Dr. Kavanaugh said he never saw so many deliberate shots without any lasting effect—he said there were ten or twelve shots. . . .

Monday, March 28, 1859

Well the chief event of to day was at night. . . . I bought me a pair of pantaloons to day at Kingsbury's at $4.50 which I wore to the ball to night. . . . We had a fine time. Howe went after Lola . . . but Howe had a row with the old lady and she would not let Lola come. I took a fancy to Charley Conclin's sister who is a very fine girl I think—I danced with her and she danced very easy. The wife of Jesus Cena was also there and very good looking. We had an excellent time.

Wednesday, April 6, 1859

I rose this morning about my usual hour and went to breakfast. . . . The blacksmith where Colorado works caught fire to day and burned down—it was the only fire I have ever seen in Santa Fe—they soon pulled it down and kept it from burning the rest of the houses close or joined to it rather. These are terrible houses to put out when they get afire and burn for a long time. I did not learn whether it caught from carelessness or by accident but the house was full of fodder which helped it along—it was about 2 1/2 O'clock when I found it out—I was playing billiards. . . .

Thursday, April 7, 1859

Well to day shall be employed in describing our fishing expedition. We started about 9 O'clock and rode about eight or nine miles up the canon directly East. We got up there about 11 O'clock. The party consisted of Howe, [J.T.] Battail, Crump, Captain Chapman and myself. We had a lunch given us by Mrs. Rencher which we eat as soon as we got up there and then all scattered along the creek which contained nothing but trout. We only caught three—I, Howe and Battail caught one a piece. Howe fell down and caught his hook in his finger which spoiled all his fun. They had a bottle of brandy but I took none nor Howe. . . .

Friday, April 22, 1859

Of all the strange and unheard of religious ceremonies—to day beats all. To day is one of the Mexican Catholic's great days and I am glad I had a chance to see everything. This morning I was on hand when the ceremonies came off and at which I am somewhat surprised. I and Willie went up . . . and got on the last house closest to the church where we had quite a fine view of every thing that was going on. The ceremonies began about 11 O'clock—there was [an] immense crowd there of between two and four thousand. . . . The church was crammed full and the outside was full [too]—at least the placita. There was one man with a comic looking cap on a horse that looked as if it had paint on it and then another who was supposed to represent Pilate. . . . There were some fifteen or twenty with long sharp poles who went on each side of the procession and kept the watchers back. First three little boys marched out abreast the middle one carrying an image of the Savior, then came the effigy of Jesus who was to be crucified borne by four strong men, with the crown of thorns on his head and bearing the heavy cross—then three or four priests one of which with two or three little boys were singing—then came the effigy of the Virgin Mary who was born by four virgins with lamps among whom was Lolita—there followed masked Mexicans—but before the front of the procession the thirtysoldiers who guarded Him and cast lots for this garments. . . . The priest made them a sermon on a raised pulpit—of about ten minutes long and then they very deliberately marched back into the church. They had a small drum which the[y] gave three expressive taps continually with short intermissions also a whistle—such is a short sketch of the first procession.

This afternoon another procession came off similar almost to this morning's except that they brought Jesus out in a coffin ready for burial. They had an effigy of some one else dressed in white with a book in his hand. . . . Barry Simpson, Howard and Windham curse the whole proceeding as a humbug and a sacrilege—they are disgusted with it. . . . After the excitement of the day I feel tired and sleepy. . . . I almost forgot to say that Charley Thayer had a fuss with a Mexican to day. And Leo Smith got drunk and got to brandishing his knife and the sheriff took him in charge.

Wednesday, April 27, 1859, 4:35 p.m.

By way of variety I have taken my seat by the window to see and write down what is passing with whatever reflections I may wish to make. I[t] snowed this morning and the clouds are now gathered round the summits of the famous Rockey Mountains which over look Santa Fe. Old Bauly is in the distance with his snowed crowned cap. . . . [Y]onder goes a man galloping a mule with a half a dozen dogs after him which is quite a common thing—a person cannot ride around Santa Fe without a lot of dogs following him. There the bugle has just sounded[at Fort Marcy;] the soldiers I suppose must run. . . . I hear an anvil . . . —I see a man here and there and here a woman. Fort Marcy is the first point that meets the eye on looking out the window which is on the first grade and lowest of the mountains. . . . I see a raven flying over the Government coral. They resort there in great numbers when it snows, and they cannot [find] anything to eat. . . . It looks a little gloomy out and cloudy and is a good time for one to reflect. . . . I wonder [what] ma and the girls are doing now—perhaps on their road to [New] Mexico—Santa Fe I hope so. . . . I hear the band playing perhaps in the plaza—I believe I will go up and see. . . .

Thursday, May 5, 1859

There is one thing which I had intended and ought to [have] commented on but which like many other things slipped my memory and that is to mention an Italian organ grinder who has been perambulating the streets for the last three or four days. . . . It is one of the worst organs I ever heard—it is large and heavy and all out of tune which makes the music miserable—they are bad enough when in good order but when out of order are almost impossible to put up with. I got my music this morning and played it with Bauer—the first page is called the Serenade. . . . The bugle has sounded so I will cease. *BUENAS NOCHES.*

Friday, May 6, 1859

Tomorrow as we say, *"Es el día por el correo"* [mail day] and which I am always glad of for I look for letters and for word from ma or some one at home so that we may know whether father and ma are on the road or whether they even intend coming or not. . . . I got my boots repaired to day by the Soldier Shoemaker. The band played in the plaza this afternoon some very good music. . . . I and Willie went over to see the [Edgar sisters] about 9 O'clock. . . . They were serenaded just as we came away by Lieut. Wilkins, George Bell and the two fiddlers who have just come to town. . . .

Wednesday, May 25, 1859

I feel very much like I was attacked by that contagious disease called "Spring Fever" in the States but I have not found out the name it goes by out here. . . . I suppose I have read fifty pages in Bayard Taylor to day which is decidedly better than nothing but when I see how much time I have it seems like I [ought] to read three or four times as much.

The days pass away very slowly now[;] I want the mail to come with father in it. . . . To day has been rather warm, but still pleasant. Howe and I went over to see the ladies this evening and intended to go with them down to the fish pond and row them over the pond but it was to[o] windy. . . .

Friday, May 27, 1859

To day has been a very lucky day. I and Howe recited our French to day at the usual hour and as we were reciting the mail came in from the East. After we finished reciting and started up to the Fonda—just as we got out the door we espied father walking cross the plaza and we both immediately broke across the plaza towards him, but found to our sad regret that he had brought none of [the rest of the family] whom we long to see. Fannie nor none came—he says they will come next Spring. He said they were all well and ma and Sis came with him as far as Madison. . . . Oh! how much I want to see Bettie—the first thing father did after sitting down was to sing "The Long, Long Weary Day." All the fellows at the Fonda say they are going to tell great "yarns" on me, but Howe and I have an unimpaired reputation. This I think is father's eighteenth trip across the plains—he looks quite ruff when he first arrived but got shaved and put on a clean shirt and now looks considerably better. . . . [In the evening] I went up to see pa and . . . we had a little chat and a song and. . . . Father wanted to know if I could speak Spanish yet which I told him I could not. I broke one of my guitar strings to night. The wind is blowing to night rather hard—whistling through the door and houses. I am going to do better with my music than I have been here lately. Father wishes me to learn to perform well on some instrument and now is my time. I have so much time. So we will make a new start tomorrow.

Monday, June 13, 1859

Well all of to day has been occupied in hunting. This morning I and Howe, Eddie, Jim (alias "Bud") and his pa all went hunting. We went about three miles South—down the creek and stopped by three large trees under which Howe sat all the time and killed the most birds which was four but we soon run out of ammunition and then we came home. I

57

did not kill a single one this morning but all the rest did. This afternoon we went again through. . . . and we had four guns in the crowd. . . . We killed eight birds this morning, six doves and two snipes. This afternoon we killed twenty-seven more[,] four of which I killed. . . . Howe killed the most—Jim the least. We had quite a nice day of it and when we came home nothing would do but that we should go over and eat supper with them—then we had a nice talk in the parlor—played two or three games of eucher [a card game]—then Howe . . . played on the guitar for them. . . . We both came home about 10 O'clock and went to bed without posting. I read none to day neither did I recite in music to Bauer.

Tuesday, June 21, 1859

We arose this morning about our usual hour and after breakfast . . . started for the long before arranged pic-nic. The weather did not look favorable at all but foreboding of a bad day for when we started it was blowing hard. . . . It was some time before I could manage my mule but he went along very well. . . . [A dozen men and six women made the trip, riding horses, mules, and traveling in wagons.] The place selected for the pic-nic was the Rio Hondo—a dry creek which is about six miles from Santa Fe which is a nice ride—we turned out of the road a short distance and went up the bed of the creek for a short way where we found two nice tall pine trees with a cool spring close by. Here the ladies got out and seated themselves in the cool refreshing shade. . . . We. . . . employed the time in playing eucher, chatting[,] taking walk[s] and rambling on the mountain sides. We had a very nice dinner . . . without anything to mar or interrupt. It was concluded by rolling a huge stone down the mountain side. . . . We got a little sprinkled but it was all wind and no rain. We hurried home helter skelter each one breaking for home. And so ended the pic-nic which was enjoyed and complimented by all.

Wednesday, July 27, 1859

I took a little "nap" this afternoon which did not do me any good that I know of. I got caught to night—while I was at the Fonda playing billiards. It rained quite hard and thundered and lightning terribly—

more than I ever heard in the States. But it did not last long for in a half an hour I came home and now it is no more than 10 O'clock.

Howe had gone to bed and it will not be so terrible long before he will have a companion [for he plans to marry soon]. . . . Howe and I have always eat together slept together and been together nearly all our lives.

My heart almost fails me when I think of leaving Howe perhaps forever but still I will not think of it now. I feel some what melancholy to night, but I do not know why. Bettie is going to be married to[o] and I do not know how many more [friends will marry soon;] Mary may be married by the time I get back home but it all goes in a life time they say.

Monday, September 19, 1859

[T]he crowning thing to day or rather to night was a Concert given by this new band which has just come out and which was splendid. Admittance was fifty cents. . . .

There were fourteen pieces and in two parts and the best of the performance I think was "a solo" on the violin [by] the best violin player I ever heard. He imitated on the violin, a flute, an organ, a fife, a Scottish bagpipe, and played the devil's dream with a perfect rush and in two or three ways different from each other. There were most of the ladies that are in town. . . . I feel like all my music is no music at all since I have heard such good—but I will go to bed—it is time. . . .

Sunday, October 16, 1859

Adíos Nuevo Mexico

This day's journal as is indicated above is a Farewell to New Mexico. As this is the last journal I expect to write in Santa Fe and in New Mexico I thought I would devote it to thoughts on the subject above mentioned. I and Jimmie Edgar expect to start to El Paso tomorrow morning in the stage and wait in El Paso for pa . . . and then we will go on. I have had some delightful times in Santa Fe and New Mexico and when I think I am going to leave it my wishes and heart fain would still remain here but it is my interest and good which will be increased by going and therefore I must go and ought to without complaint. . . . I have just finished packing my trunk and am sitting in my drawers writing, while father is sleeping. I am going to take my guitar—a present from Howe. I have given father a list of my debts which he says he will settle. I went to Sunday School, church and eat dinner and supper at Mrs. Edgar's. . . . I cannot write much to night. As I have to get up early I will now say to Santa Fe and New Mexico, Good By—Farewell—at least for two years and perhaps forever—*Adíos! Adíos! Adíos!*

John Watts had recovered sufficiently to return home to Indiana in October 1859. He studied at Indiana University, graduating in 1861. He lived in Washington, D.C., during the first years of the Civil War while his father served as New Mexico's Congressional Delegate (1861-63). From Washington, John returned to New Mexico, where he spent the next twenty-odd years as a rancher as well as a bank employee in Santa Fe. He spent the last thirty-nine years of his life in the banking business in Kansas. New Mexico's climate must have agreed with him: he led a long, generally healthy life with his wife, Susan Jane Barnes, and their only child, Loraine. John lived to be eighty-five.

KENNETH C. BALCOMB
GOING TO THE TERRITORIAL FAIR[1]

Kenneth Chester Balcomb was born on June 13, 1891, in Denver, Colorado. When he was two years old, his ailing mother took Kenneth and his older sister, Marion, to live with their grandmother in San Diego, California. Kenneth's mother died shortly thereafter. His father, who had moved from Denver to Albuquerque, sent for Kenneth and his sister so they could live together as a family in New Mexico.

Arriving in New Town, Albuquerque, in 1898, Kenneth and the city seemed to grow together. Thanks largely to the coming of the railroad, Albuquerque's population had more than tripled, from 2,135 in 1880 to 7,517 in 1900, with about eighty-five percent of the latter population residing in the new section of town near the railroad and its expanding operations. Kenneth tells of this growth from a boy's perspective, describing the activity along Railroad (now Central) Avenue, at the jail, at the fire department, by the railroad depot, and even in the forbidden Red Light district. Kenneth saved his greatest detail for the annual event he and his boyhood friends cared most about: the territorial fair.

New to Albuquerque

The train on which my sister and I arrived from San Diego slipped into the station in the dusk of a December evening in 1898. It was snowing, my first sight of snow. As we alighted on the board platform alongside the red frame depot, we were greeted by my father (whom I was seeing for the first time in my memory). . . . It was cold, and our

San Diego clothing seemed inadequate as we hurried across Railroad Avenue. . . .

My first recollection of living in Albuquerque is our having moved into a three-room frame house on Keleher Avenue. . . . In 1898, only the homes of the more affluent boasted running water, flush toilets, electric lights, and telephones. Certainly two small homes on Keleher Avenue did not. In our house, kerosene lamps served for lighting, a pitcher pump rising from the kitchen drain board served as the source of water, and a dishpan served as a sink. Disposal of dishwater was very elementary— one simply threw it out the door. The privy stood grandly on the back of the lot—a two holer complete with crescent in the door.

These crudities in living conditions probably had more of an impact on my sister than they did on me, as we had been used to more modern conveniences in my grandmother's home in San Diego. It was all a lark for me . . .

Learning About the Town

I first learned about the town when going around with my father, who was a contractor and builder, but I was later permitted to go alone. The impressions I gained of the town and some of the people are indelibly stamped on my mind. . . .

The principal improved street was Railroad Avenue, extending from High Street on the east to Old Town on the west. No streets were paved, but sprinkler wagons plied back and forth daily to keep down the dust. When it rained, all streets became muddy. I can remember enormous wagons loaded with huge sacks of wool, pulled by two, four, or sometimes six oxen struggling and slipping through the mud of Railroad Avenue— marvelous sights to a boy. Most sidewalks, where there were any, were boardwalks. Trash collected under them attracted rats, and trying to kill them furnished great sport for boys. . . .

Most of the town's activities centered around the [railroad] depot, from which business houses extended east and west. . . . The mystery of North Third Street did not at first enter the consciousness of a seven- and eight-year-old, but sly remarks of boys with whom I became acquainted soon charged me with curiosity about, and some awe of, this Red Light district. It was forbidden territory for decent folks, and especially children. . . . Other forbidden places for children were the many saloons along Railroad Avenue. . . . Although they appeared dead and discouraged by day, they were livened by electric lights by night. Many a male passed through swinging doors and into the lighted rooms amidst the sounds of music and clinking glasses. . . .

Of great interest to us were the horse-drawn street cars that ran on narrow-gauge tracks from First Street to Traction Park in Old Town. They seemed to be huge affairs, pulled by enormous fat-rumped horses driven by giant men. . . .

The arrival of a horsecar at First Street was an exciting experience for us. As it came rolling up Railroad Avenue, the driver would tramp on a pedal to clang a huge bell and draw the horse to a halt with great flourish. When the passengers had alighted, the driver would unhitch the horse and lead him to the other end of the car to be again hitched and made ready for [the return] trip. After a short wait, the great bell would again be clanged, the reins flicked, and the horse would step out at his set pace down the well-worn path between the tracks. . . . The horse seemed to know as much about the routine as did the driver. . . .

[A]cross Tijeras Avenue among cottonwood and willow trees was the city jail. Painted an unpleasant green, it seemed a pitifully small affair even to a child's eye. . . . It had ominous-looking bars at the windows and doors. We avoided the jail like a pesthouse, but took a lively interest in activities of the policemen whose headquarters were somewhere in the vicinity of the jail. . . . The police paddy wagon was a single horse-and-buggy rig that we called the "hurry-up" wagon. One would sometimes see a policeman driving towards the jail with one arrestee beside him on the seat and another one or two sitting in the back with their feet hanging out.

Our greatest interest was in the Fire Department. The fire engine and the horses that pulled it were the wonder of wonders, and the firemen were all heroic figures. . . . I vividly remember the huge black, fat-rumped horses being stalled alongside the fire engine with their harness[es] suspended above them. When an alarm sounded, the harness[es] dropped, firemen buckled the necessary straps, the bar in front of the horses would rise, and each horse, without prompting, stepped forward to his place in front of the vehicle. Neck yokes and tugs were fastened, the lines handed to the driver, and with a loud clanging of a bell on the vehicle, the horses charged into the street with firemen jumping onto their stations on each side. All this took about the time it took to count to twenty. . . .

Another alarm that had a profound effect in the lives of us boys was the "curfew bell". . . . It was rung at 8:00 p.m. as a signal for young people under sixteen to be off the streets unless with an adult. It was also rung in emergencies such as flood or fire, or on such festive occasions as July Fourth, or when there was a parade. The bell, sitting high in its derrick,. . . . seemed to carry an authority almost human. As we passed it even in daytime we looked up at it with the respect due a judge or other officer of the law.

Transportation by train was the only reasonably fast means of getting anywhere, whether to Bernalillo, Belen, El Paso, Los Angeles, or New York City. Each day people were going someplace, or arriving from a trip, and friends gathered to say good-bye, or to welcome someone home. Many days a train carried a notable whose arrival, heralded by the papers, caused a crowd to gather. We small folks tried to be on hand on such occasions, when we weren't in school.

The visible activities of train arrivals are pictured nostalgically in my mind, but memories of the sounds come back vividly also: the whistle as the train approached in the distance, growing ever louder as it neared; the engine bell ringing; steam hissing from places all over it; and brakes slipping and squealing as the train stopped unerringly in front of the depot. Immediately, organized pandemonium broke loose. Baggage trucks were pulled out, with the men shouting at one another. The Harvey House gong sounded peremptorily, newsboys called their extras, and people shouted and squealed as they greeted each other. And always could be heard the deep, resonant voice of a hotel barker booming out "Savoy Hotel." When a returning passenger heard that call, day or night, he knew he was back in Albuquerque.

Highwire act at the Territorial Fair. Cobbs Memorial Collection, Neg. No. 000-119-0729. Courtesy of the Center for Southwest Research, General Library, University of New Mexico, Albuquerque, New Mexico.

The annual territorial fair . . . was wonderful to young folks. . . . The fairgrounds, known as Traction Park, began where Railroad Avenue reached Old Town Boulevard. To the left of the great gate was the ticket window, and to the left of that was the county jail, a grim reminder to behave. To the right of the entrance were the exhibition buildings. The high board fence surrounding the fairgrounds reached almost to the river to the west. The grandstand stood along the south side, center to the half-mile racetrack which circled the field inside the fence. The area within the racetrack held a baseball diamond and room for other activities. . . .

Although the performances varied somewhat from year to year, there were always exhibits, horse races, and ball games. The races featured sulky races, both trotters and pacers. . . . Even as a child I saw something really majestic about a big, powerful animal, nostrils blowing, and frothy sweat pouring from him, hurtling along with the little sulky and driver so close behind as to look as if they were riding on his rump.

A baseball game was held every day of the fair. Since fair week occurred after the national baseball series was over, big-league players were recruited to play with the local team, the Browns, and this provided two good teams and creditable baseball. The umpire seemed always to be Tom Hubbell, the sheriff. He was a big man and always. . . . wore his shiny gold badge. His decisions were not contested.

Most years a troop of cavalry from Fort Wingate, near Gallup, pitched camp on the grounds and gave daily exhibitions of drilling and horsemanship. . . .

[But] the greatest event of the fair was a balloon ascension. The huge bag was inflated with lighter-than-air gas that was produced by pouring kerosene on a wood fire. We kids got free admission to the fair to help anchor the balloon and keep it from sailing off prematurely by holding on to ropes attached to it. As it filled, it rose majestically into the air, covered with colored streamers and spangles. A large basket was attached to the balloon; the balloonist would mount it, we would release the tethering ropes, and it would shoot into the air amid cheers, a tune from the band, and colored paper thrown out by the balloonist. After it got to what seemed a terrible height the balloonist would jump out to parachute down, maneuvering the parachute so as to land in front of the grandstand. The balloon, freed from the man's weight, would slowly turn bottom up, emitting gas and smoke and eventually crash to earth, to be retrieved for the next ascension.

One year there was a death-defying act in which a beautiful black horse climbed a ramp to the top of a tower some seventy feet high and, with a daredevil on his back, dove into a tank of water seventy feet below. One day a hundred dollars was offered to any local citizen who would ride the horse until he emerged from the tank. A grocery clerk name Riley Edwards, who was conveniently quite bowlegged, made the ride and collected. He was the town's hero for weeks.

We had several ways of getting into the fair, not counting the remote possibility of buying a ticket. One was to assist with the balloon; another was to help clean the racehorse stables; sometimes we got a job selling pillows to relieve tender derrieres from the wear of hard bleacher seats. When all other means failed, we would sneak in.

The board fence around the fairgrounds was too high for a boy to reach the top unaided, so we worked in pairs: one boy leaned over, furnishing a platform from which another could reach the top and swing up. He could then reach down and pull up another. This worked fine unless a guard happened to be there, prepared to grab someone when he jumped down. If caught, a boy would be marched to the county jail house, lectured, and finally released—necessitating his having to go through the fence-climbing routine all over again. After all, fair time was fun time for children, adults, performers, and even guards. . . .

There were no carnival concessions at the fairgrounds; these were allowed to set up in the side streets entering Railroad Avenue from Second to Sixth streets. They were open at night when all vehicular traffic on these intersections stopped. The merry-go-round, ferris wheel, and all other such attractions would locate back of the curfew [bell] at Second Street and Railroad Avenue. All daytime activity was at the fairgrounds, but nighttime revelry centered downtown around the carnival concessions. This enabled us to participate in the night's activities without having to venture into the darkness and uncertainties of the fairgrounds. It was also a boon to the downtown merchants and saloons, as they stayed open until the carnival attractions closed down.

In the carnival tents, we saw our first motion picture, *The Great Train Robbery*, first marveled at the sword swallower, the 350-pound fat lady, the living skeleton, the snake charmer, the tattooed dancer—this latter for adults only. Every night, Monday through Friday, was fair night, with curfew hours suspended, and with lights and excitement on every hand. Then, on Saturday night, Railroad Avenue was closed to traffic from First to Sixth streets; everyone was supposed to be in masquerade dress, bands played, and people danced in the street and threw confetti and paper streamers. When the hilarity was over at midnight, the street was a shambles and the people were disheveled, but as they walked home, arm in arm, some sober and some not so sober. . . . It was the end of another fun time, memorable and happy.

Kenneth Balcomb grew to maturity in Albuquerque, entering the University of New Mexico in 1912, the same year the territory finally

67

achieved statehood. As Kenneth put it at the conclusion of his childhood memoirs, the city and the boy—and the state—had made the transition from their short- to long-pants days. Kenneth worked as an engineer for the federal government during most of his professional career. He retired in Albuquerque in 1953.

5

FARMING CHILDHOODS

FRANCIS QUINTANA
BECOMING A *PÉON DE LA ACEQUIA* [1]

Farming was the main economic activity in the small villages of New Mexico for hundreds of years. Farmers relied on subsistence crops to feed their families, and, more limitedly, on cash crops to make at least small profits by the nineteenth and twentieth centuries. To water their crops, farmers used simple butefficient irrigation ditches, known as acequias, *running off main waterways, especially the Rio Grande. All water users were responsible for helping to maintain the* acequias, *clearing them annually to assure an even flow of water and rebuilding ditch banks to keep their precious resource on course. As Francis Quintana explains, these responsibilities were taken very seriously, marking a social rite of passage for youths deemed fit to help in this essential work for not only the sake of their families, but also for their entire farming communities.*

The early Spanish settlers brought the *acequia* system to northern New Mexico. The *acequias* are a rudimentary method of delivering irrigation water to the land. But *la acequia* as a concept is much more. It has developed and maintained a Hispanic cultural tradition that has survived three hundred years of constant human expansion and land development. . . .

As tradition dictates, land is passed down from one generation to the next. It makes sense that the big *ranchos* would become smaller *ranchitos* through subdivision. The operators of these small *ranchitos* still generate important supplemental income from their land. The unifying cultural force that binds these *ranchitos* is the *acequia*. The *acequia* ties the present *rancheros* to each other as well as to their collective past. . . .

As a child I looked forward to the day when I would be accepted by the *mayordomo* [ditch boss] as a *péon de la acequia* [ditch cleaning worker]. My father awaited that day, too. I would be one less *péon* he would have to hire on *el día de la acequia* [the ditch cleaning day]. The number of *peones de la acequia* a *ranchero* needed to send to *el día de la acequia* was decided by the number of acres he had under irrigation. My father had to send four *peones*.

One night in February, my father took me to the local county school building for the annual *junta de la Acequia Del Prado* (ditch association meeting). At the meeting the association [members] elected three *comisionados de la acequia* (ditch commissioners) and a *mayordomo*. . . . All business of the ditch was the responsibility of the three *comisionados* and the *mayordomo*. The *comisionados* set regulations and policy on the management of the *acequia* and the *mayordomo* carried them out.

Cleaning the ditch was the first order of business. It was agreed to clean the ditch on a day in April when the weather was warm and the ditch was dry. The allotment of irrigation water would be conducted by the *mayordomo* throughout the coming season. The *mayordomo*, a portentous looking *ranchero*, stated *las reglas de la acequia* (the ditch rules), along with some consequences for those caught in error. Chief among these [errors] was the unauthorized use of water. Any diversion of water without the permission of the *mayordomo* was considered an outright theft and would incur his wrath. The *mayordomo* had a lot of power and he was not afraid to use it. The use of the ditch was administered by him very successfully, and the community was satisfied with how the water was disbursed.

In the middle of March, the *mayordomo* sent out a proclamation that the ditch would be cleaned on the first Saturday of April. The proclamation was spread by word of mouth throughout the community, with enough time for everyone to make plans, hire workers, and ready tools.

On *el día de la acequia* the *peones* gathered at the *compuerta* (water diversion headgate) on Lino Miera's *rancho*. My father was the *primer*

70

comisionado (first commissioner). His job was to keep records of all the *acequia* business. On *el día de la acequia*, he would call out the names of the landowners who used the *acequia*. He called out the names in order of use [from the] first user below the *compuerta* and the number of *peones* apportioned to that user.

"Lino Miera, *cuatro peones*," my father called into the crowd of men. The call was immediately followed by, *"!Aquí, José Gonzales!"* A *péon*, hired by Miera, responded as he moved toward the *mayordomo* for approval. As each name was called and approved by the *mayordomo*, the *peones* fell into their individual *tareas* within the *acequia*. A *tarea* is a short piece of the *acequia*, about a yard, marked by *el segundo comisionado*. *El segundo comisionado* walked down into the *acequia* marking each *tarea* according to the degree of work needed to clean it. *"Aquí, Roberto Miera,"* the second *péon* yelled as he too passed to the *majordomo* for approval and direction. Those *peones* the *mayordomo* did not approve were sent away immediately and the *ranchero* was charged with a deficit unless he had another *péon* for approval.

This process went quickly, and before I knew it, my father was calling out his own name and I yelled, *"Aquí,* Francis Quintana," and passed to the *mayordomo* for approval. The austere *mayordomo* looked me over, asked me if I were old enough and whether I knew how to use the new shovel I was carrying. *"Sí, señor,"* I responded. *"Cuántos años tenías tú en tu primer día de péon?"* ("How old were you?") the *mayordomo* asked my father. My father looked up from the rule book and quickly surveyed both the *mayordomo* and me, then slowly, as if dragging up some long-lost memory, he said, *"Como de ese tamaño."* ("About that size.")

The *mayordomo* looked me straight in the eye and stated deliberately, "Your father has always been a hard worker. I am going to assume that you are like him, so I am going to approve you for now. If I see you cannot do the work as I require it, I will send you home. Fall in to your *tarea*."

I cleaned my *tarea* as fast and as well as I could, knowing that I was on probation. I could hear when the *peones* above me on the *acequia* were told to *dar vuelta* [work on it more]. Suddenly, the *mayordomo* was at my *tarea*. The walk from one end of the working *péon* chain to the other was a gauntlet. As I passed, the *peones* looked up from their work to jeer and taunt me for their own amusement. At first I felt all that challenging interaction was meant to harass and intimidate me. After the second *vuelta*, my *tarea* partner counseled me: *"No te dejes; diles algo para atrás! Todo lo que dicen es puro chiste."* ("Defend yourself, it's all in fun.")

At noon the word was passed down the *péon* line to take thirty minutes for lunch. Most of us sat and ate our sack lunch right in our *tareas.* Some *peones* who lived close by went home to eat. They would have to get back to their *tarea* before the *mayordomo* gave the signal to start again. After lunch, the work continued until we reached *el desagüe* (the end of the ditch where the excess water runs back into the river).

Earlier, the first and second *comisionados* had returned to the *compuerta* to divert the water from the Rio Lucero into the newly cleaned *acequia.* They would follow the flow of water down the ditch for a final cleaning. The first flood of water would pick up loose debris and cause occasional dams or clogs on sharp turns or individual *compuertas.* The flow of water would arrive at the *desagüe* just as the last *tarea* was finished.

There the first *comisionado* read the roster again to credit each *ranchero* properly, then dismissed them and their *peones.* When the water flowed cleanly in the *acequia, los peones de la acequia* congratulated each other on another good *día de la acequia* and went home. From here on the *acequia* and the use of water would be the responsibility of *el mayordomo de La Acequia Del Prado.*

Fifty years later,. . . . [m]y days as a *péon de la acequia* are gone. I have witnessed many El Prado progeny become successful *hombres* [men] under the conventional scrutiny of the *mayordomo.* Forty-five years ago, the *Acequia Del Prado* was where it is today. It is still cleaned at the same time of the year, and it still delivers water to the same land in El Prado. The *ranchos* have become *ranchitos.* The great fields of grain and hay have changed to vegetable gardens and smaller crops. There is not much production from the *ranchitos,* but the benefit in personal satisfaction is [still] well worth the effort.

Francis Quintana is a retired rancher and educator who still lives in El Prado in northern New Mexico.

ANGELICA GURULÉ CHÁVEZ & MARCELINA MIRANDA CHÁVEZ: HUMBLE LIVES FILLED WITH JOY[1]

Angelica (Angie) Gurulé Chávez and Marcelina (Lena) Miranda Chávez were children in large, rural families of the Rio Abajo, or lower region of the Rio Grande Valley, in the era 1918 to 1945. In 2001 Angie agreed to keep a tape recorder by her side to record various memories of her childhood as they occurred to her over several days. Lena did the same, albeit by recalling her memories and jotting down thoughts over many months.

The result is the combined memoir of truly happy childhoods, despite their families' general economic poverty. Their happiness in the face of adversity is a credit to their indomitable spirits and to their parents who worked hard, loved their children, and seldom let on that they were financially strapped much of the time. As Angie recalls, her family never lacked for food (repeatedly described as "delicious") and she never knew she was "poor." She and Lena were certainly never poor in affection from their families and in appreciation of their rich Hispanic heritage.

Marcelina Miranda Chávez, ca. 10 years old.
Author's collection.

73

Parents

ANGELICA GURULÉ CHÁVEZ:

I was the sixth of thirteen children born to Jacobo and Valentina Gurulé. Two of my siblings died as infants.

We had a good, patient dad, and he spent time with us. At night we'd play table games like *la pitaria* (a board game played with corn and beans) and *saca pon deja todo* (a spinning game). He believed in everything in moderation. He didn't eat too much or sleep too much or work too much. And he always wanted us to do everything in moderation. He lived to be ninety-six years old.

My dad was a person with a lot of faith who believed that everything would come out right. And it usually did. One time we were on our way to work in South Dakota in a car pulling a little trailer. We were in the middle of the Black Hills when a tire on the car wore out. My dad just patiently pulled over to the side of the road and we all went down to a little stream nearby. Right there by the stream was a tire that he could use. So he put the tire on the car and away we went. It was quite a miracle, I think.

My father had certain rules for us. He wouldn't let us say *embustera* (liar) or *mientes* (you lie). He didn't need to do anything but threaten us with a mentra (good whipping). His threat was enough. They also told us that if we said bad words the priest would put a hot egg in our mouths. I was deathly afraid of the hot egg the priest might put in my mouth, so I wouldn't say bad words.

We also had a good, hard-working mother. She was always busy cooking and sewing and cleaning. She was a very generous person. She gave anything to anybody. Aluminum pots and pans were scarce, but we had one. An old man who came to visit us admired that skillet, and mother just gave it to him. We were all mad at her because she gave away our aluminum skillet. But that's how generous she was.

MARCELINA MIRANDA CHÁVEZ:

I was one of eleven children born to Aurora Miranda and Mateo Chávez. Four of my siblings died before they were five years old. Two brothers died before they were fifteen years old. Five of us grew to adult-hood.

I was born in the community of Abeytas, New Mexico, about seven miles south of Belen. I was named after one of my grandmas, although I never knew any of my grandparents. We used to call one of my mother's older sisters Nana (Grandma) Mersedez because she was like a grand-mother to us.

My parents used to tell me that an Indian on the side of the road was giving me away so they took me. I believed them and always thought I looked like an Indian.

Houses & Facilities

ANGELICA GURULÉ CHÁVEZ:

We lived in several houses over the years. When I was very young we moved from Belen to Albuquerque. We traveled by covered wagon and stopped to sleep that night in Isleta pueblo, and the Indians there were so nice to us. In Albuquerque we lived in a two-room shack. It was papered with newspapers to cover all its cracks. It was kind of fun to read all those words on the newspapers so I didn't mind that the shack was papered with newspapers.

We had oil lamps for lighting. At night we would all gather around one lamp. They don't give off much light, but we thought they did at the time. We didn't have bills—no gas bills or water bills or any of those. We didn't even know what they were.

MARCELINA MIRANDA CHÁVEZ:

In the first house we lived in in Las Nutrias, we had a well. The water was drawn with a bucket tied to a rope. One time during a drought, my dad brought the cows to the well so we could draw water for them. It was a job trying to get enough water for all those thirsty cows. We couldn't draw it fast enough. Our arms got really sore.

By the time I was four or five years old I washed dishes. I could not reach the table, so I had to climb up on a small box and my mother would get a big pan of soapy water for me since we didn't have a sink. When my

Drawing water from the family well. Neg. No. 000-289-0218. Courtesy of the Center for Southwest Research, General Library, University of New Mexico, Albuquerque, New Mexico.

sister would leave me to clean the kitchen by myself, my mother would call me "La Cinderella."

Once we visited some friends who had a small pump on their kitchen counter. We wished we had one so we wouldn't have to carry water from the well. Water was kept in a bucket hanging from the wall or from a tree outside to keep it cool.

Long ago when our father asked for water, we took him some and stood with crossed arms until he finished drinking. It was a sign of respect.

Sotera D. Martinez and Genovera M. Ortiz carrying water, Chimayo, New Mexico. Prudence Clark Collection, Accession No. 1975.001.034. Courtesy of the Menaul Historical Library, Albuquerque, New Mexico.

ANGELICA GURULÉ CHÁVEZ:

When we moved to our house in Belen we had a water pump, but the water was so hard that we couldn't wash with it. If you put soap to it, it would just get sticky, instead of foamy. So I was the one who had to carry city water from way across Main Street. We had to carry the water to wash and to use for everything for several years before we got city water.

At Casa Colorada our house had hard clay floors. They knew how to mix the mud with the clay and sand so the floors were just as hard as cement. We never had to scrub those floors, and they lasted for years.

MARCELINA MIRANDA CHÁVEZ:

Our adobe houses stayed pretty cool in the summer, especially if a room was kept dark through the day. My mother and sister and I took naps every afternoon in such a room. We slept on the cool floor with no rug.

We had dirt floors in our house. To sweep them, you had to sprinkle them down with water first. My dad grew the straw for the brooms we made and used to sweep.

The dirt floor in the entrance to our house would constantly wear down with everyone going in and out. I would make some mud and fill up the hole. Then I'd cut a piece of cardboard and place it by the door. After the mud dried, it almost felt like having a new kitchen floor.

There were a lot of winter storms where we lived so we would put blankets over the windows. One time I remember that it was so cold that not even the blankets helped much. We were scared we might freeze, *pero gracias a Dios que todavía estoy aquí* (but thanks be to God that I am still here).

In the summer the kitchen was very hot because of the wood stove. In the evenings we sat outside, but the mosquitoes were bad. In order to keep them away, we built a fire with *bunigas* (cow manure) in a big can. The smoke kept the mosquitoes away, but we all smelled like smoke until our next baths.

Every morning we took a big cloth to chase the flies toward the screen door to get them out. You can't imagine how many flies came in, even though we had a screen door, because we went in and out so often. There were probably so many flies because our corrals were close to the house. I tell you, we did not give a thought about germs back then.

We hung our rugs on the clothesline and beat them to shake the dust out. Four of us would hold a rug by its corners and shake it, since vacuum cleaners were unknown.

Sometimes we slept outside in the summer, watching the stars in the sky. The boys slept outside all summer long on mattresses laid on the ground. Later on they slept under a *carpa* (tent). One night my younger brother was sleep walking outdoors. He started walking toward our garden, but woke up when the goat head weeds started pricking him. He said he was scared to death when he woke up in the middle of nowhere. He ran all the way home. My mother always worried that it might happen to him again.

We slept on *colchones* (mattresses) that were spread out on the kitchen floor. We slept in a row: first my father, then my mother, then my sister Ramona, then me, and then my brother Pedro.

My mother made our mattresses by sewing two long strips of soft cloth together and putting small strips of cloth inside, about twelve inches apart. Then we put wool inside and tied it as we went along. Each mattress was about a yard wide. Every morning we took the mattresses, pillows, and blankets outside to be aired.

ANGELICA GURULÉ CHÁVEZ:

Our mattresses were about six inches thick and at night we'd just throw them on the floor and sleep on them. In the day we'd pile them on the bed. But the mattresses were very comfortable. On wash day we didn't have sheets to wash because we slept on the bare mattresses. After a while, mother would take the wool out of the mattresses and wash the mattresses. She took the wool out and beat the wool with sticks called *barras*. Then she'd put the wool back into the mattresses. You had to be sure that you spread the wool out evenly in the mattresses or the mattresses would look funny and be uncomfortable to sleep on. Every once in a while mother would also wash the wool. She had to wash it in the summertime or else it wouldn't dry before it was time to sleep on it again that night.

Food and Cooking

ANGELICA GURULÉ CHÁVEZ:

People were very poor, but we always had a lot of things to eat. We always had milk and eggs and chickens. In the summertime my dad had a garden. He grew lots of melons and cucumbers. The neighbor kids always loved to come to our house in the summertime because we always had melons and their parents didn't have melons, but we always did.

Every family had its own *chile* patch. We had to depend on rain and water from the *acequia* (irrigation ditch) to water the crops. One particularly dry year there wasn't enough water from the rain or the ditches so my dad put a hand pump in the middle of our *chile* patch. We each had a bucket and a tin cup and after we drew water from the pump, we'd give a little water to each plant just to keep it alive until the rains came. We were kept busy keeping those *chile* plants alive. We could lose much of the other crops, but we had to save the *chile* because everyone needed their *chile*.

For cooking we had very few pots and pans. We had an iron skillet. We used to make our *chile* and our *chaquegue* in it. We really treasured that one cast iron skillet. Otherwise, we had mostly enamel wear, the kind that chips all the time. We didn't have anything breakable because they would have been broken pretty quick. (We were usually out of glasses because they got broken.) So we had mostly enamel wear. It was really grand to have something aluminum.

Everyone cooked beans every day. The first thing the adults did when they got up was to clean the beans and put them to boil for about three hours.

MARCELINA MIRANDA CHÁVEZ:

We only had a small, four-burner wood stove. When the *peones* (hired field help) were working for my dad or when we had company, my mother started cooking from early in the morning. We didn't have a refrigerator, so we made fresh beans and *chile* for every meal.

ANGELICA GURULÉ CHÁVEZ:

When we ate beans and *chile* we didn't need any silverware. We made our own silverware out of tortillas by making *palitas* (little shovels) and using them to dip into the beans and *chile*. We had less silverware to wash that way.

We used to roast *chile* in the hornos, and then we'd peal the *chile* and dry it. We didn't have any freezers. We dried the red *chile* and made it into *ristras*—real *ristras*. Now if you get half a *ristra* they call it a *ristra*, but it isn't. We had really big *chile ristras*.

In the winter we'd have ground *chile* that we had ground with the *machinita* (little machine). Everyone ate *chile*, even the little ones when they were old enough.

Everything that could be dried was dried up in the summertime so we'd have lots to eat in the winter. We dried many fruits like apples and peaches. We also dried beef into *carne seca* (jerky). I remember they'd pound the jerky with a hammer and a little piece of rail, and then they used to make *chile*. Oh, it was so delicious. Everything that was made with pounded jerky was delicious.

MARCELINA MIRANDA CHÁVEZ:

By the time I was fifteen I had made my share of *tortillas*. I had started at a very young age, with my mother telling me the measurements and giving me instructions. My mother was a good cook, and I learned so much from her. Her *tortillas* were especially delicious. Sometimes in the middle of a meal the big pile of *tortillas* was almost gone and someone would say *"estan doblando."* This expression came from the old tradition that when someone died, the church bell would be rung slowly several times. In our house it meant that the *tortillas* were finished, or coming to an end.

ANGELICA GURULÉ CHÁVEZ:

We always had *tortillas*, and we'd put *chile* on them or beans or just plain lard with sugar for a dessert. My mother was an expert at making corn *tortillas*, making them three times a day. She made the best corn *tortillas* because when she was growing up her family had a lot of corn, but could not afford to buy much white flour for flour *tortillas*. When we'd fuss about cooking, she'd say, "I don't know why you fuss when it's time to cook. As long as you have something to cook." She was just grateful to have something to cook.

I also liked white cheese. They made *cuajada* of milk. They'd heat the milk and pressed it and make it into white cheese. That was a real treat.

For dessert and snacks we had parched corn, dried apples, dried peaches, or a sweet rice pudding. My dad used to buy *miel* (corn syrup) that was really a delicacy. We went through a gallon of *miel* in two days, we all loved it so much.

MARCELINA MIRANDA CHÁVEZ:

When I was very young we used a *molino* (grinder) to make coffee. We'd put the coffee beans in a little door in the grinder and hold the *molino* between our legs as we sat on the floor and ground the coffee by hand. At times I'd get sores or a rash on my legs. I didn't know ground coffee was sold in the stores. It would have been too expensive for us anyway. We made coffee in those great big coffee pots every day. We kept adding ground coffee every day, not emptying the old grounds. At the end of the week we would wash the pot and make coffee with new grounds. We did this to economize.

Hygiene

MARCELINA MIRANDA CHÁVEZ:

A bath was a must every Saturday. We had no indoor plumbing so in the summer we heated our bath water on our wood stove. The tub we used was so small we could barely fit in it. Our neighbors had a big oval tub, and we wished we had one, too. We never did. Sometimes we took baths in the *acequia*, but it was scary because the water was sometimes rushing very fast.

We washed our faces in a *bandejita* (small basin). We did not have many hand towels so we shared what we had. By the time I got to wash my face in the morning, I could not find a dry spot on those little towels.

We didn't have toothbrushes. We used a piece of white cloth with baking soda as toothpaste and salt water to clean our teeth. My father never owned a toothbrush and, except for one molar, still had all his teeth to the day he died at the age of seventy-five.

ANGELICA GURULÉ CHÁVEZ:

Every house we lived in had a piece of a mirror inlaid in a wall. It was placed too high for some and too low for others, but we'd adjust. Hung close to the mirror would be a horse tail and that was where we kept our combs. Everybody in the family would comb their hair at the mirror and then they'd put their combs right back on the tail.

MARCELINA MIRANDA CHÁVEZ:

We went outside to the privy, regardless of the weather. We used catalog pages for toilet paper. We threw cinders in the privy to keep it from smelling. We really didn't mind it. We were young.

Treating the Sick

MARCELINA MIRANDA CHÁVEZ:

My dad planted a lot of herbs that we used to treat sicknesses. For fevers, we used asafran. for stomachaches, we used *yerba de manzo*. And so on and so on.

ANGELICA GURULÉ CHÁVEZ:

My Tía Valentina knew a lot about herbs. If you had a stomach-ache or other ailment she'd pull up her long skirt and find the right herb from a bag tied around her waist. She always wore a black shawl over her head and long skirts with herbs in a bag.

MARCELINA MIRANDA CHÁVEZ:

We hardly ever went to the doctors because they were so far away (although some made housecalls) and so expensive. My dad didn't go to the doctor because he was never sick until three months before he died. My mother only went to the doctor when she was seriously ill with arthritis and was often very weak and sleepy. I suspect she had what I have: diabetes. She went into a coma in 1944 and died soon after. The doctors back then never discovered what was wrong.

Shoes and Clothing

MARCELINA MIRANDA CHÁVEZ:

I only had two dresses for school when I was in the lower grades. When I got home each day, I would take off my dress and hang it up or wash it for the next day.

ANGELICA GURULÉ CHÁVEZ:

My mother made most of our dresses on a treadle machine. Everyone had a treadle machine. We had a dress to wear to school, and we'd come home and change into an old dress. We used to have one needle. Every time my mother needed a needle she'd say, "Where is the needle." And we had white and black thread. There was no such thing as colored thread back then.

One time my sisters and I ordered some dresses from the mail-order catalog. The dresses were three for a dollar, and I'm sure we specified the sizes for the three of us to each have a dress. When the package finally arrived, we went to the post office to get it. We were so excited that we couldn't wait to get home to open the package so we opened it on the way. But the dresses were all the same size. We were so disappointed because that meant that they would only fit one of us.

MARCELINA MIRANDA CHÁVEZ:

One day my mother said I could choose a new dress from the store.

Instead, I cut out a picture of a dress I wanted from a mail order catalog. Usually, my parents ordered what I asked for, but if the catalog store was out of a particular item, they'd send another. If I did not like the dress they sent, I made it a point to wear it out so I could order a new one as soon as possible.

Whenever I got a new dress, my mother would measure it, pin it up, and hem it below my knees. Later, I'd move the pin a little higher. She never noticed, but my brother José would say, "Look, mother, where Lena is wearing her hem." José noticed everything we girls wore, including if our slips were showing or if our nylon stockings were crooked. My brother Eduardo never noticed these things, and could have cared less.

I always dreamed of having wide red ribbons for my *chongos* (braids). My dad used to say, *"Te vamos a comprar unos listones rojos."* ("We will buy you some red ribbons.") The day never came. He could not afford such luxuries. Instead, I used a strip of cloth for my braids and also to tie my hair back.

We traveled to Las Nutrias to a little grocery store. We'd buy some hose there. In those days that was a luxury just to have something new. I used to wear out my hose on the knees so on a certain day I would have to leave them home so my mother could patch them. When mended, it felt like I was wearing a new pair of stockings. When I was about fourteen or fifteen years old, we bought a pair of nylon hose and one pair of socks each for my sister and me.

My shoes were bought at Conant's store in Bosque. My older brothers wore shoes made out of pieces of tires.

Boys with little, if any, footwear. Photograph by Russell Lee. LC-USF 33, Neg. No. 12805-M4. Courtesy of the Library of Congress, Washington, D.C.

ANGELICA GURULÉ CHÁVEZ:

We had one pair of shoes each.

In the summertime we kids would go bare footed a lot. So when my parents said that we were all going to Casa Colorada, we'd all start looking for our shoes. "Where's my shoes? I can't find my shoes," we'd all say because we all lost track of them when we went so many days without shoes.

When it came time for our first holy communion, mother made our white dresses and veils, but we couldn't afford to buy shoes. So my parents bought us some white high-top tennis shoes and mother cut off the tops and put bias tape around the raw edges of each tennie. So we wore fancy dresses and veils and tennies. It was a letdown. Now I think if I knew of a girl making her first holy communion who didn't have money for shoes I'd buy her some shoes.

Work and Money

ANGELICA GURULÉ CHÁVEZ:

When we lived in Albuquerque, my older sisters worked as maids and my dad would buy and sell things. My sisters and I picked wild asparagus by the river and bundled them up to sell them to the Anglo people for five cents a bunch. We felt so rich. Everywhere we went people would buy them. The Anglos really went for them. That's how we made it in Albuquerque.

My dad did a lot of jobs, including farm labor in other states. Recruiters from South Dakota and Colorado and other places would get workers from places like Belen and Las Vegas and Taos. We all went with my dad for three years, twice to Colorado and once to South Dakota. We thinned beets and picked cucumbers, tomatoes, and green beans. We went to Colorado in a Model T truck and, later, in a car pulling a little trailer. One summer in Colorado we stayed by the tracks in a big tent my dad owned and cooked outside on an oil stove. We could take home all the green beans we wanted, and when trucks full of cantaloupes went over the tracks lots of cantaloupes would fall out and we'd go pick them up. We just had plenty of everything, but we did work hard. I'd write letters home to my friends and relatives. Writing and receiving letters was one of our favorite pastimes. I remember that stamps cost two cents each back then.

Until I started recalling these things about my childhood I never realized *how* hard my mother worked and *how* much my dad had to struggle to keep us fed and clothed. He didn't have his own land so for a while he planted a *tercio*, which meant that two parts of the crop were for him and one part was for the owner of the land. The land owners weren't always nice people. One year by dad had a really good crop of melons. The land owner came and took the best melons as his one-third of the crop.

My dad did pretty well anyway. We always had corn, and one time my dad sold tomatoes to the Becker-Dalies mercantile store in Belen. Other times he would take his *chile* and apples to sell up around Mountainair. He'd come back with beans and pumpkins, and maybe a sheep or a goat.

Money was very scarce. If you happened to have a nickel you were very rich. You'd make sure everyone knew you had a nickel, and you'd gloat, and they'd envy you. Probably you wouldn't sleep in the night thinking of what you'd do with your nickel.

We didn't think we were poor. All our friends and neighbors had the same conditions, customs, and the same food. We had everything alike. We didn't think we were any different or any poorer.

MARCELINA MIRANDA CHÁVEZ:

The men worked in the fields all day. My dad grew a lot of corn, feed for the animals, wheat, vegetables, *chile*, watermelons, melons, pumpkins, *caña dulce* (sugar cane), and other crops. The men came home for lunch, but in the afternoon my sister, Ramona, and I would take a big can of hot coffee and sweets or *sopaipillas* for their break. We probably walked about a mile or so to bring them their food and drink.

School

ANGELICA GURULÉ CHÁVEZ:

When some of us kids were ready to go to school, my dad traded some of his land in the mountains for some land in Veguita (which used to be called San Juan). That's where we started going to school. I was probably about four years old—not old enough to go to school, but they needed to fill a quota so I went to school early. We lived close to the school house, but we had to climb a little hill to get to the school, so we were always late.

When we moved to Belen the fathers would take turns driving the neighborhood kids to school in their wagons. The horses were fine until trains came by. Then they'd become alarmed and very agitated. For that reason, I always feared going to and coming from school.

We spoke English in school. If you didn't know English in the Belen schools they sent you to Miss Sanchez's classroom to learn it. She was a very kind, good teacher. I already knew English because my older sisters taught me, and I had learned it in my first year at the school in Veguita.

It was a rule that you had to speak only English in the Belen schools for fear of being punished. I never saw anyone punished for it, though.

For lunch at school, we brought green tomato jam spread on *tortillas*. I got to where I hated green tomato jam for many years. Now I love green tomatoes and can't get enough.

We had our childhood diseases. When one of us had whooping cough, everyone had whooping cough. When one of us had measles, we all had measles. When one had chicken pox, we all had chicken pox. The only good thing about it was that they would quarantine our house when we were sick, and we didn't have to go to school. So it wasn't bad having those childhood diseases.

MARCELINA MIRANDA CHÁVEZ:

I started school in Abeytas when I was about eight years old. When we moved to Las Nutrias I went to school there also. Apparently, there were not enough classrooms in our little school building so I attended school in a room of a local family's house.

In kindergarten we had a chart that showed pictures of different things, such as apples. The teacher would point with a ruler to see if we knew what each picture was. Sometimes we watched movies without sound and just used our imaginations as to what was going on.

When I was in the sixth grade we moved into the regular school building. I have only good memories of my teachers, including Mary Sanchez, Eulalio Barela, and everyone's favorite, Mrs. Jaramillo, the school superintendent's wife.

In grammar school we had to walk about a mile each way. Once, when my sister and I were walking, we begged my brother to let us ride our horse, Blue, home. He let us, although we later regretted it because Blue had no saddle. It was worse than sitting on a board. We asked my brother to let us down, but he wouldn't do it. Finally, he did and we gladly walked the rest of the way home.

On very cold days the boys would build a fire with tumbleweeds about half the way to school. We warmed our hands and kept on going. We wished we could at least have had a *caro entoldado* (covered wagon).

I liked school so much that I never missed a day. As a reward for my good attendance, one of my teachers gave me a little wax bottle filled with drinking soda. It was only about an inch high, but it was a thrill to me.

We brought our lunch to school, but never *tortillas* because we didn't want the gringos to see us. We took mostly fried potato sandwiches and almost choked to death if we didn't have water with them because they were so dry.

Meanwhile, at home, my mother enjoyed the quiet with no one fighting. She said that when we left for school the house was *sordo* (deaf, meaning there wasn't any noise). I don't know why we fought so much. I guess we were a normal family.

My mother would always see that there was something made for us to eat after school. It was often *tortillas*, but if there was nothing else we would peel a raw potato and eat it with salt.

At night, when I'd do my lessons, I worked by the light of our oil lamp or by the light of our wood stove. I had to help my younger brother, Pedro, and when he did not understand what I was trying to teach him, I would smack his head. My mother would get after me for this.

No one could help me with my homework. My older brothers were often gone and my parents knew very little English.

My dad was so strict that he did not allow us to wear lipstick. When I was in high school the girls would put some lipstick on me. When I was almost home I would start taking it off, but the more I tried, the redder my lips got. Fortunately, my dad did not notice. When I was twenty-one I wore lipstick and my dad stared at me, but did not say anything.

Animals and Pets

ANGELICA GURULÉ CHÁVEZ:

My dad always had at least two horses and a lot of times we had a cow, but not always.

MARCELINA MIRANDA CHÁVEZ:

My father and all my brothers rode horses. Once, one of my brothers was trying to tame a wild bronco named Rocillo. My mother almost had a heart attack every time he put blinders on the horse and prepared to ride him. No sooner was my brother on when he would be bucked off. Rocillo was really wild.

We also had Blue. He was very tame and listen to this: his real color was red. It never dawned on me why he was named Blue.

We had a favorite cow named La Canela (Cinnamon). We all loved her. She was very gentle. One time all the men were away at work, and my sister and I tried to milk the cow. She was very tame, but we tied her hind legs and she got mad and started kicking all over the place. We never got to milk her that day or ever.

ANGELICA GURULÉ CHÁVEZ:

We also had several chickens so we'd have eggs for breakfast.

Boy caring for chicken. Neg. No. 000-289-0259. Courtesy of the Center for Southwest Research, General Library, University of New Mexico, Albuquerque, New Mexico.

MARCELINA MIRANDA CHÁVEZ:

Sometimes we didn't find all the chicken nests and the chickens would surprise us with as many as a dozen *pollitos* (chicks). They were the cutest things—all different colors. The mother would call them to eat, shielding them under her wings, just like a mother. To feed them we had to grind the corn so they wouldn't choke.

When a cow or sheep gave birth and the mother died, their newborn offspring were called *pencos* (orphans). We had to feed them milk from a bottle. We made the nipple for the bottle out of the inner tube of a tire. If it was during the winter, the borregito (lamb) or becerrito (calf) was wrapped in a blanket and laid by the stove. I used to hate that because it sometimes cried all night. It also stunk.

My sister loved dogs and cats. Sometimes she would bring a puppy inside, and it would whine all night. Then she always forgot to feed these pets. So yours truly always fed them because I could not stand to see a hungry dog or cat. We had several dogs at different times: two Fidos, a Kino, a Turko, and so on. I would even pull off their fleas. We had a big, beautiful dog and one time a porcupine got a bunch of quills in him. We tried to remove them, but couldn't and we finally had to shoot him. I felt so sorry.

Sharing

MARCELINA MIRANDA CHÁVEZ:

My father gave everything to anybody. He never took advantage of anyone. He was honest, kindhearted, and compassionate. But he expected others to respect his property. For example, he would not let our cows into somebody else's property, and he expected the neighbors to do the same with their cows and his property. My father used to say, *"El que anda por pies siempre le va bien."* ("He who walks in a right path will never be in danger.")

When I was very young a lot of homeless men known as tramps used to stop at our house to ask for food. I believe the reason we had so many men stop by was because we lived by a highway. My mother always fed them, but outside. Once my parents let a man who rode a horse stay in our house for about three days. At night we were afraid, and we would try to secure the flimsy door between our bedroom and his. He began to talk to himself so my dad told him he had to leave.

Another tramp threw his food away. Apparently he wasn't very hungry.

Then there was the tramp we called *madamas* who came around every year. He wore many layers of clothes and was very raggedy. Whenever we looked raggedy, my mother would tell us, "You look like *madamas*."

One tramp gave my brother, José, a little dried plant. When we put it in a bowl of water, it opened up and came alive. We had it for a long time.

A neighbor borrowed half a cup of beans from us every day. My sister and I would gripe, but my mother said she did it for the woman's kids. The neighbor just sat in the shade all day.

Peddlers

MARCELINA MIRANDA CHÁVEZ:

A fruit peddler often came by, although his oranges were usually dried and mixed with red *chile* in a box. We seldom bought from him, but when we did we would trade with *cueros* (skins) that my dad had dried from the cows.

One peddler used to sell different medical products. We did not especially care for him because he was so persistent. One time we saw him walking up to the house, and we locked all the doors and pretended we were not at home. (Otherwise, no one locked their doors in those days.) We had three outside doors facing the same direction, and all the screens were locked from the inside. He knocked, tried all the doors, and peeped through the windows. We heard him say, *"No estan aqui y todas las puertas atrancadas por dentro!"* ("Nobody's home yet all the door are locked from the inside!") We laughed at ourselves for being so dumb, but we never did open the doors for him.

Gypsies used to stop by all the time. When we saw them we locked the doors because my parents believed they would steal everything they could. My mother did not believe in fortune tellers, but they took her hand and predicted her fortune. She did not pay them for their trouble.

Fears

ANGELICA GURULÉ CHÁVEZ:

When my oldest sister, Tillie, wanted to get rid of us younger kids she'd say, "Here comes the *patipalo* (hobo with a peg leg). We were deathly afraid of the *patipalo* and under the bed we'd all go. She'd keep us there for hours until she got good and ready and then she'd say, "He's already passed by. You can come out now."

I was always afraid of thunder and dark rooms. Oh, it was really horrible for me to go into a dark room.

Family going to market. Courtesy of the Historical Society of Valencia County, Belen, New Mexico.

MARCELINA MIRANDA CHÁVEZ:

When we lived in Abeytas, we used to go to Las Nutrias in an *ambulacita* (horse-drawn buggy). My parents would sit in the buggy's high seat, while my sister and I stood in the back, holding on to the seat, or sat in the back with our feet dangling out of the buggy. We had to cross the Rio Grande, and to me it seemed scary because the river was deep. Before we would cross, I would be brought up on the seat with my parents, but not my sister. One time the water was so high that it covered all the back of the buggy, and my sister got her legs all wet. I don't know why she was not brought up to the seat with us. I think it was probably because the seat was not wide enough.

One time we had a rattler in our house. We found it hanging from the ceiling. We did not kill it, but we didn't go into that room. Finally, my brother killed it when he found it on the floor. I don't want to tell how he killed it, but he did.

Another time there was a snake in front of our kitchen door. Our house was shaped like an L, with all of the doors facing one side and all of the windows on the other side. So I jumped through the opposite window to avoid the snake. Those were the days when I could still jump and climb roofs.

Play and Entertainment

MARCELINA MIRANDA CHÁVEZ:

My sister and I each owned a cloth doll with a porcelain head. They cost thirty-five cents each. When we were pretending to baptize my doll by our well, my sister accidentally dropped her and cracked her head. I got really mad and went home. We also enjoyed playing hopscotch. We used a pretty piece of glass from a broken bottle to toss into the squares we drew on the ground.

ANGELICA GURULÉ CHÁVEZ:

We didn't have any dolls when we were growing up. Dolls were too scarce. We used to roll up a towel and make it into a little bundle. We'd wrap it in a blanket and that was our baby. We never picked those babies up—they'd just lie there.

We also played with paper dolls cut from the catalogs—ladies or men or children. We'd stand them up and cut clothes for them from the catalog and cut out furniture and make little rooms with the furniture. We really felt rich with all that pretty furniture from the catalog.

Our neighbors had a phonograph. I remember standing outside their open window and listening. If you had a phonograph it was really something.

MARCELINA MIRANDA CHÁVEZ:

I used to play marbles with my younger brother, Pedro, and jacks with my sister, Ramona. We played jacks with pebbles until one day my mother bought real jacks from a peddler that came to the house with things to sell. They cost five cents, and we were really excited.

I always wished for a swing like some friends had: an old car tire hanging with a rope from a tree. One day my wish came true. The tree we chose for the swing was a little ways from our house. That's where we always played house.

ANGELICA GURULÉ CHÁVEZ:

When we lived in Los Lecos there was a ditch nearby. For fun we'd go wading or swimming—depending on how much water there was in the ditch. We'd take a bar of soap and take a bath there. We used to spend so many hours in the water that sometimes our skin would get wrinkled. It was so much fun. All the neighbor kids got together and we'd say to their mothers, "My mom said if your kids could go swimming, we can go too." And then the neighbor kids would go to our house and say to our mother, "My mom said if your kids could go swimming, we can go too." We were kind of tricky that way.

My dad and mother never smoked and nobody in my family smoked, but when I was little I thought it was cool to see somebody smoking. So I used to roll my own paper and put it in my mouth. I thought the reason the *cigaro* got small was because the smokers bit it off every time they put it in their mouth. So I'd put it in my mouth and bite a little of it off and then take another little bite until it got small. I never did become a smoker.

Visiting

ANGELICA GURULÉ CHÁVEZ:

We used to go to our grandparents' house in Casa Colorada. We'd all pile into the wagon and it was a really nice trip. We didn't get to go very often. I remember grandma had a big box—I guess they call it a larder now—where she kept all the goodies. If she had *biscochitos* she'd have them in there, and she kept the sugar in there and the dried apples or peaches. The mice didn't have a chance with that box. I liked going to grandmother's house, and she'd sometimes give me biscuits or *biscochitos* or some treats like that.

Sometimes we'd go to my *madrina*'s (godmother's). I was her god-child. I remember going to spend time with her and sleeping over there and she loved me so much and I loved her so much. I remember that she saved a cabbage for me one time. I liked cabbage, and it was a special gift for me.

When we lived in Veguita I liked to visit my Tía María, my great-aunt. There were all adults in her house—two old maids and a bachelor and the father and mother—and I was pampered because I was little. They'd give me an egg and I'd take it to the little store and the man would give me a candy for it. Oh, that was a lot of fun. Candy was as scarce as dolls!

I also liked to spend time at my Tía Valentina's house. Her husband was always away taking care of someone's sheep so she was alone most of the time, and I'd spend time with her. She had the sharpest eyes and the sharpest ears you ever saw. She could hear something a mile off so we had to be really careful when we said something because she always heard it.

And she could predict the weather. One time Tía Valentina said, "Girls, you better bring in plenty of sticks and wood for the fire because tomorrow it's going to snow." Of course we laughed because we thought, "how does she know it's going to snow?" Well, sure enough the next morning there was snow. How she knew I don't know.

MARCELINA MIRANDA CHÁVEZ:

I especially liked to visit one of my mother's friends because she had a rocking chair. When we arrived and we knocked on the door, I would get ahead of my sister so I could sit in the rocking chair first.

ANGELICA GURULÉ CHÁVEZ:

I miss not having the time to visit. Now we seem too busy to visit anymore. Maybe it's because of the telephone. You can get on the telephone and visit. The more conveniences we have today, the less time we have to visit. I miss that.

MARCELINA MIRANDA CHÁVEZ:

When my parents had company we weren't allowed to stay in the room where the guests were. I used to peep through a crack in the door to see what was going on. I liked to listen to what they were saying. You could say I was a brat, but I was just curious.

We always served our guests coffee and pastries or jelly and *tortillas*. Cookies were hidden for whenever we got company. I always managed to find them in a trunk under all the clothes, and I would eat a piece every chance I got. When our company came my mother couldn't find the cookies and would ask us who ate them. Everyone would say they didn't know. I said I didn't know either. My mother did not get mad.

We had so few treats that we used to save our chewed gum, sometimes under the table, sometimes in the cupboard. You see, we couldn't afford to throw it away.

Our neighbor came to visit my parents nearly every night. He talked about the same things all the time and stayed until midnight. None of us could go to bed until he left because the mattresses had to be spread out on the floor in that particular room. Also, we had to say the Rosary and our prayers after he left. We never said anything to him because he was a widower and was probably lonely.

Dances and Dating

MARCELINA MIRANDA CHÁVEZ:

There were dances every Saturday night. My two older brothers would want to go so my father usually sat by the kitchen wood stove with his hat over his forehead. One of my brothers would go by and motion to us that my dad was mad. My brother would then tell me (I was in my teens by then) to ask my dad if they could go to the dance. He would say no. Then in a little while he would say, "Tell them to go, but don't get in trouble *y no se esten hasta que raspen*" ("and don't stay until it is finished"). They got ready, and I would always button their sleeves for them and shine their shoes for a dime. My mother ironed their shirts with starch and pressed their dress pants with cleaning fluid.

When I was very young we only went to a dance once a year for the community *fiesta*. I did not know how to dance, so I sat with my mother. Later, when we were about fourteen or fifteen years old, we were allowed to dance, but my father would sometimes go with us. Once, at a dance in Veguita, my sister was dancing with the boy she later married. My father saw her talking to him and would you believe he walked to the middle of the dance floor and told her, "Let's go home. You know how I don't like for you to carry on such conversations." Embarrassed, my brother and sister and I left.

ANGELICA GURULÉ CHÁVEZ:

When I was older, we wanted to go on dates, but Spanish people didn't allow their girls to date without permission from the girls' parents. But we managed to date anyway. We would say we were going to work, and we would go on a date instead. Sometimes my dad would be going to bed and we'd hear his shoe drop and we'd wait around and listen till we heard the other shoe fall. Then we knew it was safe to sneak off to meet our boyfriends. Maybe that's where the expression "waiting for the other shoe to fall" came from. We sure had a lot of nerve.

Special Days and Events

MARCELINA MIRANDA CHÁVEZ:

Once a year the *maromeros* (entertainers) came to our small community, and we really got excited. My parents always took us. It would cost about twenty-five cents each, but my father used to trade a cow skin for tickets for our whole family. The *maromeros* performed in a big dance hall. We saw magicians, clowns, acrobats, and one particularly fat man named *El Tamborino*. We were amazed at the performers' tricks, such as pulling rabbits out of hats, eating fire, and cutting a woman in a box in half. Later, the box would be opened and she'd jump out all in one piece.

Audience at a traveling show. Photograph by Russell Lee. LC-USF 34, Neg. No. 37109-D. Courtesy of the Library of Congress, Washington, D.C.

Once, our neighbor invited my sister and me to go to the circus in Belen. Our neighbor rode the camel, but we didn't. It would have been really nice, but the circus people got into a big fight and soon the camels, elephants, and other animals were running loose all over the place. The circus people hit each other with the pipes that held up the tents. We left in a hurry.

ANGELICA GURULÉ CHÁVEZ:

Let me tell you about the *fiestas* in Belen! The Belen *fiestas* were every fourteenth and fifteenth of August. There was really a lot of action then. A lot of people would come from California, and they'd bring their brand new dresses for *fiestas*, and they'd show each other their dresses. Whenever you tried to go anywhere in town the streets were wall-to-wall with cars because people came from everywhere to the Belen fiestas. There was a lot of traffic at our house. People came from Casa Colorada—all the relatives came to stay at our house for *fiestas* and there was a lot going on. The women used to make bread and *biscochitos* and *empanadas* and *tamales* and everything that was good to eat. It was really a big thing. There was no carnival back then. There was a lot of eating and dancing under the *carpas* (pitched tents) and people had lots of fun.

MARCELINA MIRANDA CHÁVEZ:

On Christmas eve we hung a little match box from the *vigas* (eves) outside our house for Santa Claus. We did not have stockings to hang, although I always wished for some. Later I would check the box, and all I would find was a *biscochito* (cookie). I would say I didn't want a *biscochito* because we already had a lot of them in the house. My dad would say that Santa Claus was very poor that year.

But on Christmas morning we would each find twenty-five cents in our shoes. It was very exciting. We would count all the things we could buy with that money: an ice cream cone for five cents, candy, little bottles of soda, and still have change left.

On Christmas eve and on Christmas day we went to church. When we walked to church, my mother called me her *bordoncito* (little walking cane) and held on to me. I was very, very young.

When I was small, I would always fall asleep on my mother's lap in church, but not on Christmas because I was too excited. After church on Christmas, my sister and I went from house to house asking for treats, which was the custom then. We got a lot of candy and *empanadas* (fried pies) and *pastelitos* (little square pies).

When my brother Jacobo was fifteen, he was very sick and my parents bought a Christmas stocking to hang at the foot of his bed. On Christmas day he found lots of candy in the stocking. He divided it with the rest of us. He died a few weeks later, on January 13, 1937.

For Easter, we did not decorate eggs. Instead, we made a small hole at one end of each egg and emptied it out. Then we filled the eggs with jelly beans and hid the eggs. Whoever found the most eggs got a prize. It wasn't much of a prize, but it was exciting to us.

Eduardo Chávez, Lena's older brother, asked Angie's father for formal permission to date his daughter in 1940. Four years later Angie married Eduardo in Belen, thus becoming Lena's sister-in-law. Eduardo and Angie raised four children of their own: two boys and two girls, including Rena, for whom this book is dedicated. Eduardo and Angie continued many of the customs of their Rio Abajo childhoods. But, as a mother, Angie made sure that her children were never afraid of thunder. In fact, to this day Angie and her children enjoy hearing thunder because it often means that precious rain is on the way.

Lena graduated from La Joya High School in 1945. She worked for the Community Action Program in Grants and Los Lunas for twenty-five years. Now the sole survivor of her large family, she lives in retirement in Rio Communities, New Mexico.

LULA COLLINS DAUDET & RUTH COLLINS ROBERTS
HOMESTEADING ON THE PRAIRIE[1]

Lula and Ruth Collins were sisters in a farming family of twelve children, eleven of whom lived to adulthood. Their parents, the Reverend James S. and Effie Blanche Collins, were living in Oklahoma when they heard glowing reports of the opportunities for homesteading in northeastern New Mexico. Homesteaders filed for sections of government-owned land with the understanding that they would live on the land and develop it ("prove up") over a period of five years. If they were successful, the property was theirs to keep. If they failed, the property reverted to the federal government. Some families succeeded, but many more failed because the odds (in natural and economic forces beyond their control) seemed stacked against the average farmer with his meager means.

Ruth Collins, the family's third child, was five and Lula Collins was just a baby in 1915 when their courageous parents took on the challenge of starting a homestead and "proving up" in Union County. The girls later recalled some of their fondest memories of their homesteading lives in a new, often hostile land.

Boxcar Home

In the early part of the second year in our new country, an abandoned railroad car was moved to the site of the homestead and became home to the family with their few belongings. Mother deserves laurels for the home she made in that boxcar.

Trying to fit a family of seven into a boxcar house took some doing, but Mother was ingenious. Soon three iron bedsteads were fitted into the corners—one, a double bed for Mother, Daddy, and Baby Louise; and two small ones where two children would sleep in each. On the big double bed went the feather mattress. Thin cotton mattresses were put on the two small beds. Around the double bed wires from the ceiling held another wire on which was draped a curtain. The parents must have privacy. A big cook stove, a homemade table, some trunks, a water stand made from a box, a dressing table (also a box), and a small mirror on the wall above the dressing table: these comprised the necessary furnishings. Two luxuries—a sewing machine and an heirloom secretary [writing desk]—had come all the way from Oklahoma by train and then had been carted by wagon over the rough roads. They were highly prized. . . .

[But our] most precious possessions were our books. Two sets of encyclopedias were stored safely on the shelves of the secretary. . . . The Bible, the *Denver Post*, and some religious magazines were our other reading materials. We had no money to buy newer books. . . . . We were delighted when Mama had time to read to us. . . . Our books added not only physical beauty to our stark homestead shack, but they also added enrichment to our simple lives. . . .

The inside of the boxcar had been papered with durable pink building paper, and the outside was covered with heavy tar paper. Where the cracks were wide and drafty, extra strips of the tar paper doubled protection against strong winds and blowing snow. . . .

This boxcar shack was completely isolated on the prairie. It had not even a barbed wire fence to protect it from the range cattle that roamed freely over the country until roundup time. The ranchers had arrived first and claimed the land for their cattle. Mama used to be very nervous when she would feel the shack shaken by the huge red bulls rubbing against the walls to scratch themselves. . . . . The first improvement Daddy made on the homestead was to build a fence around our 320 acres. . . .

In the ten years we lived on the homestead the boxcar house took on a different character from the lone little gray shack standing starkly on the prairie. After our first good crop, . . . Daddy built a long addition to the east side of the building. There were two rooms, one to be a new kitchen and the other, a long dining room. Later, another room was added to the north and it became a bedroom for our parents. Privacy at last! . . .

We dug flower beds by the south and east windows and planted sweet peas and hollyhocks. Water was too precious to be used for flowers only, so they were given bath and dishwater. They grew well and certainly brightened the walls of that gray little shack. . . .

Farm & House Chores

The very first chore I remember having to do was hauling of fuel for heating and cooking. Jim was barely old enough to drive the team of horses hitched to the wagon. We would drive over endless prairie and pick up cow chips. We could afford a little coal, but it had to be hauled from Des Moines, fourteen miles away. Mixing coal and cow chips kept a good hot fire going in both heater and cook stove.

We hauled water from lakes nearby. Our drinking water we hauled from the well of a neighbor about two miles distant. Winter water hauling became a great game. We would drive the wagon, loaded with five barrels, out onto the thick ice. One of us would stand on the wagon and the other on the ice near the hole which we had to chop with an ax. The dipper would fill up a three-gallon bucket of water, hand it up to the one standing on the wagon, and he would pour it into the barrels. The bucket would quickly wear a thin coat of ice which had to be broken off by slamming it against the side of the barrel. . . . As we dodged the flying ice we would scream with laughter. . . . If we took too long to get home, Daddy seemed to know our game had gotten out of hand and would walk to the lake and persuade us rather roughly to get on with it.

Jim was a cheerful worker as well as a fun-loving fellow when there was time for play. He and I rode our horses many miles on Saturday during the winter when we could hunt rabbits and check the traps he had set for coyotes and skunks. The prairies, snow-covered most of the time, would reflect the bright sunlight. After a long day's ride, we would come home with sunburned faces. We often put lampblack under our eyes to protect them from the glare of the sparkling snow.

Getting up at four o'clock on a winter morning is not exactly fun, especially when the bedrooms were cold and one has to dress quickly and get to the fire in the kitchen. There wasn't much time to linger around the comforting fire, for finishing the chores and getting to school on time was the business of early morning.

Milking a herd of dairy cows morning and evening was a long and tedious task. Each of the five kids had to milk from two to five cows.

Then the milk had to be separated and the pails and separator cleaned before we could get ready for school in the morning or in the evening before we could settle down with our homework. But . . . we made games of our work. It was always a part of the milking job to haggle over who would have to milk the cows that always gave us trouble. Some of our cows would never submit to being milked without first being hobbled and tied securely to the manger. We had a barn, but the rain and snow sometimes made the lot and barn . . . into such loblollies of mud, manure, and straw that we had to wear rubber overshoes; and during the most inclement weather we would mire down on our way into the stable. . . . The slippery ground inside the barn made our work doubly hard. Passing behind some of the cows to reach others involved a risk of being kicked painfully. . . .

Work was a necessity for every member of the family. Even the smallest toddler could wipe dishes and dust. One thing that could be said for Mother. She could organize her work forces for maximum production. She knew who was working and who was shirking, and it took her a very short time to convince the shirker to join the working class. She did not tolerate sloppy jobs, and we learned early that doing something right the first time was better than having to do it over a second or third time, for she never relented until she was satisfied that we had done our best.

Months of summer away from school were anything but a vacation for us. As soon as the first crop peeped over the ground, little weeds peeped too, and then was the time for all of us who were big enough to hold a hoe to begin our summer work. No matter the crop, if there were weeds they had to be chopped down. In the row crops each of us took a row to hoe. I was always behind the others; and when Jim and Laura would reach the end of their rows, they took my row, one each for themselves and another for me, coming back to meet me. I could never stay even with them. They were patient with me and never scolded because I was so slow. . . . Sometimes we would finish hoeing one field only to start all over the same area, for the weeds seemingly grew right behind our hoes.

Children weeding a garden. Neg. No. 000-289-0244. Courtesy of the Center for Southwest Research, General Library, University of New Mexico, Albuquerque, New Mexico.

By the end of the weed season, some crops were ready for harvest. . . . Pinto beans, our chief crop, were ripe and ready to be harvested in September. The beans had to be pulled by hand from the hard ground. By harvest time the ground was baked dry. Eventually the farmers discovered that they could plow the ground, cutting the roots of the beans; then the vines could more easily be picked from the loosened soil. . . .

Picking corn was a rough, exhausting job. We often worked all day to pick a wagon load of ears, which were shelled by hand on a crude device. . . . The shelled corn was excellent feed for chickens and pigs. The corn cobs were stored in a dry place to be used for kindling fires. Nothing went to waste. . . .

Daddy Was a Methodist Minister

A minister is a minister is a minister! Although Daddy left his little church in Oklahoma willingly, he was still concerned because the people in our new pioneer communities had no one to hold Sunday worship services or to establish Sunday schools. So he did something about it. [Each surrounding community had] its own schoolhouse. Daddy would send word to a leading citizen to pass the message along that he would be at [a] schoolhouse to preach at eleven o'clock on Sunday. He did not have any means of transportation. . . . He was too considerate of his [work-horse] teams which had worked all week pulling a walking plow, so he would turn the horses out to pasture [on Sundays] and then walk to his appointment, some as far away as ten miles.

He would take a few songbooks and lead the singing himself without accompaniment most of the time. However, some of the one-room schoolhouses were proud to own a hand-pedaled organ; and someone in the community could play it, often poorly and with many wheezes from the worn instrument. Services ended promptly at twelve o'clock. Daddy always said that he thought twenty minutes was long enough for a minister to preach. "In that time a preacher can say everything he needs to say about his chosen topic once, and there is never a need to say it twice."

After the services were over, everybody usually gathered outside to eat the food which had been prepared and brought in huge baskets to be spread on tablecloths on the ground. Great quantities of many varieties of salads, meats, vegetables, and desserts would be served. Women vied with each other in cooking and baking. It was very important to remember that every lady wanted to be told how great her food was. . . . Although the men ate voraciously of all the food, each lady was made to believe that her own delicacies were preferred above all others.

After gorging ourselves to the limit, we all stood around visiting, reluctant to leave the fellowship of our neighbors and the people we met in the distant communities. Some of the men would like to have played ball, but Daddy never condoned Sunday games and the men always deferred to the preacher. They respected him highly and depended upon his service in sickness and in health. The children would run and play, and the teenagers slyly flirted with each other.

On long summer days, the people often gathered, after the festivities, to sing together.

These weekly events relieved the monotony of the long weeks of hard work, and we looked forward to being with our friends. . . . [In the afternoons we often] roamed the prairie for hours, enjoying one day of freedom from farm work. In our little homestead house we were very crowded, and our parents had little time to themselves. I think they always encouraged our taking long walks and leaving them alone. I often suspected that most of us were conceived during those long Sunday afternoons.

Being the only licensed clergyman for miles around, Daddy was often called upon to perform marriage ceremonies, baptisms, and funeral rites for complete strangers. Sometimes a couple would just happen by and ask to be married. The ceremony would be performed with Mother as official witness and always us children as curious spectators. Then the newlyweds would drive off in their buggy with no thought of reimbursement for the favor, because they probably had no means either.

After having lent his services freely time after time, on one occasion Daddy remarked to the couple, "You know, I have to mail in your marriage certificate to the county court house and it costs money."

"How much?" inquired the brand new groom.

"At least seven cents for postage," answered Daddy, whereupon the young man handed him exactly seven cents. The next couple who came solemnly handed Daddy seven cents at the end of the ceremony with no questions asked!

Holding funerals for friends as well as for many totally unknowns was sometimes a very difficult task for Daddy. We often went along to furnish the music. . . .

I think early religious sects based their disciplines entirely on the "thou shalt nots" and proceeded to add many taboos of their own, but some of the members at least took as their motto, "Thou shalt love thy neighbor as thyself." Daddy and Mother made it a rule never to turn away an itinerant traveler who would ask for shelter or food. The many times they and we took food to sick neighbors, helped with chores, and tried to minister spiritually have impressed me deeply throughout the years.

One time during my teens, when I had been left in charge of the younger children, I had to make the decision about helping the needy. At that time we had moved into Des Moines and here our home was a short distance from where the trains stopped and the many tramps got off to work the town. Some message seemed to have been left by sign or word of mouth, for these hobos always headed directly for our door. When one fellow came for a handout, I abruptly sent him on his way down the street.

I thought it was about time we sent out a different message. Looking out a few minutes later, I saw him empty-handed, coming dejectedly back down our street. Sam was a little boy, and I sent him out to see if it were the same man and to tell him to come to the back door for food. Sam ran out and shouted, "Hey, are you that [same] tramp? If you are, my sister said to tell you to come to the back door and she would feed you!"

Grinning unashamedly, the man said, "Well, I guess I am and I will."

I fed him royally, trying to atone for my not responding to his first request. Daddy was always very sure that if he was merciful to the poor and needy that somehow his family would be cared for. He often quoted, "I was young and now I am old and I have never seen the righteous forsaken nor his seed begging bread"; and although we never were rich, there was never a time when we were hungry or destitute.

Wild Animals

In the country where we lived were all kinds of wild animals and birds. Hawks, eagles, and other winged creatures would soar through the air creating intricate and artistic patterns in the blue cloudless sky. Ground squirrels, prairie dogs, badgers, and other rodents made their homes burrowed under the grass. Coyotes roamed the prairies, foraging at night and often howling forlornly, thus provoking nightmarish ideas in the minds of children. I remember being sent on an errand to our neighbor's house early one morning. After having been awakened in the middle of the night by the howling coyotes, I was so scared that I walked through the midst of a herd of wild range cattle for protection from the coyote which I imagined must be nearby.

Although we never saw a mountain lion or wolf and only one bear, we knew that they made their homes in the high reaches of the mountains surrounding us. A rancher had captured a black bear which had strayed from his mountain lair and was running in the pasture. The man had roped the small animal and staked him out in the yard where the bear became a curiosity for all the neighbors to see. Poor bear! One Sunday he was on exhibit all afternoon, and everyone for miles came to pay him a visit.

Skunks flourished in that area, as well as rattlesnakes, two most undesirable creatures. . . .

Pets

Our farm animals worked for us and we in turn lavished upon them all the personal affection in our child hearts. Horses, cows, and even chickens, goats, and dogs had pet names. We grieved for days when anything happened to one of our beloved animals.

When Laura joined the 4-H Club, she received a little calf which she had to care for until he was grown when he would be exhibited along with the animals of other 4-H Club members. She named him Money because of his glossy golden coat. One morning she noticed Money out in the garden methodically eating row after row of her prized vegetables. . . . Grabbing the nearest weapon, a garden hoe, she ran out and whacked Money on the head between his short horns. The handle of the hoe was more powerful than she had thought it would be, and heaving a long sigh, Money fell to the ground. Laura was so alarmed she ran crying to the house. "I've killed old Money!" she wailed to Daddy, With a big grin Daddy said, "Aw, tut! Look back in the garden!" Laura looked back and there stood a recovered Money, calmly demolishing another row of vegetables.

Fritz was a beautiful riding pony that Daddy had bought especially for James. He had been a racehorse and could glide sure-footed across the rocky prairie as swiftly and smoothly as the shadow of a cloud driven by the strong wind. . . . We not only loved Fritz, we admired him. He was a magnificent, spirited beauty. Because of his volatile nature, we sometimes called him Firecracker. When riding him, we had to be alert to his lightning-like movements, especially if he should suddenly spy a rattlesnake in his path or a large burrow. He could sidestep those dangers so quickly that he could easily unseat his rider, then go merrily on his way.

Jim loved him dearly and rode him as if the boy and horse were one. [But tragically Jim was killed in an accident while riding Fritz.] For weeks after the accident, Fritz would stand for hours in the pasture, his head down, looking so dejected just as if he were reliving the tragedy and regretting his part in it. But the sight of him was too much for Daddy, and he was soon sold. . . .

Tip was our dog. How we loved him! He was clever. We trained him so well that we thought he could almost talk to us. An unkind rancher harshly put an end to his life with poison. The inane excuse was that Tip was killing his calves. We knew that was not true, and the rancher soon discovered that Tip had not been the culprit. It had been the wolves coming down from Sierra Grande. But it was too late for Tip. I don't think we ever forgave that rancher for his hasty, fatal act.

Dust Everywhere

Blizzards, droughts, hail storms! Nothing seemed to daunt these hardy settlers. [There had to be] worse hardships than these to drive them away. The sterner their existence became the more adamant they grew, determined to make their permanent home in this land.

Then one spring after a very dry year the wind became more ferocious than ever. It was angry! Dark clouds would appear to look like rain clouds but would turn out to be dirt whipped up by the wind and by its centrifugal force become a whirling mass of soil to be deposited in drifts around every object: barns, houses, fence posts, rocks, shrubs. It was impossible to keep the house clean and even to keep the dust out of our food.

One Sunday when the wind was howling and swirling tons of dust in the air, we had to leave the house, take our food in tightly covered pots, and go around to the protected side of a hill in order to be able to eat.

Women despaired. Strong men lost their minds, health, many entering early graves, some becoming alcoholics, and others becoming the victims of suicide. Many people feared that we were in the last days of time. A neighbor boy about fifteen years of age went hunting one Sunday. He bagged a couple of jackrabbits and was taking them home when a storm suddenly blew up, engulfing him in darkness and suffocating dust. He became so frightened that he actually thought the day of judgment had come. He later was to tell us that he immediately threw away the rabbits because he feared to be caught hunting on Sunday when the judgment day had arrived!

Week after week, these phenomena would occur. Later in the season the wind would subside, but no rain or moisture would fall so that the tragic cycle was repeated year after year.

Finally, one by one the settlers gave up, leaving their shacks and their fields to the ravages of time and the violent weather. Hardly a trace of all that excruciating human endeavor remains. The prairie, the scene of all that warfare against the elements, is now a lovely, quiet domain for great herds of cattle. On our homestead site stands a lone sentinel, a sturdy cedar hitching post, staunchly defying the elemental forces which have obliterated every other trace of man's effort to tame the prairie. . . .

The Collins' homestead fell victim in the terrible Dust Bowl of the 1930s. James Collins became the pastor of the Methodist Church in Des Moines, New Mexico, until he and his family finally returned to Oklahoma. Both Lula and Ruth finished college, earned advanced degrees, taught school for many years, and married. They also became accomplished poets, as reflected in Lula's poem entitled, "Heritage."

> *I am part prairie to my bones.*
> *I spent my childhood*
> *Roaming a lonely, high prairie*
> *Seeking out its treasures*
> *To carry in my heart for unknown years to come:*
> *The tawny gold of the morning;*
> *The violet of the twilight shadows;*
> *The wind—always the wind—*
> *Singing a happy, sad song.*
>
> *Once a playground for children*
> *It has returned to its pristine state. . . .*[2]

6

RANCHING CHILDHOODS

FABIOLA CABEZA DE BACA:
WAITING FOR RAIN—AND STORYTELLING—ON THE *LLANO*[1]

Fabiola Cabeza de Baca (1894-1991) was born and raised on the
llano, *or plains, of eastern New Mexico. The Cabeza de Baca family ran*
thousands of head of livestock on the open range, struggling to make a
living in an arid climate that brought sufficient rain and good grazing in
some years, but serious dry spells and little grazing most of the time.
Fabiola's family was more fortunate than most, but, as the following pages
reveal, they were always at the mercy of the weather. It permeated their
thinking, their prayers, their yearly calendar, and even their view of the
moon and its heavenly travels. Rain, or the lack of it, thus dominated life
on the llano *and, as a result, Fabiola's childhood on her family's ranch in*
New Mexico.

We had just finished branding at the Spear Bar Ranch. For a whole week we had been rounding up cattle and branding each bunch as they were brought in from the different pastures.

As we sat out on the patio of our ranch home, I watched Papá leaning back in his chair against the wall of the house. He always did that when he was happy. The coolness of the evening brought relief from the heat and dust in the noisy corrals during the day.

The hard dirt floor of the patio always had a certain coolness about it. Just a few nights before, the boys had been in the mood to renovate it.

They brought a load of dirt, which we sprinkled with water and spread over with burlap sacks. We had such fun trampling it down. We made it a game by jumping on it until the soil was packed hard. This was repeated until we had a solid, even patio floor. Around it the boys built a supporting wall of rock filled in with mud.

Our home was a rambling structure without plan. It was built of the red rock from the hills around us, put together with mud. The walls were two feet thick. Viewed from front, the house had an L shape, but from the back, it appeared as a continuous sequence of rooms.

We had pine floors in the front room and dining room and the other rooms had hard-packed dirt floors. The *despensa* occupied a space of twelve hundred square feet. This room served as a storeroom, summer kitchen, and sleeping quarters when stray cowboys dropped in on a snowy or rainy night. The windows had wooden bars and so had the door.

The *cochera* adjacent to the *despensa* was a relic of the days of carriages and horses. When automobiles came into use, it became a garage, but we always called it the *cochera*. The front had two large doors which opened wide for the carriage to be brought out, and the hole for the carriage tongue always remained on the doors to remind us of horse and buggy days.

The roof on our house was also of hard-packed mud. Many years later, it boasted a tin roof. The dirt roof had been supported by thick rectangular *vigas*, or beams, which remained even after we had the tin roof.

All the rooms were spacious and our home had a feeling of hospitality. We had only the most necessary pieces of furniture. We had Papá's big desk in the front room and dozens of chairs with wide arms. Over the mantel of the corner fireplace, in the dining room, hung a large antique mirror. Grandmother's wedding trunk, brought over the Chihuahua Trail, stood against a wall. It was made of leather, trimmed with solid brass studs. We had no clothes closets, but there were plenty of trunks in every room. Mama's wedding trunk, made of brass, tin, and wood, was the shape of a coffer. Papá's trunk was very similar. We all had trunks.

The most necessary pieces of furniture were the beds. Of these, we had plenty, but many a night three of us slept in one bed, and if we were inconvenienced we were recompensed. Our sudden guests came from different *ranchos*, and they always had wonderful tales and news to relate.

Tonight we had no guests, We were a happy family enjoying the evening breeze with hopes for rain. The cowboys did not need chairs; they were stretched out on the ground with their hands clasped behind their heads as a protection from the hard dirt floor of the patio—a typical relaxation from the day's labors.

I can never remember when Papá was not humming a tune, unless his pipe was in his mouth. Tonight he was just looking up at the sky. As the clouds began to gather towards the east, he said, "We may have some rain before morning. Those are promising clouds. If rain does not come before the end of the month, we will not have grass for winter grazing. Our pastures are about burnt up."

From the time I was three years old—when I went out to the *llano* for the first time—I began to understand that without rain our subsistence would be endangered. I never went to bed without praying for rain. I have never been inclined to ask for favors from heaven, but for rain, I always pleaded with every saint and the Blessed Mother. My friends in the city would be upset when rain spoiled a day's outing, but I always was glad to see it come. In the years of drought, Papá's blue eyes were sad, but when the rains poured down, his eyes danced like the stars in the heavens on a cloudless night. All of us were happy then. We could ask for the moon and he would bring it down.

Good years meant fat cattle and no losses, and that, we knew, would bring more money. We had never been poor, because those who live from the land are never really poor, but at times Papá's cash on hand must have been pretty low.

If that ever happened, we did not know it. Money in our lives was not important; rain was important. We never counted our money; we counted the weeks and months between rains. I could always tell anyone exactly to the day and hour since the last rain, and I knew how many snowfalls we had in winter and how many rains in spring. We would remember an unusually wet year for a lifetime; we enjoyed recalling it during dry spells.

Rain for us made history. It brought to our minds days of plenty, of happiness and security, and in recalling past events, if they fell on rainy years, we never failed to stress that fact. The droughts were as impressed on our souls as the rains. When we spoke of the Armistice of World War I, we always said, "The drought of 1918 when the Armistice was signed."

115

We knew that the east wind brought rain, but if the winds persisted from other directions we know we were doomed. The northwest wind brought summer showers.

From childhood, we were brought up to watch for signs of rain. In the New Year, we started studying the *Cabañuelas*. Each day of January, beginning with the first day, corresponded to each month of the year. Thus, the first of January indicated what kind of weather we would have during the first month. The second day told us the weather for February and the third for March. When we reached the thirteenth of January, we started again. This day would tell us the weather for December. After twenty-four days, we knew for sure whether the *Cabañuelas* would work for us or not. If the days representing the months backward and forward coincided, we could safely tell anyone whether to expect rain in April or in May. The *Cabañuelas* are an inheritance from our Spanish ancestors and are still observed in Spain and Latin America.

From the Indians we learned to observe the number of snowfalls of the season. If the first snow fell on the tenth of any month, there would be ten falls that year. If it fell on the twentieth, we would be more fortunate: there would be twenty snowfalls during the cold months.

We faithfully watched the moon for rain. During the rainy season, the moon had control of the time the rains would fall. April is the rainy month on the *llano*, and if no rain fell by the end of April, those versed in astrology would tell us that we could still expect rain in May if the April moon was delayed. There were years when the moons came behind schedule.

Whether these signs worked or not, we believed in them thoroughly. To us, looking for rain, they meant hope, faith, and a trust in the Great Power that takes care of humanity.

Science has made great strides. Inventions are myriad. But no one has yet invented or discovered a method to bring rain when wanted or needed. As a child, prayer was the only solution to the magic of rain. As I grew older and I began to read of the discoveries of science, I knew that someday the *llano* would have rain at its bidding. On reaching middle age, I am still praying for rain.

My mind still holds memories of torrential rains. Papá would walk from room to room in the house, watching the rain from every window and open door. I would follow like a shadow. My heart would flutter with joy to see Papá so radiant with happiness.

Often before the rain was over, we would be out on the patio. I would exclaim, "We are getting wet, Papá!" "No, no," he would say. He wanted to feel the rain, to know that it was really there. How important it was in our lives!

After the rain subsided, off came my shoes and I was out enjoying the wetness, the rivulets. The arroyo flood would be coming down like a mad roaring bull. Papá and I would stand entranced, watching the angry red waters come down. The arroyo, usually dry and harmless, would come into its own, defying all living things, enjoying a few hours of triumph. A normally dry arroyo is treacherous when it rains.

If the rain came at night, we were cheated of the pleasure of enjoying the sight. Yet there was a feeling of restfulness as we listened to the rain on the roof. The raindrops on the windows showed like pearls, and to us they were more valuable than the precious stones themselves.

A few rains and then sun, and the grass would be as tall as the bellies of the cows grazing upon it. And Papá was happy.

A storm on the *llano* is beautiful. The lightening comes down like arrows of fire and buries itself on the ground. At the pealing of thunder, the bellowing of cattle fills the heart of the listeners with music. A feeling of gladness comes over one as the heavens open in downpour to bathe Mother Earth. Only those ever watching and waiting for rain can feel the rapture it brings.

Papá never saw the lightening. He was too busy watching for the raindrops.

On the *llano*, although rains come seldom, the cowboy is always prepared with his yellow slicker tied on the back of the saddle, always hopeful and waiting for rain. The straps on the back of a saddle were put there to hold the rider's raincoat.

As we sat on the patio that evening, the wind suddenly changed and the odor of rain reached our nostrils.

El Cuate, the Twin, who was the ranch cook, spat out a wad of tobacco as he said, "I knew it would rain before the end of the month. The moon had all signs of rain when it started. The signs never fail."

We were always glad when El Cuate spat out his tobacco. We knew he was in the mood for storytelling. What stories he could tell! There were stories of buffalo hunts, Indian attacks, about Comanche trade, of rodeos and fiestas.

El Cuate was an old man, and he had a history behind him. He was a real western character reared on the *llano*. To me, he seemed to have sprung from the earth. He was so much a part of the land of the *llanos* that he might have just grown from the soil as the grass and the rocks and the hills.

Looks, he had none. He was short in stature, blind in one eye, with an aquiline nose and sensuous mouth guarded by a long tapering red mustache. His skin was tanned by the sun of the prairies and the wrinkles on it portrayed the endurance and hardships of his life. His hair was gray with signs of sandiness in it. His hands were rough and wrinkled, showing that his life had not been idle. He used his hands for talking as well as for working, so they were always in evidence; they were interesting hands.

My brother, Luis, rose from the ground and started to leave saying, "I am going to hit the hay. Today has been a day. I am too tired even to listen to you tonight, Cuate."

El Cuate laughingly answered, "You young fellows are soft, you can't take it. Take your Papá there, although he is still a young man he and I have seen some tough times. Branding today is play. You should have been part of the rodeos I experienced."

I could never let an opportunity pass of hearing his adventures when he showed signs of talking.

Before he had time to take another chew of tobacco, I said, "Please tell us about life on the *llano*, Cuate."

We knew we must make ourselves comfortable, for it might be months or years before he would be in a storytelling mood. Even Luis forgot he was tired and resumed his resting position.

Papá was a man of few words. The only time he became talkative was after a rain and then he would compete with El Cuate.

Tonight Papá was happy. The clouds were gathering in the east. This was a sure sign of rain before morning, so he made himself comfortable by leaning his chair against the wall. I knew then that he meant to stay up with us until the first raindrops came. Listening to El Cuate would help pass away the time.

I watched El Cuate take a chew of tobacco as I heard Papá start him off. "I believe it was in this spot or just where the east windmill stands that I was initiated into my first rodeo. I was fifteen years old and fresh from school."

"Yes, sir," replied El Cuate, reminiscing, "I remember that rodeo," and as if prompted, began a tale of a lifetime.

Fabiola, her Papá, El Cuate, and everyone on the llano *were thrilled by the prospect of rain and good grazing. Unfortunately, good years were the exception and two devastating droughts (in 1918 and from 1932 to 1935), combined with over-grazing and poor conservation practices, nearly destroyed ranching on the plains. Fabiola's father fell victim to these tragedies. But as Fabiola wrote in the final chapter of* We Fed Them Cactus, *"the land which he loved had sucked [his] last bit of strength. . . . Life so cruel and at times so sweet is a continuous struggle for existence—yet. . . . [o]ne has not lived who has not experienced reverses. Papá had a full life."[2]*

Fabiola studied at New Mexico Normal School (now New Mexico Highlands University), the Centro de Estudios Historicos (in Madrid, Spain), and New Mexico College of Agriculture and Mechanic Arts (now New Mexico State University). Earning her degree as a home economist in 1929, she spent her thirty-year career working among the residents of northern New Mexico villages. She died in 1991 and is buried on her beloved llano.

AGNES MORLEY CLEAVELAND
LIVE AND LET LIVE IN CATTLE COUNTRY[1]

Agnes Morley was born in Cimarron, New Mexico, on June 28, 1874, the daughter of William Raymond and Ada Morley. Her father was the chief construction engineer for the Atchison, Topeka and Santa Fe Railroad when that railway system built its tracks over Raton Pass and through New Mexico from 1879 to 1881. He later served as the manager of the controversial Maxwell Land Grant and as the editor of the Cimarron News and Press. *He died of an accidental gunshot wound in Mexico in 1883, leaving Ada a widow with three small children to raise. Moving to land her husband had purchased before his tragic death, Ada built a home and ran a cattle ranch in the Datil Mountains of western Socorro County.[2] As clearly reflected in the following pages from Agnes's autobiography, Ada taught her children to be brave, independent individuals on an often wild ranching frontier.*

Agnes Morley Cleaveland. Courtesy of the New Mexico Farm and Ranch Museum, Las Cruces, New Mexico.

120

If your home is in a canon it won't be long before you climb out to see what's on top. One day shortly after our arrival, Ray and I climbed the mountain at whose base our log cabin sat, confident that from its top we should look out over the wide world. We were disappointed. Another and higher mountain overshadowed the one we had so painfully scaled. We hadn't heart to begin the conquest of another just then.

"And you'd have found still another mountain back of that one," Henry Davenport told us on our return home, footsore and weary. Henry was supervising the building of [our] new house. "I'll take you up on the highest of 'em all some day when it's not so cold. It's Sierra Madre and we'll have to go horseback most of the way."

Sierra Madre proved to be not only Mother Mountain but pinnacle of enchantment. Rising baldly ten thousand feet into the sky, its peak above our local timberline, it hovers over its brood of lesser hills, the Datil Range. From its top we did indeed look out over the wide world according to the standards of our childish experience. . . .

"It's an awful big country." Ray had no better words to express his enthrallment. I had no words at all. I was taking that scene into my heart and soul as *my country* for so long as I should live. . . .

Building our new house was itself an adventure. It began immediately after our arrival. The logs were felled on the nearby mountainsides and dragged by ox teams to the site in the canon bottom, itself 8,300 feet above sea level.

Four expert axemen—superb craftsmen—had been brought from Michigan logging camps to hew the logs. The original ten-room house still stands, although, log by log, it has been moved to another site and enlarged, serving now as a tourist "motel." . . .

When the house was finally done, furnishing followed. First there came the library, begun by my great-grandparents, and added to subsequently by other generations of the family. Books came out to the ranch in wagon load lots. Walnut and rosewood furniture . . . arrived. There was the old Steinway in its rosewood case, and my mother's box of music. Itinerant piano-turners appeared only at long intervals, and soon the piano got so badly out of tune that my mother's trained ear could not tolerate its dissonance.

One day before my mother hid the key to the piano, a party of uncouth-looking men stopped and asked for water and general trail directions. By what they did *not* volunteer, we knew that they were undoubtedly an outlaw band passing through the country.

As they were preparing to leave, one of them, who was in every way as rough-looking as his fellows, spied the piano through the open door.

"Madam," he said, turning to my mother, "with your permission I should like to put my hands upon that instrument just for a moment." His voice had become that of an educated man. He strode to the piano, and then there burst from that long-silent box a flood of harmony filled with all the suffering-through-to-victory that makes music great. He played on and on. I remember the enthralled look upon my mother's face and the respectful silence of his companions.

Finally, with a crashing chord that seemed to cry defiance to the world, he arose and thanked my mother.

"You cannot know what this has done for me," he said. "I had quite forgotten—"

He did not finish his sentence, but bowed and walked out to where his horse stood with the others. Once he looked back as though to return, but, instead, squared himself in the saddle and, surrounded by his evil-savored companions, rode away.

But it was not merely the dissonance of the piano that accounted for its gradual disuse: more pressing but less aesthetic occupations soon engrossed my mother. Before we had been very long in the Datils she discovered how tragic had been the mistake of her second marriage. My stepfather vanished; and she who believed more than anything else in education and culture found herself marooned with three young children on a desert island of cultural barrenness, with no means of escape that would not sacrifice her entire investment. We became a sort of Swiss Family Robinson without a Rather Robinson to meet emergencies. She resumed the name of Morley, and the ill-fated husband's appearance upon the stage of our family life became a gradually receding reality.

Faced with the supervision of a well-stocked cattle range of a good many thousand acres, she rode and did her indomitable best to keep herself informed about what was happening to her livestock; but she was unable successfully to cope with the cattle rustlers who abounded and with the proclivities of open-range cattle to wander. That she survived the years that followed speaks volumes for her courage, her stamina, and her self-sacrifice. It would have been so very easy to sink under the all but overwhelming flood of hardships and disappointments that were hers.

For us children, however, the new life was from the beginning a sort of glorified picnic.

We had been but a day or two on the place when a stranger appeared. He was something of a shock to all of us. He looked as if he had been through some scathing ordeal, and his horse was an even more pitiable sight—staggering, hollow-eyed, and breathing with difficulty. In spite of the cold, he was sweat-caked, and as his rider all but fell off him, it appeared that the horse would go down too. I was standing close by, wide-eyed with interest mixed with pity. The man turned to me.

"Here, little girl," he said, "will you ride this horse around a few minutes so's he won't cool off too fast?" And without waiting for an answer he picked me up and set me astride the horse. "Just walk him about easy."

No one asked the man any questions. He ate in silence. At the close of the meal, he spoke with complete matter-of-factness. "I'll git a horse back to you if you'll let me have one—and how about trading hats with somebody?"

One of our less valuable horses was saddled for him, somebody gave him another hat, and he was in the saddle and gone, all within a few moments. "The little girl can have that horse," he called back, as he set out, a little too briskly for a man who wasn't afraid.

It was my first introduction to an outlaw. We were often to see others: western Socorro County, because of its wilderness, was sanctuary to many a man "on the dodge." . . .

I was walking on clouds. . . . The horse never recovered sufficiently to be of any value, but the experience was momentous for me. I had earned the horse by not screaming in terror when a fearsome-looking stranger set me for the first time on a horse's back.

A Morley child on burro. Cleaveland Family Collection, Neg. No. RG94-046. Courtesy of the Rio Grande Historical Collections, New Mexico State University Library, New Mexico State University, Las Cruces, New Mexico.

In addition to the outlaws, we had another uncertain neighbor—the Indian. If anyone imagines that the early settlers, by maintaining a proper attitude, could have lived in amity with the Indians, let him consider how little amity existed between the various Indian tribes themselves. From time immemorial, American Indians had lived by raiding, whether of the natural bounty of the land or the garnered resources of their neighbors. . . .

There were always rumors of Indian attacks, and frequent evidences that they had indeed attacked. On my first visit to the Los Esteros Ranch, our secondary headquarters over the Datil Divide, I was taken several miles "up the crick" to see "where the Injuns kilt them Mexicans."

With the physical eye, there was little to see—just two grave-shaped mounds of loose rock with rough wooden crosses at their heads and beside them a litter of iron junk, rims of wide-tired wheels, hub casings, bolts, those parts of a wagon that would not burn. . . . This is what the physical eye saw. The mind's eye saw the sudden dash of yelling savages from the timber beside the dim wagon tracks that were the "road," . . . saw the swift, terrible slaughter of the surprised and helpless men; saw the oxen driven away to their own later slaughter, leaving behind them the remnants of what had been human bodies and a fire that blazed fearsomely—with no one to see. Now I was seeing it through eyes that should not have been looking upon such sights. We mounted our ponies and rode away in silence.

While we were still living in the cabin, the Indian menace suddenly became very real. The Apache warrior Geronimo was making one last despairingly futile gesture of defiance to the white invaders.

One afternoon, a courier dashed in on a lathered and dust-caked horse.

"Geronimo is this side of Quemado!" he cried. "Gimme a fresh horse. I got to warn the folks in Nester Draw."

Ten heavily armed men were at the time engaged in laying up the logs for the new home. All out-of-door work was done heavily armed, and it would have appeared on first glance that no safer place could be found than behind those foot-thick logs guarded by crack marksmen supplied with ammunition to withstand prolonged siege. But unfortunately the half-finished house stood at the base of a steep mountain, and that mountain-side was strewn with boulders ranging in size from a water bucket to a boxcar. . . . . So, against the advice, even the pleadings, of the men, [mother] insisted upon taking her children and going down to Baldwin's [ranch], which sat well out in the open.

There had been but three horses in the horse pasture and the courier had taken one, so no mount was available for an escort to accompany us. I well remember the disapproval in the faces of the men as we set forth. But my mother was firm.

It was a ten-mile ride fraught with the ultimate of physical and mental misery. Two on a horse is never comfortable, less so when the pace is an unrelieved high trot, which was as fast as we could force our ponies to go. Lora, riding with my mother, valiantly stifled her moans, and the robust nine-year-old Ray gouged his fingers into my midriff as he clung to me, muttering child profanity under his breath as he bounced up and down on the stiff saddle skirts which projected beyond the cantle.

At the end of what seemed at least a century, we arrived at Baldwin's, battered and bruised and so exhausted we had ceased to care whether our end was brought about by an Apache tomahawk or by one more jounce on a pony's back. Lora's legs were bleeding where the leather had rubbed them, Ray's were black and blue, but no more so than my own waistline, where he had clung to me with that amazing strength. . . .

But we had reached safety—we hoped. Other settlers had already come in from distant ranches, and the place was overflowing with terror-stricken families. The younger children occupied all the beds. The next older group, of which I was one, were put down on folded comforter pallets on the floor. The women, with white, strained faces, wandered restlessly about. It was while lying on my hard pallet, aching to the very marrow and unable to sleep because of the pain, that I overheard the discussion in the adjoining room where the men were making ready their guns and ammunition.

It was carried on in subdued tones, and, moreover, we children were supposed to be asleep. But if I had had no disposition to sleep up to this moment, which I had not, certainly there was none afterward. I heard old Jim Wheeler delegated to use his next to last cartridge to shoot me in the head in the event the Apaches' ammunition outlasted ours. The last was for himself. . . .

But the Apaches did not go our way, after all, and with daylight came news that they were far to the south, heading for the Mexican border, having left a trail of unspeakable carnage behind them.

Also, with daylight came a new world to a child benumbed in spirit and in body, a world wherein life itself loomed as a blessing so great that nothing again has ever seemed very important by contrast. I rode back to the site of the new home a quite different person from the one who had passed over that trail a few hours before. . . .

[B]efore I leave the subject of adventures with Indians, I might note one of my own. First, the setting. The north face of the Datils breaks off sheer, in bluffs hundreds of feet high. At their feet lie the rough brakes of the Alamosa Creek watershed, gradually smoothing out into less broken country, with wooded patches pleasantly interspersed with small parks and swales and long gentle draws. . . .

I emerged from a juniper thicket into an open space; on my small buckskin pony I was a speck of humanity in a vast region of solitude. From the timber on the opposite side of the park a band of Indians rode out, in single file. Feathered and buckskin-clad, they came toward me with no break in the stride of their ponies. Although only a twelve-year-old, I was so enchanted with the pageant that it did not occur to me to be afraid.

Arriving at the spot where I waited—for I had stopped when the first Indian appeared—the leader of the band looked at me with an air of puzzlement and then circled his horse slowly around me. Each Indian that followed did the same: in a moment I was the center of a ring of horsemen who rode slowly around and around. Even though I had heard of this encircling maneuver as something Indians did before they attacked, it still did not occur to me to be frightened. I was as interested in the Indians as they were in me.

Finally I realized that the object of their interest was my blonde hair, which had come unbound and was hanging down my back in long wind-blown taffy-colored ripples; they were doing the equivalent of standing in line, that each might have his turn at a close-up view. After some moments of this silent riding in a circle, during which no word had been spoken on either side, the leader broke the ring and resumed the straight direction in which the group had originally been traveling, followed each in his place by the whole forty of them. I had even taken time to count them.

Almost fifty years after the event, I met an old and withered Indian garbed in a pair of faded Levi Strauss overalls and a frayed custom-made shirt, discarded by some white man. He could talk a little halting English. He asked me if I remembered meeting him and his band that day Piñon Flat. I grabbed his hand and pumped it, to his mild embarrassment. Navajo dignity precludes such behavior. But I was so delighted to meet the old patriarch that I forgot my manners.

Then he told me that mine was the first woman's blonde hair any of them had ever seen and that it had fascinated them beyond words. He looked at my graying short-cropped thatch and shook his head disapprovingly.

To change the embarrassing subject, I asked him how old he was. A faraway look settled in his dim eyes. His scrawny hands came up in a gesture of encircling a sphere the size of a grapefruit. "When I boy, the moon thees beeg," he said solemnly.

I could make my own calculations.

Ray Morley graduated from Columbia University (where he be-came a football legend) and returned to the Datil Mountains to expand and manage his mother's cattle holdings. Though well respected and successful for many years, his operation could not withstand the prolonged drought and economic problems of the 1920s. Heartbroken, Ray died an early death in the 1930s.

After attending Stanford University, Agnes married Newton Cleaveland in 1899 and lived in California for many years before finally returning home to New Mexico. She became an esteemed author of books, of which No Life For a Lady *(first published in 1941) is her most famous. She died on her beloved ranch at the age of eighty-three.*

WILBUR FRANKLIN COE
BRAVELY DEFYING HIS HANDICAP[1]

The Coes were a pioneer family. One generation of Coes had mi-grated from West Virginia to Missouri in the 1850s. The next generation migrated down the Santa Fe Trail to New Mexico. Frank Coe arrived in the territory in 1871, first settling in northeastern New Mexico and, by 1875, in Lincoln County. Unfortunately, Lincoln County was a powder keg about to explode into the territory's most famous county war.

Although he befriended William Bonney (Billy the Kid), a central figure in the war, Frank survived the conflict and continued his life as a rancher. Frank met seventeen-year-old Helena Anne Tully in 1880 and married her the following year. The couple had four daughters before the arrival of their first son, Wilbur Franklin Coe, in 1893.

[Frank Coe's] four girls grew, as he often said, like weeds on the banks of an irrigation ditch. Three years after the birth of Agnes, when Helena Anne knew her fifth child was on the way, she hoped and prayed that it would be a boy. Strong arms and bold hearts were needed on the frontier. To the joy of everyone, on October 4, 1893, I was born. Immedi-ately, I became the center of an adoring family even though I could not have been much to look at. I was named Wilbur Franklin, partly after my father, who began at once to make great plans for me at the ranch. My mother, who was deeply devoted to all her children, gave me all the care and attention possible. Josefa, the faithful servant who had been nursemaid for the older children, hovered over me in delight, I have been told, pouring forth endearments in her soft, mellow Spanish.

To understand better the illnesses of children, Mother continually studied her mail-order medical guide, *The Home Book of Health and Medicine*, for the services of a doctor were hard to get on the frontier. Her extensive knowledge was eventually drawn on over a wide area. When sickness struck, Mother was the first person called. Taking off with her guidebook and an interpreter, if necessary, she hurried to give whatever aid she could, and by prescribing simple home remedies, and urging stricter sanitation, she saved many lives in a settlement that had its unhappy share of diarrhea, dysentery, consumption, and other diseases that were often fatal to infants.

At home her children received routine doses of castor oil, which she constintently administered for all internal ailments—and woe to any of us who backed away from the spoon. For external troubles her stand-by remedy was coal oil, generously applied to scratches, bruises, bites, blisters, burns, and rusty-nail injuries. Although a strict dry, Mother would recommend whiskey for medicinal purposes; to make sure it was used only for that, she kept it locked in a cabinet. As regularly as the first green apples appeared, "cholera morbus" doubled us up with pains in our stomachs, so she had ready Jamaica ginger mixed with castor oil.

But there were many diseases against which Mother's home remedies were powerless. This became tragically evident after an epidemic of spinal meningitis struck the entire area of the three valleys. Since there was no known treatment for it the victims died like flies; Indians, Mexicans, and Anglo settlers alike. Once the disease struck, it was usually fatal. The Coe mothers, like all parents in the settlements, were deeply concerned.

At the time I was six months old. Before anyone else in the family noticed something wrong with me, Mother became aware of it. She studied her medical book constantly, waiting with terrified heart lest any symptoms of the dread disease appear. When spots began to appear on my body and I started having convulsions, the heartbreaking truth became known.

All she had to rely on was the medical book, for the nearest doctor was ten miles away at Fort Stanton. He could not make calls except in extreme cases. With the disease so prevalent, my case was only routine. Following the directions in her medical book, Mother put me into a tub of hot water, a treatment similar to that of Sister Kenny years later. This procedure went on day after day. Unquestionably, this way of caring for me, added to her dogged determination to save my life, brought results even though at one time my heart stopped beating. Mother, however, was one who preferred to render unto Caesar the things that were his and to God the things that belonged to Him, thus maintaining her deep belief in the efficacy of prayer, which probably saved my life.

As soon as possible the doctor from Fort Stanton came to the ranch. He could only marvel, as he looked at my feverish emaciated body, that there was the breath of life in me. At the time he prescribed nothing more than the treatments Mother was already giving me. At a later date he suggested that an electric current passed through my body might stimulate the lifeless muscles of my legs. To get me to endure the tickling sensation, my sisters joined hands with me in a circle while someone turned the crank which spun a coil inside three magnetos. The faster it turned, the more power it generated and my sisters and I screamed and tugged, trying to let go of each other's hands. I cannot say by what miracle it ever came about, but my body from the waist up was spared the ravages of the disease. And I retained partial use of my stricken lower limbs.

It was Mother who conceived the idea that the hot mineral baths of Pagosa Springs, Colorado, might be beneficial to me, so after another baby, Edith, was born in 1895, she decided to take me there. The springs are just over the New Mexico line not far from where the Tully family lived. This enabled her to visit with her family at the same time. At it was too much for her to make the trip with me alone, she took sweet-natured Winnie, who was only eight, to help look after me. Baby Edith was left with Aunt Phoebe. Dad took us in the carriage for the long, dusty four-day trip to San Antonio, New Mexico, to catch the train. When we reached Durango, Uncle Fred met us.

At the time of our visit Pagosa Springs was famed more for its mines than for its health-giving waters. Because there was more money in ore than in mineral water, promoters had done little to develop the facilities there. Coming from the underground extremely hot, the spring water had been piped into a trough to cool and from there it flowed to the bathhouse, which was little more than a shack containing some private baths and a steam room. No living accommodations worthy of the name had yet been constructed, so Uncle Fred fixed up some sleeping quarters for us in an abandoned schoolhouse. He rigged up a tent adjoining the schoolhouse to use as a kitchen.

In order to take all the advantage possible of her visit, Granmaw and Aunt Edith went to the springs with us and we made a family party of it. Granmaw Tully was suffering from inflammatory rheumatism, but she was too modest to go to the public pool where the rest of us splashed together so she soaked her aching joints in a private bath, wearing an old house dress over her underclothes and her long cotton stockings. With Winnie and Aunt Edith, Mother's younger sister, to look after me, I was taken to the public baths, where special care was taken to see that my muscles were exercised as much as possible. On ropes stretched across the water I began then to develop strength in my arms, which later became prodigious. But it always took considerable effort to swing my legs and walk. . . .

When our stay at the springs was over, we boarded the train for San Antonio, where Dad met us to take us to the ranch. . . .

As soon as my sisters were old enough, Dad taught them to ride and round up the stock. Annie early showed signs of becoming an excellent rider. To my mother's dismay, the girls preferred riding to doing ladylike tasks around the house. Although they cared little for books, Mother saw that they spent some time with them and with their musical studies, which at first was guitar and the rudiments of music theory.

Memories of Granmaw's piano were dear to my mother. She often yearned to run her fingers over its keyboard again. . . . One year Dad sold some crops to Fort Stanton at a higher price than he had expected and so he had some extra cash on hand. He asked Mother what she would like for the house. As she looked around at some of the boxes and crates that served as furniture she saw the obvious need for some new pieces. Yet the thought of depriving herself and her family of a piano any longer was an unpleasant one. She chose the piano and immediately wrote to her brother Kivas to select one and have it sent to El Paso, Texas, by railway freight.

After weeks of anxious waiting, the piano arrived in El Paso. Dad and Timio drove a four-horse team hitched to a heavy wagon the 170 miles to get it. . . . When the box containing the piano was safely loaded on the wagon, they started home. . . . Dad and Timio had no trouble on the return trip until they reached within a mile of the ranch. There had been torrential rains for several days and pulling up the last hill the wagon wheels bogged down to the hub in the heavy mud. The horses pulled and tugged as best they could but were unable to move the wagon. It was getting dark, so Dad and Timio unhitched the tired teams, mounted two of the horses, leading the other two, and rode bareback the last mile home.

Mother was glad they had arrived home safely but was disappointed that the Steinway grand piano would have to stay on the wagon overnight. Early the next morning Dad took fresh teams and brought the wagon and its precious load safely home. . . .

[T]he piano was unloaded and set up in the parlor. Mother immediately began to play and sing. This was the first piano in the valley and it brought pleasure to her family and to the entire community for almost fifty years. . . . [Somehow Mother] found time to give the oldest of us piano lessons. We all loved music. It was not only a means of passing lonely hours where ways of recreation were few, but also a part of living itself. . . .

About this time a dismal tragedy brought lasting and indescribable grief to the family. I was still quite young at the time. Dad had just returned from Fort Stanton in the afternoon with the mail. Part of his job was to carry the local mail to the fort to be put on the stage headed east; on his return trip he brought back the mail for the settlement. As he turned the sack upside down to empty it, he saw a yellow Western Union envelope that was used to mail telegrams that could not be delivered otherwise. It had on it the San Antonio, New Mexico, postmark, our nearest railway station.

I was playing at the woodshed with an old gristmill when Annie and Winnie came running to tell me the news. I could tell by their faces that something terrible had happened. Annie told me that Aunt Edith and Uncle Fred were dead. . . . It was some time before the circumstances surrounding their deaths were made known to us. The telegram was a week old when we received it.

We found out later that Aunt Edith . . . had set out with Uncle Fred in a light wagon to go to Aztec, a small village about twenty miles away, to transact some business. Their route lay across a ford of the Animas River, which at the time was very high. Even though they were both good swimmers, Fred must have surveyed the rushing water carefully before urging his team into it. But he evidently miscalculated the swiftness of the current and forced the horses into the deeper part. Too late he discovered his mistake. With a tremendous rush the swirling water overturned their wagon and engulfed them both. . . . From the evidence put together it was concluded that, in overturning, the wagon bed had been torn loose from the running gear and gashed Fred on the head, either killing him outright or knocking him unconscious. Edith doubtless was pinned beneath the bed and was drowned.

After Mother had partially recovered from the shock, she sent her brother Jim, who had come to Coe Ranch sometime previously to work as a cowboy, to Farmington to get Grandmother and bring her back to live with us. Part of Granmaw had died with the two children. . . .

At the end of her tiresome journey from the San Juan Valley, Granmaw walked stiffly from the wagon into the outstretched arms that awaited her at Coe Ranch. When I gave her the biggest hug I could, she kissed me on the cheek and said I was as strong as an old bear, which pleased me very much.

The day after Granmaw's coming, the family gathered in the parlor with joy and anticipation to welcome her into our musical circle. Although I was too young to join it yet, I waited impatiently for the performance to begin. After Dad had tuned up his fiddle, he turned to Granmaw and said, "It's been a long time since you played for us, Granmaw, and we're pleased to have you join the Coe orchestra. We'd like for you to take your place now at the piano and start us off with my favorite march."

Within her sorrowing heart Granmaw was carrying a grief that she took to the grave; yet she was determined not to allow it to cast a shadow over the lives of her children and grandchildren. Smiling bravely, she walked over to the piano and twirled the stool until it was the proper height. As she sat down she said, "When I had to leave my own piano behind, it was a great consolation to know I would find another at Coe Ranch. Thank you for inviting me to become a member of your orchestra."

From then on Granmaw was a participant as well as a strong promoter of music in our valley. She was strong in her belief that it was a binding force that helped hold people together. No matter how much the men wrangled over water rights or fences during the week, come Saturday night the people would all get together for a dance. On Monday they could take up their arguments anew. . . .

While still not old enough to take much of a part in the musical performances, I had my own problems, some of which were knotty ones. Mother had seen to it that my life was made as nearly normal as possible, so I took part in all the games and sports my sisters and I could devise. But I always had to strive hard to do the things other children did easily. Despite Mother's fears that I would be hurt riding, I was put on a horse as soon as I could hold on to the saddle horn. From that moment it must have been my unswerving ambition to become a cowboy. But not until I was tall enough to reach the saddle horn and had sufficient strength in my arms to lift myself over the horse and into the saddle was I able to make much progress.

To take part in games, I had to learn to handle my partially paralyzed legs well enough to keep up with the other children, and in everything except a foot race I could hold my own. In haying time we climbed up to our cupola playhouse in the hay shed, accessible only after the fresh, fragrant alfalfa had been piled as high as the hay fork and pulley horse could stack it. By grabbing hold of the rope on the pulley track, we were able to shin the rest of the way up to the cupola, which was floored around the sides and open at the center. We took with us our dishes, dolls, kittens, and anything else suitable for a playhouse.

The tougher the game was, the harder I tried to keep up with the others. If Annie, in playing "follow the leader," took us around the edge of the hayloft, where to keep from falling we held precariously to the cracks in the walls and at the same time kept our feet on the narrow side of a two-by-four, I would sweat it out. Or if we found the swallows nesting in the comb of the roof and wanted to dislodge them by tearing down their nests, I was the first to reach them because this involved swinging by the arms on the rafters and here, with my strong arm and chest muscles, I had the advantage. To get down, we just dropped to the hay below.

Getting to the . . . [one-room] schoolhouse a mile away presented a problem that I tackled with all the ingenuity I possessed. My first year I trained a team of dogs to pull a little red wagon over the trail through a little canyon. But the uphill stretch was too much for them so I had to walk or ride my "stick-horse," pushing as best I could with my legs. It was a speedy method. Uncle Austin once told my dad he had seen me "skedaddle off across the mesa faster'n a jack rabbit," a comparison that pleased me even though I knew it would have to be a crippled rabbit he was talking about.

In bad weather I rode my pony Kate. But she had to be tied up and fed, so I preferred the dogs, Towser and Tag, hitched to the wagon. I even tried a team of goats. They were so hard to handle I ended by picking out a husky calico-colored wether and putting shafts to my wagon. But I still had to walk up hill. So I sought out old Miguel Sedillo, our goat herder, who had a couple of burros he used for packing camp gear. We always called him "Hoso" because, like a bear, he liked to eat raw meat. ("Hoso' was our own pronunciation of the Spanish *oso*, meaning bear.) As he didn't need his burros at the time, he let me try out my scheme. This necessitated making a larger wagon, which brought on more difficulties than I had anticipated.

One of Hoso's burros was slow, lazy, and stubborn while the other, though faster, was twice as obstinate. As I never like to be late anywhere and since I could not predict the burros' moods, I left early to allow for them. On the uphill climb, their added pull made my trips pleasurable until a contrary streak hit them just as the cart and I were slanted at a sharp angle. This happened once when the very stubborn one balked and sat down, so I gave him a sharp crack with my stick. He jumped as if he had been stung by a bumblebee, breaking the single tree and turning the wagon over on top of me. Then they both pulled loose from the wagon tongue and started for home, leaving me to get there as best I could.

But I did not give up. Not much later as I was leaving the ranch in a hurry to get to school, one of the burros took a stubborn spell just as Hoso happened to be coming along. He watched me for a while, grinning through his yellow teeth which were pointed like a bear's, and then said, *"Picale la cruz,"* which meant to take the sharp point of my stick and punch the burro in a tender spot where the color of the hair on top of the shoulders forms a cross. It worked like magic. But it was so sudden it turned over the wagon and I landed on my head.

I decided then that if two burros could give as much trouble as those had caused me, one would make only half as much. After hours of work in the shop I fastened a pair of shafts to the cart and drove a single burro. This was a fairly dependable system, and to share my success some of the other kids sat across the rear end and dragged their feet in the dust. . . .

By the time I was old enough to go to school, the Coe children and a few others belonging to nearby settlers nearly filled the room. . . . making a grand total of nineteen Coes! Learning was never taken too seriously by any of us. But in our family hooky was not frequent because of Mother's stern ideas about the importance of education. Miss Ward, the teacher when I started to school, was also an example of correct demeanor to my sisters. She was so painfully modest that it was embarrassing for her to get on a horse for fear she would show her ankle or maybe the calf of her leg. Once primly mounted on her sidesaddle, she would blushingly pull down the long skirt of her riding habit so that only the tips of her shoes showed. To make sure none of us kids saw her mount, she would leave very early for school, and by the time the children arrived, she'd be changed into her regular clothes. I doubt she approved of my sisters in their divided skirts riding astride a cowboy saddle. Obviously her desire to be a lady was greater than her wish to be a good horsewoman, for her riding did not improve.

During vacation Mother kept Miss Ward with us so we could go on with our studies. However, at the end of the second session she left us, greatly to Mother's sorrow, for she knew it would be hard to find another such ladylike person to take her place. But losing such a fine teacher was only one of Mother's educational problems. The Coe school was becoming overcrowded as new settlers came into the valley. Overage and indifferent to learning as some of them were, they did what they could to make life miserable for the teacher. In time Mother knew she would have to find other means to get us the kind of education she wanted for us.

She had tried to do this on a previous occasion with disastrous results. When Winnie and Annie were in the fourth grade, she took them to Roswell to put them in school. There the specter of Billy the Kid arose, as it did on many occasions, and put an end to her plans. Well-meaning friends of the family with whom the two girls were boarding advised them not to harbor any of Frank Coe's children under their roof. It was unthinkable that anyone related to a McSween sympathizer be sheltered there.[2] Chagrined and angry, Mother brought them back to the ranch and enrolled them in the Coe school again.

When that season ended, Mother began her routine "house cleaning," which entailed setting up living quarters down by the river not far from the house. To this spot we took our bedclothes, cooking utensils, and food staples. We made an arbor where we cooked and slept during the renovations. Mother and Josefa, with whatever help they could get from Timio and Fabian, scrubbed, painted, put new straw in the bedticks, washed and ironed curtains, and did other things necessary to get the house ready for another year.

When the wind blew the cupola off the hay shed, Dad had it moved down by the river. Mother used it for a summerhouse. Tents were set up nearby to sleep in. When weather permitted, the cooking was done outside. We children peeled tubfuls of peaches and pears, which were cooked in the big iron pots and put into large glass jars to be stored away for winter use. We were always sorry to return to our regular quarters.

Wilbur Coe was fortunate to have a loving, supportive family and good friends to help him cope with his handicap; many other children with physical, emotional, or psychological handicaps in New Mexico— and the world—were not as blessed, suffering terrible abuse and discrimination in their youth and throughout their lives. With the support he received and his personal strength, Wilbur continued to lead an active life. Graduating from high school in Roswell, he went on to college at Stanford University, earning his degree in 1916. He returned to Lincoln County to become a successful rancher, apple farmer, and community leader. He married Louise Holland in late 1918. Six years later, Louise became the first woman ever elected to the New Mexico state senate. Reelected four times, she remained in politics until 1942. Wilbur wrote his family's history, Ranch on the Ruidoso, *in the 1960s. He died in 1968 at the age of seventy-five.*

RAPLH REYNOLDS
BRANDING CALVES AND SAVING A COW[1]

In his words, Ralph Reynolds was "conceived, gestated, birthed, weaned, reared, and matriculated into the world from a log cabin" in rural Catron County, New Mexico, starting in 1930.[2] Born into a family of seven, Ralph was nicknamed the Luna Kid, if only because his family lived and ranched in the Luna Valley. Ralph explained that when World War II "depleted the countryside of workers [who had gone off to war], rural cowboys of [the] Luna Kid's generation had to grow up a little quicker than most. Though mere boys, by the time the war was in full swing [in the early 1940s], their. . . . legs were already bowed from sitting in the saddle, and. . . . [t]hey'd grown tough as rawhide. . . . The Luna Kid was a member of this gifted class."[3] He engaged in many cowboy chores, not the least of which was branding.

The time has come to speak of branding calves. But before we proceed, it seems useful to lay to rest any notions regarding the innocence of the victim. Please bear in mind that before the rural cowboy approaches a bound and helpless calf with his diabolical instruments, the cowboy has likely been dragged, butted, bitten, slobbered on, crapped on, and perversely and roundly kicked in several tender areas. In fact, in his advanced years, Daddy, a legendary rider of wild broncs, suffered such a calf-kick to the inside of his right knee that a broken ligament hobbled him for life.

Let us shed no tears, then, for the writhing little beasts who become the brandee and much more in this strenuous and rather messy

Ranch children, Sacramento Mountains, New Mexico, 1909. Green Edward Miller Photographs, Neg. No. Ms101. Courtesy of the Rio Grande Historical Collections, New Mexico State University Librry, New Mexico State University, Las Cruces, New Mexico.

encounter. After all, the poor animal suffers it and displays no great resentment afterwards. Maybe this indicates an innate stupidity on his part, or perhaps it's just that he has plenty of reason to feel grateful that it's over and happy that he's still alive.

The Luna Kid would enjoy the roundup at branding time. It's warm and damp now in rainy season, and the air is brightly clean, washed of its dust. The pines smell good. The grass, weeds, bushes, and flowers, bursting and swollen with sudden frantic growth, seem brighter in color and twice their usual size. Cattle are scattered this time of year—so the Kid gets to go off alone.

It's grand to be on horseback and alone in the bright morning. He kicks Bludog into a trot across Trout Creek and up the trail to the broad ridge between Snider Place and Steele Flat. Daddy said the Kid would find Redgut and her calf by the state-line fence. He is to drive her back toward the Steele Flat, picking up any other cows along the way. There may be some lone yearlin's up there. If so, leave 'em be. Watch specially for that brindle cow they'd bought from Uncle Dorf last fall. She might have lost her calf. The mule cow with the tore ear was likely up on the ridge, too. She had an early calf, and it better sure get branded now, or it'd be a chore to wrestle down later.

The Kid trots on alone. He picks up the brindle cow first and pushes her along, but she doesn't want to go. She slows to a walk and bawls. A calf answers and pops out of the brush, a dandy little whiteface bull, lively and hungry. He stops the brindle to suck, impatiently butting her teats, demanding. The Kid yells, "Git on. Git on." He rides up close and whacks the calf with the knot on the end of his rope. Bludog grabs with his teeth for the tailhead of the cow. She bursts away in a trot, the calf running backward, still trying to suck. Kid yells again, and Bludog is already in a high trot.

It's grand, really grand, to be a cowboy and alone in the woods, punching a wild cow off through the brush, yelling and spurring. . . .

He goes on a ways and picks up Redgut with her calf. The calf doesn't want to drive. It takes off back toward Trout Creek. Bludog whirls after it, hitting a bouncy sprint, the Kid holding on, feeling wind under his hat, ducking low branches of ponderosa. They turn Redgut's calf, and it dashes back toward its mother. Bludog pounds to a stop, throwing the Kid's thighs up against the swells of Lamar's saddle. He yells again at the calf, mostly in exuberance now.

That's cowboyin', and the Kid wishes it would go on and on. But at the Steele Flat he meets Dave, who's driven in from Underwood Mesa. They hear bawling and see Daddy has a bunch coming through the slot from Commor Draw.

They've got forty-five or fifty cows now. Some are McFate's. The herd moves compactly down Trout Creek toward the ranch. Dave and the Kid drive them around the fence to the corral because there're oats planted in the fields. The cattle foolishly crowd through the gap in the corral, nervous and bawling, once inside pressing back against the poles and rolling their eyes. The older cows may remember what's ahead, having suffered it once and witnessed it six or eight times.

Pitch pine starts quick and hot, with smoke the blackness of malpais rock. The fire is big because it takes plenty of hot coals for the running irons, which are made from pokers or thick steel rods bent into a J.

Daddy lays out his instruments on a flat rock near the fire. There'll be hell to pay if the boys let a calf run across that rock. From a soiled canvas bag, he draws out a stubby pair of dehorners. Old Faundeer's calf was late last year and didn't get dehorned. Might need the nippers. Next, there's an oily box about ten inches long. It has the vaccinating needle and some vials of blackleg serum. Then there's a black pint Mason jar with a lid. Daddy finds a stick and ties a strip of bandanna around it. He drops the cloth end into the stinking concoction called kersilic. Then he opens his Barlow pocket knife and lays that out. The irons are hot, and the rural surgeon, who doesn't know an antiseptic from an anesthetic and can't spell either, is ready. Bring on the calves.

There's more than one way to catch a calf. If it is big, approaching yearling, the best roper will catch both hind legs in a loop thrown from horseback. Then he will stretch out the calf 'til its body is suspended between its front legs and the tight rope. One strong cowboy merely grabs the calf's tail and pulls him over onto his back. Others grapple the lethal hooves and quickly tie all four legs together.

For a little smaller calf, a roper lassos the head from horseback. A flanker then follows the tight rope down to the calf and throws the wildly kicking little fellow by grabbing his neck in the left hand, his opposite rear flank in the right, and rolling him down one knee to the ground. Sounds systematic, but it's about as easy as lifting a Kawasaki upside down while the motor runs and the wheels spin.

This year's calves are small enough to rope and hold from on foot. But that makes the flanking even tougher because the roper sometimes gets dragged about before he can take a good half hitch around a post.

Max is doing the roping. He shakes out a stiff loop and stalks a calf. Makes no difference, now, which one. Cows glare at him, sometimes lowering their horns, and calves run behind their mothers. Each time he approaches a bunch, they split apart. He throws two loops that miss. The cattle are starting to run around the fence now. If he misses again, Daddy will make him give up the rope to Lamar.

Then the noose settles around the head of Redgut's little bull. Max braces the rope around his hips and drags the bucking calf out of the herd, excitedly demanding help. Kid rushes in. They fight the rope over to a post, and Max loops it for mechanical advantage, still holding the end to allow slack in case the calf chokes. Lamar and Dave ease down the rope to the calf. He's a tough one, bellowing and leaping. The dust boils up. Dave gets his handholds and lifts. Nothing doing. Calf won't budge.

He's choking now, tongue hanging out one side of his mouth. Max gives some rope. Dave tries again. Calf gets a breath and charges right out of his grasp.

Kid looks around and notices that Daddy is grinning. Dave is swearing at the calf. He's limping from a hoof against his ankle. The corral is filling with dust and smoke, and there's a frantic chorus of bawling and mooing. Daddy is yelling instructions in his piercing voice. Dave has a better hold now. Calf jumps. Dave pulls up strong against the flank. Calf goes crashing down on his side with a bellow. He's trying to get up. Dave is grabbing for a front leg, has it. Calf still struggling. "Git yur knee in his belly," yells Daddy. It's more command than instruction. Dave moves his knee across calf's back and drops his weight there. He's ahold of the front leg. Calf is pinned.

Daddy walks in with a piggin' string, puts his shin up against the rear legs, and grabs the front ones. He loops the leather thong and draws it tight as Max gives rope to loosen the choke at the neck. They stand back, panting. The calf bawls and struggles. His mother runs up to check him with her nose. They shoo her away. The Kid checks the irons. That's job. They're hot.

Daddy kneels at the back of the calf. "Hand me the knife." The calf's sides are heaving, his eyes rolling in terror. Daddy grabs the scrotum, stretching it out away from the testes, and whacks off its end with a single thrust of the knife. He pushes against the calf's stomach and white testicles pop out the cut end. He grabs one. The calf's stomach convulses. He scrapes off the cord attaching it. There's almost no blood. The other testicle has slipped back inside. He has to press the stomach again to bring it out. He scrapes it loose. A clean cut would cause bleeding. He hands both testicles to the Kid. "Lay 'em over on the fence. Fetch the kersilic."

Branding a maverick near Silver City, New Mexico, 1907. Dr. Thomas K. Todsen Collection, Neg. No. Ms0223.0086. Courtesy of the Rio Grande Historical Collections, New Mexico State University Library, New Mexico State University, Las Cruces, New Mexico.

     The testicles are slick and firm. They feel like big warm beans. By the time the Kid lays them across the corral pole, they're sticky to the touch.

     The calf lies there, neck stretched out. His eyes are rolled back but not glazed. The Kid is glad for him because that part is over. He dabs the open wound with kersilic. Calf doesn't show any pain now. Daddy grabs the left ear by the tip and stretches it. He cuts off two inches with a quick slash of the Barlow and tosses away the hairy triangular segment. A little blood bubbles out from the cut edge. Calf feels the knife, bellows and threshes, but again his eyes do not glaze. Daddy reaches around and grabs the left ear. The operation here is less deft, for he must cut a notch out of the lower part, deep enough to be noticeable even years from now. A brand is a legal mark, but it is the ear notch, varying between ranchers who share a range, that is most useful for quick identity. Daddy whacks out the notch, using none of the care displayed in castration. His hands are bloody now for the first time.

The Kid steps back, knowing and hating what comes next. Nothing doing, Daddy motions him over to the head of the calf. "Hold his nose." The Kid grabs the frothy nose and ducks his head just in time to miss the thin red stream that arches out to puddle on the dusty ground ten feet away. With about the same stroke you'd use to slice a carrot, Daddy's knife has whacked off a budding horn at the base. Calf is fighting against the Kid's hand, moving his head enough that the brothers, who've been standing near, have to dance about to avoid the bloody arch.

Daddy looks up to say something, but Dave, anticipating, is ready with a hot iron. He hands it to Daddy. There is a sizzle. Smoke boils up and the arch stops. The calf bawls, and its mother sticks her nose in close to the still-hot iron. In a moment, blood bubbles out again, and the iron touches down a second time. Sizzle and smoke, and the bubble stops. They turn the calf and duck again. A second stubby horn lies on the ground, and there's another bloody arch and sizzle and smoke again. The Kid carries over the syringe. Daddy lifts the skin of the front shoulder and sticks in the needle. The dumb calf indiscriminately bellows again.

Now the calf is on his right side, and Daddy reaches out a gloved hand to brush caked mud and manure off its rib cage. That's the signal. The Kid heads back to the fire for one of the pink-hot irons. This comes last because the brand has to stay clean. The Kid doesn't like the smell of blue smoke rising from the burned hair and hide as Daddy prints out an eight-inch F and then a slightly larger Y next to it. What the Kid hates most, though, is the bellowing of the calf as Daddy goes back over the brand with a second hot iron.

Our new little steer lies there with heaving sides in the corral dust, which has been muddied here and there with his blood. His tongue is sticking out the left side of his mouth. His eyes are rolled back. His white hair reveals numerous bloody rivulets, and his red hair is wavy with sweat. In a few traumatic moments, his sex has been scraped away from his belly, and a significant portion of his ears has been removed. A part of his head has been cut away on each side and the resulting wounds scabbed with hot irons. He's been stuck with a needle, and his burned-in owner's [brand] stings across ten square inches of his young hide, not to mention that the little fellow has been harshly choked, thrown down, and kneed in the neck and gut. But when that piggin' string is removed, stand back, because he's going to come off the ground like a stepped-on rattler. He runs bawling, heels kicking, and tail swinging to his mother. She licks at his bloody forehead and sniffs the scorched hair around his new brand.

By the time smoke from the next branding wafts across the corral, he's hungry and butting against his mother's teats as a signal to let him down some milk. His torture is over, but for the rural cowboys in the little corral, the bruising, dusty, bloody business at hand is just beginning. Hours later the corral floor is littered with pieces of ear and cut-off horns. It's over.

Miller Time never came to the old FY [ranch]. But along toward the end of every branding day, Daddy would pick the firm little testicles off the fence and throw them rather carelessly into the dying coals of the branding fire. They would cook and swell and finally burst like marshmallows. The rural cowboys would fish them out of the coals with sticks and summarily, if wearily, eat them. Without beer.

Branding is an inescapable duty of a rural cowboy, right? Well, it ought to be, but the Luna Kid, in all his days as accessory to the fact, never branded a calf. He sometimes slashed the ears, whacked off horns, and even gingerly cauterized the bleeding wounds. But not once did he allow himself to touch that hot iron to the heaving sides of a little calf, or a big one. Not that the Kid was any kind of Caspar Milquetoast in his contacts with animals. Once he smashed twenty-eight lizards with stones in a grisly little contest with Sonny Boy who, losing, accounted only for twenty-two. Many times did he ax the heads off chickens without batting an eye, and one early morning he buried a stiff boot deep into the paunch of a gentle-eyed old milk cow after she swished a crap-laden tail across his face. But even the Iron Kid had his limits, and in a cop-out so cunningly concealed that it would surprise his brothers even today, he never once branded a calf.

The Kid used to watch the brander apply that searing iron to the gentle side of a baby animal and wonder what the man himself felt. And gradually over time the realization came. Nothing. The Kid's Daddy and others of his age and persuasion felt nothing of the quivering anguish caused by their hot iron. But that kind of pain was transitory and came to an end. Did they feel anything of animal pain? Ever?

One day the Kid and Daddy are driving toward Jenkins Creek to put out salt and gather a pickup load of wood. It is late in the high grazing season. All the cattle along the way are sleekly fat, until they come on a lone cow, barely standing, gaunt and drooped, about fifty yards to the left of the road. "Look at that," says Daddy.

"What's wrong with her?" asks the Kid, noticing a pastel-brown and wettish-looking streak along her curly white face.

"Looks like a horn's curved down and is growin' into her head," says Daddy. His shoulders move in something akin to a shudder. "That's a hell of a thing."

"Glad she ain't one of ours," says the Kid.

"It's Frank's cow," says Daddy. "looks like she's lost her calf. Well, she's an old cow and no account."

He peers in silence and finally says, "Too bad we ain't got a horse."

They drive on, drop off the salt, and load up with a tangle of pine branches. On the way back, the cow stands there still. Daddy stops again and stares. Her head drops near her knees. Now and then a rear leg gives way, and her whole frail carcass jerks up to keep from falling over.

Finally Daddy says again, "I shore wished we had a horse." He sits peering at the cow and brooding. The Kid commences to fidget. He doesn't want to look at the old cow. His head aches just thinking about her. He is hungry and wants badly to get on home. After all, they'll have to unload the wood and do chores before supper.

"I got an idea," says Daddy. "There's a chute by the cabin at the Steele place. Son, go see if you can chase that old cow into the Steele Flat. I'll open the gate and help shoo her on into the chute."

The cow is weak with hunger and exhaustion, but wild with pain. It takes more than an hour of chasing on foot to get her penned in the loading chute. The sun is going down by the time they get a close-up look at her ingrown horn. It has dipped down and penetrated maybe a half inch into the skull just above the eye. It is aimed perfectly to go right on through her brain. Blood and pus have blinded her eye, and a warm pink swelling distorts fully half her face.

"That's shore a fright," says Daddy. "There's a hacksaw in the tool box under the wood. You'll hafta unload to git at it while I tie her head down."

Unloading the wood, the Kid can hear noises of a fearsome struggle at the chute. There's thudding and crashing. The cow grunts and moans and once or twice emits a bellowing scream. If Daddy swears or raises his voice once, the Kid doesn't hear.

Slowly and carefully, the saw cuts into the horn, but each tiny vibration can be seen in the rolling pain-maddened eyes of the cow. Daddy is sawing as gently as a roughened rancher can saw. And he is talking supplications to an old cow who is so sick the Kid has to stand back in revulsion from the foul smells of her.

Afterwards they load the wood again and start home in the dusk. "I reckon that hole in her skull's gonna heal," says Daddy. "She'll git better."

"Yeah. Good," says the Kid.

"She sure perked up the minute we pulled that horn out of her head," says Daddy.

"Yeah," answers the Kid, thinking what it'll be like to do chores and again unload the tangled pile of wood, this time in the dark.

Daddy switches on the headlights of the pickup. "Too bad we'll be gittin' in so late," he says. He sounds almost apologetic, even though Daddy was never known to apologize for anything. The Kid nods.

"No need to unload the wood tonight," Daddy goes on. "That kin wait 'til morning. I'll do the mikin' when we git in."

The Kid has reason to be surprised, but somehow he isn't. He stretches with pleasure in the warm cab. He feels drowsy. His head doesn't ache anymore.

After growing up in southwestern New Mexico, Ralph Reynolds entered military service, went to college, taught high school ("which proved to be no less strenuous than branding calves"), married, and had four daughters, "all bright and beautiful enough to be troublesome at times."[4] Professionally, he was the editor of an international magazine and an award-winning author. Now retired, his advice to young people is not to take themselves too seriously and avoid seeing "glitches in life as somehow either tragic or romantic, when in fact they're most likely just ridiculous."[5]

LINDLEY J. STILES
THE TROUBLE WITH RATTLESNAKES[1]

*Lindley J. Stiles was born—weighing no less than twelve pounds—
in 1913 in Tatum, New Mexico, west of the Caprock Cattle Ranch, where
his father Dave served as a respected ranch foreman. A proud Texan,
Lindley's dad once told his son to "never ask a man where he comes from.
If he is from Texas, he will tell you; if he isn't, it doesn't make any difference."[2] Despite this strong bias, the Stileses lived on New Mexico cattle
ranches throughout Lindley's satisfying childhood. A deeply religious man,
Lindley believes that he survived many harrowing experiences (including
several described below) because God was always at his side, meaning
that he never rode alone.*

I n the semi-desert country in which my dad's cattle ranches were
located, rattlesnakes were almost as common as jackrabbits. In win
ter, they hibernated under rocks or in prairie dog holes. The lava
flows from ancient volcanoes near the Grants area were full of them.
When the warm days of spring arrived, they emerged by the thousands,
it seemed, shed their skins, added a rattle to their tales, and began to
hunt for food.

Rattlesnakes are most dangerous when they are shedding their
skins. The shedding is necessary for the snake to grow larger and longer
since their skins do not stretch as do those of [other] animals. The snake
literally crawls out of its skin, and, for a time it is blind as the loosened
skin of the head moves across its eyes. During this time of blindness,
which may last for several days, the snake will strike at any noise it
hears. I have seen many abandoned snake skins, completely intact with

mouth and eye holes, everything but the rattles, which the snake takes with it leaving a hole at the tail end. People used to think that the number of rattles a snake had indicated how old it was. Actually, a snake may grow more than one rattle a year, as the end rattles get broken off.

Baby snakes are born, rather than hatched. One day Dad and I came across two snakes creating the babies. They were wrapped together like strands of a rope, unaware of our presence. Dad took a rock and smashed both their heads at one time. We took sticks and unraveled their bodies; their private parts were still interlocked.

Survival in ranch country, for human beings as well as horses and cattle, required learning how to avoid getting bitten by a rattlesnake. Animals had the advantage of their sense of smell to help them to know where the snakes were. People, if they were wise, took their cues from animals and learned to anticipate where snakes were most likely to be found: under rocks, in bushes or prairie dog holes, in lumber or wood piles, around hens' nests (snakes eat eggs), or anywhere in the shade on hot days.

Early in our years in our . . . home near Grants, New Mexico, Shep was barking like mad outside the kitchen door. Mother opened the door and looked out. There on the step was a rattlesnake, coiled but facing out toward the dog, which kept its attention. Mother told our dad about it: "If it hadn't been for Shep, I might have stepped on it."

I remember a time when Mr. Stacey was drilling a water well for us. Some neighbor children were visiting, and all of us decided to take a walk out to see the well-drilling rig. As we wound our way through the sage bushes, old Shep ran ahead and found a big rattler ahead in the direction we were walking. When Shep started barking to warn us of the danger, the snake coiled itself and began sounding off with its dozen rattles on its vibrating tail. Someone called to Mr. Stacey who was nearby tending his drilling machine. He came with his pistol and shot the snake's head off. Then he warned, "Stay back until I get a rock and crush that head; it can still bite you." . . . [H]e told us about a time when his dog had sniffed at a snake's head which he shot off and been bitten by it.

Most often horses and cows were bitten by snakes when they were grazing. Such bites could be fatal immediately if they hit an artery in the neck or head of the animal. It is a myth that rattlesnakes always give a warning rattle before they strike. Likewise, it is untrue that a snake has to coil in order to strike. Its purpose in coiling up is to give it the advantage of striking out for several feet, raising up on the lower end of its body. But if a snake happens to be in the grass where an animal is grazing, it will bite without coiling or rattling.

When on a trail drive with a large herd of cattle, I remember seeing the moving animals separate, leaving an open space of perhaps fifteen feet in diameter, as they walked around rattlesnakes which were in the herd's path. Sometimes four or five such indicators could be seen at one time. Riders would move their horses into the herd where they would find the snakes coiled. They would dismount and kill the snakes with the large knots they kept tied at the end of their saddle ropes. The technique required swinging the rope with the knot aimed at the snake's head, then slowly withdrawing it before making another swing. Novices who swung their ropes in a rapid circle risked the possibility of hooking the snake and pulling it into themselves. When rocks or large, long sticks were available, these were used as well as ropes. Whatever was used to crush the snake's head, the rider always finished the kill by placing his boot heel on its head and pushing it deep into the ground.

It was a tradition that riders would report the number of rattlesnakes killed each day on a trail drive to the cook of the outfit, who kept the tally by marking notches on the wagon or on a "snake stick." Fifteen or twenty was a typical number, but on one drive along a caprock type formation, a record number of eighty-seven snakes were killed on one day.

It was on this day that I found myself surrounded by a den of snakes and was lucky to get out alive. I knew all the older riders were killing large numbers of snakes among the volcanic rocks which jutted out from the caprock, by which the herd was moving. I wanted to be able to report some that I had killed. I purposely rode Frankie up into the rocks where I could hear snakes rattling. One was coiled right in the trail ahead. I dismounted, took my rope and approached the snake to make the kill. As I prepared to swing, I became aware that Frankie was stomping his feet, snorting, and backing away along the path we had come. Then I realized what he was warning me about. Snakes were crawling from both sides of the path in a pattern which would let them surround both me and Frankie. With fear and trembling I quickly ran back to Frankie, mounted him, and let him have his head as he picked his way out of the snake ambush.

When reporting time came that night at the chuck wagon, I kept real quiet. I was thanking God, and Frankie, that I was there to listen to the success stories of the other cowboys.

The closest I ever came to being bitten by a rattlesnake happened one day when Dad left me to keep the water troughs filled while he rode out in search of some lost cattle. The herd was watering in a series of rows of water troughs, arranged about twenty feet apart so that the animals could drink from each side. They reached out from the windmill like the sections of a fan. Each row of troughs had been constructed so that water would flow from one to the next, with as many as six or eight troughs in a row. They were constructed of wood, with each trough sitting on a base about four inches high.

The windmill pumped water into a large steel holding tank. From it water was let out into each of the lines of troughs by large shut-off valves which were worked with wheels about six inches in diameter. My job was to watch the level of the water in the various lines of troughs and to keep them filled. When all the troughs were full, I had time to sit on one of the several rows which were not being used, and read a dime novel I had brought from the ranch house.

After filling all the troughs on one trip to the holding tank, I returned to where I thought I had been sitting on the cross brace on one of the empty troughs. I was reading a particularly interesting part in my book as I walked back. By mistake, I approached a different empty trough from the one I had left. As I stepped into the trough I heard a rattle and looked back to see the open mouth and fangs of a large rattler just miss the foot I was pulling after me into the trough. I was so frightened I couldn't move. My book, which I had dropped outside the trough, lay under the snake which had recoiled and was rattling loudly as it turned its head eyeing me where I sat about two feet away in the trough. I realized it could attack me again whenever I moved. I sat trembling, scared to try to escape. Finally, after what seemed like hours, I regained control of myself, and quickly moved a few feet down the trough. Then, because the trough was full of holes and tumbleweeds—the reason it was not in use—I crept cautiously down its length, jumping from one section to the next until I reached the end of the row. I stood on the last trough brace and jumped as far as I could and ran to where Frankie had been tied. I got on him and sat still, shaking until Dad returned.

When I told Dad what had happened, he immediately asked me to point out the trough where the snake was. "I've got to kill it; we don't want it biting our cattle," he commented. I told him it was the one where my book was lying. He found a long two-inch-by-four-inch [board] and routed out the snake and killed it. My book was covered with the snake's blood and, I suspected, the venom it had aimed at me. Dad picked it up and wiped it off on some grass and held it out to me. I couldn't touch it. I didn't even remember the story I was reading. Dad tossed the book on the dead snake, and we rode for home.

"One more step and you're dead," came a voice out of the dark, rainy night. Dad and I had ridden in late to one of his ranches six miles north of Pueblo Bonito where the famous Anasazi-built pueblo [still] stands today. We had unsaddled our horses in the corral, which was about one hundred yards from the adobe ranch house and started walking up a slight hill on which the house stood. "Put that gun away, Jim. It is just us," Dad said to Jim Farmer, an old cowhand who was looking out for the ranch by himself at the time. "Oh, Mr. Stiles," Jim said as he recognized my dad's voice. "I am sorry to throw down on you, but I don't want anyone sneaking up on me at night. Next time call out so I'll know who it is."

That was the beginning of an eventful night. When we got to the one-room adobe ranch house, which had been built by a Mexican owner years before and showed its wear, Jim lit a lantern and said, "This place is full of rattlesnakes. I'm sleeping in the wagon. You can join me there if you want. There is room for all of us." He went on to tell us about how that morning he had started to reach for a stick of wood to build a fire and found a rattler coiled in the wood box. "The adobe walls are filled with holes the mice have dug," he explained. "The snakes come through them into the house."

About then, the rain which had been threatening all evening began to fall in big drops. Jim said he had rather get wet than snakebit and headed for the wagon. Dad unrolled a bedroll and spread it out on the only bed in the room. Because the roof was leaking in several places, he took a heavy tarpaulin and spread it over the bed roll. He and I climbed into bed, pulling the tarp up over our heads. It was late, and we both were tired. Soon we were sound asleep.

Sometime later, I was awakened when Dad put his hand over my mouth. Quietly, he whispered, "Don't move or make a sound. There is a snake crawling across our bed." Terrified, I could feel its weight against my hips and hear the rustle of its movement over the tarp. Then I heard the snake drop off the bed onto the dirt floor. I let out a big sigh, but Dad's hand suppressed it. I immediately felt the weight of a second snake following the path of the first across our still forms under the tarp. "Where there is one snake, there usually are two," Dad told me the next day.

I never knew what time it was, but I hardly breathed or slept for the rest of the night. It was a night of wakeful nightmares. I needed to get up and go outside to relieve myself, but I didn't want to take the chance of stepping on a snake. At long last, daybreak came. Dad, who usually was up with the first light of dawn, broke his long tradition and snuggled close to me as morning came alive. Finally, we heard Jim Farmer call in from the door, "Mr. Stiles, are you all right?" Dad eased back the tarp from over his face and said, "Jim, clear the snakes out so we can get up." Jim cautiously entered the room, looked around, and said, "I don't see no snakes. Come on out." "Check our clothes," Dad requested. Jim did, found nothing, and handed them to us. We both dressed on the bed and only when our shoes were on did we finally venture to slide out and [gratefully] put our feet on the packed dirt floor.[3]

Lindley graduated from Farmington High School and attended both Fort Lewis College and the University of Colorado. To this day, he claims that his success as a noted author, poet, and college educator was firmly anchored in his boyhood experiences in rural New Mexico.

7

TROUBLED CHILDHOODS

BILLY THE KID'S TEENAGE YEARS IN SILVER CITY[1]

By any measure, be it newspaper coverage, narratives, novels, or modern movies, William Bonney—better known as Billy the Kid—was the most notorious criminal in New Mexico history. Rightly or wrongly, he was accused of crimes ranging from petty theft to cattle rustling and murder. But how did this young man become involved in such increasingly serious crimes on the New Mexico frontier? Although literate, Billy had no chance to write his own memoirs or compile a collection of revealing writings in his short, twenty-one-year life. We are therefore left with the opinion of others who knew "the Kid" or studied his life long after the fact. The eminent historian, Robert M. Utley, has drawn on the opinions of Billy's contemporaries to provide the following explanation of how an erstwhile good youth went tragically wrong in his teenage years.

Until the final few months of his life, the youth destined for immortality as the West's most famous outlaw was known not as Billy the Kid but simply as "the Kid." He acquired the label as a teenager, when he first began to associate with men. To the day of his death, his boyish face and slim figure stamped him as a kid. So did his behavior, uniformly characteristic of youth, untouched by adult maturity. A kid he remained throughout his short and violent life, ended by a bullet at twenty-one. More than any other trait, youth shaped the personality and directed the life of Billy the Kid.

The Kid's origins are shrouded in mystery. . . . That he was in Santa Fe, New Mexico, on March 1, 1873, is indisputable. On that day, as a lad of thirteen, [Billy] stood with his brother Joe as witness to his mother's marriage. The ceremony took place in the First Presbyterian Church, with the Reverend D.F. McFarland administering the vows as William Henry Harrison Antrim, age thirty, took in marriage the widow Catherine McCarty, age forty-three. . . .

Bill Antrim and Catherine McCarty had known each other since 1865, when they met in Indianapolis, Indiana. A Civil War veteran, Bill drove a hack for an express company. How, when, where, and by whom Catherine had been widowed are disputed questions. Almost certainly she had moved with her two young sons from New York City, but why to Indianapolis is not known. She told the compilers of the Indianapolis city directory for 1868 that she was the widow of Michael McCarty.

Without much doubt, Catherine and [Michael McCarty] were Irish immigrants. . . . [Their sons, Billy] and Joe, therefore, probably lived their first years in the impoverished Irish ghettos of [New York City]. . . .

In 1870 both [Bill] Antrim and [Catherine and her two sons] turned up in Wichita, Kansas. With Bill's help, Catherine had lifted her family from ghetto origins. Both [Bill and Catherine] grew sufficiently prosperous to acquire real estate in the infant frontier community, and Catherine ran a successful [laundry] business in the heart of town. . . .

Abruptly, however, in June 1871 the widow McCarty sold her property and two months later vanished from Wichita forever. Antrim left too. . . . Almost certainly, a diagnosis of tuberculosis prompted Catherine to search for higher, drier, more healthful climes. The little group made its way to Denver, Colorado, and from there soon turned south to New Mexico. . . .

[Bill Antrim] with Catherine and the two boys settled first in New Mexico's capital city. . . . From Santa Fe, shortly after the marriage of Bill and Catherine on March 1, 1873, the Antrims turned south. . . .to make their new home in Silver City. . . . In Silver City the Antrims established themselves in a log cabin at the head of the "Big Ditch," the stream bed that ran next to the town's main thoroughfare and carried runoff from mountain storms. . . . Bill worked at odd jobs while indulging a lifelong compulsion to search for the elusive strike that would bring mineral riches. Catherine supplemented the meager income by taking in boarders. "Mrs. Bill Antrim was a jolly Irish lady, full of life and mischief," remembered a neighbor. . . .

[Meanwhile, Billy] ran with the other boys and did little to set himself apart from them. He was "a scrawny little fellow with delicate hands and an artistic nature," recalled a schoolteacher, "always willing to help with the chores around the school house. Billy. . . was no more of a problem in school than any other boy growing up in a mining camp."

The New Mexico climate failed to head off Catherine's tuberculosis, and gradually she grew weaker. Bedridden for four months, she died on September 16, 1874. . . . The funeral took place the next day in the Antrim cabin, with burial following in the town cemetery.

After Catherine's death, Bill Antrim. . . .exercised little parental oversight. In fact, he may have been absent for months at a time. With other restless [residents] of Silver City, he was drawn by the new mineral strikes in Arizona. . . .

"Billy was one of the best boys in town," recalled [one of his young friends] years later. "He was very slender. He was undersized and was really girlish looking." "I never remember Billy doing anything out of the way any more than the rest of us," he added. . . . "He was quiet, I remember," related another friend, Chauncey Truesdell, "And never swore or tried to act bad like the other kids.". . .

During these youthful months, [Billy] grew passionately fond of music. He and other boys formed a minstrel troupe that played to appreciative audiences at Morrill's Opera House. "Billy was Head Man in the show," commented a fellow thespian. For the few years remaining to him, he would love to sing and dance.

Besides music, noted [a friend], "Billy got to be a reader. He would scarcely have his dishes washed until he would be sprawled out somewhere reading a book. . . . Soon, books gave way to lighter reading such as dime novels and the *Police Gazette*, which may have filled the young mind with fantasies of which his mother would not have approved.

Whether incited by the *Police Gazette* or simply by the absence of parental restraint, [Billy] drifted toward petty thievery. "His first offense," recalled Sheriff Harvey Whitehill in later years, "was the theft of several pounds of butter from a ranchman by the name of Webb, living near Silver City, and which he disposed of to one of the local merchants. His guilt was easily established, but upon promise of good behavior, he was released."

"He was a good kid," declared another friend, Louis Abraham, "but he got in the wrong company." The wrong company was George Shaffer, locally known, because of his headgear, as "Sombrero Jack." According to [Sheriff Whitehill's son], "Every Saturday night, George would get drunk. But he thought a lot of Billy and Billy used to follow him around. This fellow George liked to steal; he had a mania to steal and was always stealing."

And so, thanks to Sombrero Jack, [Billy] took his first big step toward a life of crime. One night a year after his mother's death, [Billy] accompanied his inebriated friend on a foray against the local Chinese laundry. They made off with a bundle of clothing. [Billy] hid the loot at the home where [his] family now boarded. The proprietress, Mrs. Sarah Brown, discovered it and turned the boy in to Sheriff Whitehill. Hauled before the justice of the peace, [Billy] found himself in the toils of the law.

"It did not amount to anything," observed [a local friend], "and Mr. Whitehill only wished to scare him." The sheriff's son agreed: "He didn't want to put him in a cell. He was just a boy who had stolen some clothes. . . . He didn't want to be mean."

[Billy] did not regard the matter this lightly. With the combination of cunning and sincerity that marked his later escapades, he persuaded the sheriff to let him have the run of the corridor outside the cell. "And right there is where we fell down," conceded Whitehill. The sheriff left the boy unguarded for half an hour. "When we returned, and unlocked the heavy oaken doors of the jail, the 'Kid' was nowhere to be seen." Not for the first time, the slim, wiry youth had climbed up a chimney to safety. . . .

The escape stamps fifteen-year-old [Billy] as clever, resourceful, and daring—traits that would carry him through many a scrape in the next few years. It also betrays the first stirrings of a reckless temper, together with a determination to do as he pleased. The death of his mother, for whom he later voiced an abiding affection, had freed him from parental influence. He got along well enough with Bill Antrim, who treated Catherine's sons with kindness and consideration but did not attempt to impose authority. As [Billy] grew into adolescence, therefore, he also grew increasingly free willed and independent. The escape from Sheriff Whitehill's jail was the ultimate assertion of independence, cutting all family and social ties and, in his own mind at least, making him a fugitive from the law. Now on his own, with a mixture of anxiety and resolve. . . , he fixed a westward course [to Arizona] into the unknown [future].

Space does not allow a recounting of Billy the Kid's short, but complex life from 1875, when he escaped from Silver City, to July 1881, when he was shot by Sheriff Pat Garrett in Ft. Sumner after several infamous escapes and gun battles. While there are literally hundreds of histories of Billy the Kid, Robert Utley's 1989 award-winning biography remains the best for readers young and old.

JIMMY SANTIAGO BACA
FINDING A PLACE TO STAND[1]

Jimmy Santiago Baca was born in Santa Fe, New Mexico, in 1952, the youngest of three children in a dysfunctional family plagued by violence, drunkenness, betrayal, and parental abandonment. Despite terrible abuse, Jimmy loved his family and spent much of his childhood harboring the vain hope that he might be reunited with his parents and siblings in his father's village of Estancia, or wherever they could settle peacefully. As the following excerpt from Jimmy's autobiography shows, the chances of his dream becoming reality grew dimmer and dimmer over time. Without family solace in his childhood, Jimmy would grow into a disillusioned adolescent with little to guide him toward a healthy emotional future.

I was five years old the first time I ever set foot in prison. A police man came to the door one night and told Mom she was needed at [the] jail. She took me with her. When we arrived at the booking desk the captain asked, "You married to Damacio Baca?"

"Yes."

"He was arrested for drunk driving. His bail's a hundred. . . .."

The captain. . . led us past holding cells to the drunk tank. It smelled like urine and whiskey vomit. I held tightly to Mother's hand. The corridors were dark and gloomy, and the slightest sound echoed ominously in the hall. We stopped in front of a cell where men sat and stared at the wall in front of them. Some were crumpled on the floor where they had passed out.

[T]he captain. . . banged the bars with his baton. The inmates glanced at us with hung-over disinterest, and one shook my father awake. He rose in a groggy stupor. Cautiously stepping over bodies, losing and regaining his footing, he approached the bars. He rubbed his face and blinked his red eyes.

"Did you have to bring *him*?" he asked accusingly. Then he added, clearly hurt that I was there, "I don't want him seeing me like this. Get me out of here."

"No," Mom said.

He stared at her. "Listen, you, don't—" Shaking with rage, he looked at me and made an effort to control himself.

We stood in silence for a few seconds. Then Mom cried, "Stay away from us!". . .

"Get back here!" My father's voice was strained by both aggression and self-pity, but Mom opened the door and we left. . . .

For weeks afterward my father's voice from behind bars echoed in my head as I moped around our yard or slept at mother's side in our narrow bed. I had nightmares of violent forces hurling my father through the air; I tossed and turned but could never reach him. . . .

When I was a boy, my father always wore a pained expression and kept his head down, as if he couldn't shake what was bothering him. He snapped irritably at the slightest infraction of his rules and argued continuously with Mother. He drank every day and she sank deeper into sadness and anger. To escape their fighting, and the gossiping of villagers in my Grandma Baca's kitchen, I often bellied into the crawl space under our shack to be alone in my own world. I felt safe in this peaceful refuge. . . .

I don't remember much before the age of five; my memories are of Grandma and Grandpa Baca in the kitchen, whispering. . . about Father's drinking, concerned about Mother's absence, and worried that there's never enough money. People come and go; behind their conversations, a Motorola radio under the cupboards by the sink drones Mexican *corridos* [ballads] or mass rosaries. . . .

Whether we were [living] in Estancia or Santa Fe, Dad would still come in late at night, smelling of whiskey and perfume. When I was six or seven, I was usually in bed right after sundown, but I stayed awake, waiting for him to come home. I would brace myself for a fight, as anything could happen when he was drunk. Many times I hid under my covers, my body tense, as he threatened my mother, hurling a spindle-back chair at her and roaring.

Mom would scream at him to get out. I often wept with fear, hoping he would not hurt her. Some nights he rushed drunkenly into my room and yanked me out of bed. . . . Mom usually hid, afraid for her own safety. He would toss me into the car and drive away. I never knew where we were going. We usually drove for hours on country roads. . . . The hum of the engine, the drone of the heater, and the wind blowing past his open window made me drowsy, and eventually I would fall asleep, helpless and sad.

On good days he tried to be conciliatory, promising to stay home more and not drink or womanize. . . . Often, after sharing good news with us, he'd say he had to run errands and would be right back. And just when I thought he might be sincere, he would return hours later, drool-ing drunk and crying with remorse. . . . I didn't know which was worse, eagerly expecting him, but never knowing when he might barge drunk-enly through the door late at night to fight with Mom, or fearing he would never come home again at all. . . .

[My Mother began to see a rather well-off man named Richard.] Riding around in the car Richard had given her, she'd point to white-skinned, blue-eyed children and say I should be like them. When she dressed us, she mentioned that we should look like normal American kids. . . . [W]hen Richard was around,. . . . [he] would get mad when I asked for beans, *chile*, and *tortilla*, saying, "It's time you started eating American food." I know Mom was trying to impress him with her "white ways," but it made her look silly.

It wasn't so with my father; he spoke Spanish and used English only when he had to. He listened to Mexican music, and all his friends were Mexicans. I never saw him with an Anglo. He never said anything bad about them, but he made a point to stay away from them. . . . I sensed that if he was around them, he'd be placing himself in harm's way. Ever since I could remember, my Baca grandparents mistrusted whites. When they came to Grandma's with official papers, we hid in the back rooms. . . .

[Later, we kids] lived with Grandma and Grandpa Baca. Grandpa said it was only temporary and reassured us that our parents would return to pick us up once they settled into our new home. I looked forward to that day, fantasizing about how happy we'd all be. Little did I know that my mother had eloped to San Francisco with Richard, fleeing into a white world as "Sheila," where she could deny her past, hide her identity, and lie about her cultural heritage. . . . [W]eeks after she left, a box arrived with our clothes and toys in it. She was not coming back. There was no language, no prayer, no medicine for the pain and loneliness. . . . I was also ignorant of my father's alcoholic oblivion, in which he pawned every last possession to get a bus ticket to San Francisco to try and find her. . . .

Then suddenly, Grandpa died [of a heart attack while scrubbing floors at the local school where he worked as the janitor]. Except for my immediate family, I had loved him the most. When my parents left, it was Grandpa who kept life stable as possible for us. He was always reassuring me that things would turn out fine. . . .

[At Grandpa's wake] Uncle Julian grabbed me and forced me through the crowd and. . . into the yard. He took me to the shed and smacked me across my head and shoulders, ordering me to stay there until morning. He kept saying, "It's your fault! It's your fault! All the worry you cause!"

"My fault?" I asked, not understanding.

He glared. "Grandpa died! And you're to blame, always worrying him!"

I yelled back, "I didn't do it! I didn't do it!"

Julian locked the shed and left. I peeked at him through the board cracks and looked around, expecting Grandpa to come out of the shadows. . . .

Before I could come to terms with Grandpa's unexpected death, [my older brother] Mieyo and I were taken to St. Anthony's Boys' Home in Albuquerque. [My sister] Martina stayed in Estancia to help Grandma. It was June 1959. . . .

Thinking we were going to join [my parents], Mieyo and I were driven instead to an orphanage and dropped off. Nuns escorted us up a flight of stairs into a dark, creaky third-floor dorm with kids in cots lined up on each side of the long room. I was scared and confused, weeping and cling to Mieyo, begging to be taken back to my grandparents' in Estancia because my parents were coming to get us. . . .

In a snap of a finger I found myself in a different world, among hundreds of strangers, with each minute planned out for me. The first few months, we slept on the condemned third floor. It rained almost every night, and the roof was leaking everywhere, soaking the bedsheets. . . . Thunder roared and lightning revealed me weeping on my bunk at night. Mieyo would come and cradle me, and I clung to him as if we were one person. . . .

When I asked the nuns if my parents were coming back, I was told the matter was in God's hands and children shouldn't ask such questions. . . . I felt lost and confused around grown-ups. They never told the truth. They were always hiding something that would eventually hurt me. . . .

I wait[ed] every Sunday by the gate next to the grotto of our Sacred Mother. From the gate I [could] see arriving families getting out of cars, carrying bags of clothes and candy for kids they [came] to visit. Every Sunday I wait[ed] there for my mother to appear. Children's names [were] called over the loudspeakers, and after their visits I [saw] them coming out of the main building to my left, smiling and carrying gifts.

[One Saturday I thought I saw my mother arrive so I went to the visiting room. Sister Anna Louise found me there and screamed that I should go back to where I was supposed to be.] She slap[ped] me until my cheeks [went] numb, saliva forming at her thin lips, her eyes narrowing with rage. . . .

Attempts at placing me in a foster home. . . failed. When prospective parents [came], my brother and I were never chosen. Our hair, our color, our speech—everything [was] wrong about us. . . .

I must have run away from the orphanage a dozen times, and each time an aunt or an uncle would take me back. The last time, however, instead of calling St. Anthony's, as they had in the past, they notified the police, who took me to the detention center. . . .

I celled with six other Chicanos. The fluorescent lighting made the apprehension in their faces obvious, but they concealed their curiosity about who I was, where I came from, and what I was here for with a hard-faced indifference. I wasn't prepared for their stony silence. Estancia kids. . . had a kindheartedness that invited spontaneous participation in play or idle talk. Even the kids at the orphanage generously included you in games and asked you to play; they hadn't lost hope. These boys worried about revealing any information that others might take as a weakness or use against them. Suspicion helped them to survive, as did denying their feelings, especially fear. At night, a heaviness lay over the cells; the kids, perhaps sensing their lives falling apart, were distressed and withdrawn. . . .

[D]uring the night. . . .the halls echoed with the ominous reports of the guard's boots as he checked to see if we were all in our bunks and counted. I felt sorry for the kids in for murder, grand theft auto, or drug possession, because they were headed for Springer, a prison for teenagers. Low-Blow [a friend] was going their for assault with a deadly weapon, and even though he said he wasn't afraid, I knew he was. . . .

Life at the D-Home was as predictable as it had been at the orphanage. New kids came and went. We woke up at the same time every day and went to bed a the same time every night. Every weekend visitors came and visited their loved ones for an hour. And just as I had done at the Boys' Home, every night, before falling asleep, I'd imagine my mother's voice whispering good night to me. I'd think of my father and brother; I'd. . . .gradually. . . fall asleep, pretending that tomorrow would be the day when everything was going to turn out well in my life.

Like almost every dream of his youth, Jimmy's dream of reconciliation with his family was never realized. Instead, his life spiraled to increasingly low depths as he engaged in crime, was arrested for drug trafficking and attempted murder, and spent five years in a terrible Arizona state prison.

Jimmy survived the brutality of guards and fellow inmates in two main ways. First, he largely taught himself how to read and write. By escaping into books and writing, he was "able to reach out and find a finger hold on the fragile ledge of hope."[2] Eager to learn as much as possible about Mexican and Indian history, art, and religion, he "began to feel. . . fused to thousands of years of culture. It was as if this new knowledge was peeling off layers of wax paper from my eyes. I had a clarity of thought and feeling I'd never experienced."[3] As he put it looking back at his prison term, "In a very real way, words had broken through the walls and set me free."[4]

Jimmy also escaped the horrors of prison life by remembering his childhood, with all its sweet and bitter memories. As he remembered the few happy times in his childhood, he was "safe and joyous again. The darkness of my cell glowed with the bright dawn light of Estancia. The walls of my cell slowly disintegrated into trees and a pond and village people coming out of their houses."[5] By remembering his past, "my memories were saving me from becoming a zombie in this place of no color, no stimulation, nothing to feed my senses."[6]

Rather than be consumed and defeated by the nightmare of years in prison, Jimmy emerged from his prison walls to discover a "place to stand" in a world that had never offered him an identity, no less a meaningful future. He became a renowned poet, writing five books by 2000 and winning numerous awards for his highly expressive creative works. Most importantly, he grew in spirit and self-respect, formed in the crucible of an abusive childhood and years of institutional incarceration.

8

MINING CHILDHOODS

JAMES K. HASTINGS
BOYHOOD IN A FRONTIER SILVER MINING CAMP[1]

*We know very little about James K. Hastings beyond what he re-
vealed about his childhood in a 1951 article that appeared in the* New
Mexico Historical Review. *But perhaps that is all we need to know about
this perceptive, sensitive boy who grew to manhood not only to describe
the silver mining camp he grew up in, but also to realize that there were
both wonderfully good and terribly bad men and women in every group—
white, Indian, Hispanic, black—on the New Mexico frontier.*

In April 1880 we were living in southern Colorado, at Trinidad. Father was in New Mexico at Silver City, near the Mexican border, and
it was decided that we should join him.

New Mexico, with its 121,666 square miles of area, may have had
possibly one resident per square mile at that time. There was snow on
the ground as we started south through the newly completed Raton tun-
nel, just over the line in New Mexico on the Santa Fe [Railroad]. When
we reached Albuquerque on the Rio Grande, we went into that town on a
construction train, said to be the first one into town. Spring had come by
that time and there was a riot of roses in the old town. We lay there some
days at a Mexican hotel until we could get a coach going south. I can
remember seeing a Mexican plowing in the river bottom near Ft. Craig
with a pair of tiny oxen and a forked stick for a plow. We had no Indian

trouble going down although they passed near us one night. We crossed the "Jornada del Muerto," or Journey of Death with its ninety miles without water. There were stage stations every twenty miles or so on the Jornada. One we stopped at had a high adobe wall surrounding it and there water hauled from the Rio Grande was always kept for travelers. . . . We reached Silver City on May 1, 1880, and father met us there.

Father was the superintendent of a quartz mill that crushed the silver ore from two mines, named the '76 and Baltic, located a few miles above town in a small valley on the Continental Divide, known as Chloride Flat. The ore was hauled down from the mines by four and six mule teams, in giant wagons with boiler plated beds. Silver reduction in a stamp mill is much like any other manufacturing business. The mill ran twenty-four hours a day for seven days a week, for about ten months in the year; in the heat of summer they laid off for repairs. The men worked twelve hours a day and drew good wages. . . .

The silver on coming from the retort was pure and was in danger of being stolen before being cast into the great bricks [of three hundred pounds each. These were unwieldy and smaller ones would have been more convenient, but also more easily stolen.] It was often moved to our house in the night for safe keeping. I can remember walking beside my father carrying his Colt's revolver as he and a trustworthy man carried the silver in a hand barrow. Of course if we had been attacked father, and not I, would have used the gun. One night someone evidently drunk tried with a steel bar to pry off our front door and get at our cache of silver. Father stood at the head of the stairs ready to shoot if the man gained entrance. . . .

Two express companies, the Adams and the Wells-Fargo, ran Concord coaches from our town to carry the mail, express, and passengers to the railroad at Deming, where it had reached within fifty miles of our town. The morning after we. . . cast a brick, one of these [coaches] would stop at the mill and take it to the railroad. Once a 350 pound brick broke through the coach floor on the desert and all the driver could do was to drive off and leave it. It was safe there for no pack mule could carry it away and a wagon could be traced by a fast posse. The abandoning of a $5,000 silver brick in the road did not bother us any, for when it was once signed for by the Wells-Fargo driver, it was their baby.

The. . . Apache Indians, under Victorio and Geronimo, were raiding at that time and kept us wondering when they would strike next. Many a rancher was picked off in that day but they never attempted a raid on our camp. . . . All [of our] food beside range beef, including the staples of flour, potatoes, sugar, and such, had to come from the railroad. While the mail coaches could go there and back in a day, sometimes under heavy guard, always changing horses every few miles, the "bull trains," as they were called, took plenty of time to make the round trip. They were owned and run by Mexicans [who] were easily frightened by an Indian rumor. When they got to good grass and water they would sometimes imagine danger. There they would park their wagons in a great circle and all drivers would guard and graze the cattle by day and yard them in the circle of wagons by night. No appeal from a hungry people had any effect to get that food started towards town. They wanted a cavalry escort, but the cavalrymen were busy elsewhere.

Most of us lived on a corn-bread diet at such time and had for dessert, sack pudding; neither was there any sugar. I can remember my three-year-old sister going to the bird cage and getting a lump of sugar from between the wires and scraping her teeth across it, and with a shake of her curls putting it back with the apparent thought that she must not rob the bird.

Those freighters had good cause to be cautious about the Indians. The saddest sight that I ever saw in a long life was on a Sunday morning when two soldiers came down the street in our town, the end of the coach line, driving two broken down cavalry horses hitched to a coach filled with bullet holes and covered with human blood. The Apaches had jumped the coach about sunrise, near Ft. Cummings, a six company post. The Indians had hid behind the tall Yucca stumps and killed every mortal on the coach. Of course they took the horses and every scrap of leather in the fore and aft boots, and leather mail sacks, probably to patch moccasins. They got away, although the post bugler blew "Boots and Saddles" at the first sound of gunfire. Our mail the next day, from those mail sacks, showed plenty of blood on it.

It was thus that the Southwest was settled. Guards were often carried on the coaches when needed. I remember riding all afternoon on top of a swaying Concord coach between two infantrymen dressed in blue, with their Long Tom rifles at hand, while away to the north on a flat-topped mountain signal fires talked to someone. An Indian of that day could do a lot with a blanket and a smoky campfire. He could have dots and dashes galore.

Many men of that day belted on their guns before they drew on their boots mornings, but they did not wear those traffic-cop belts; rather they were broad cartridge belts, and never drawn up snug, but the gun hung low on the right hip and there was no pulling a gun unless you meant to use it.

Our mill being so far from the others had a complete shop attached, with a carpenter, blacksmith, and molder. Stamp shoes were always wearing out with the incessant pounding, and so we ran a cupola to melt our scrap iron with charcoal made back in the hills. One of my jobs, when they melted, was to man the hose on the roof to see that no sparks started a fire. The men generally drenched me down first so as to not get the shirt burned off me. Sometimes they let me help load the cupola furnace with successive layers of charcoal and iron.

I realize now that I must have been a pest about the mill; with no school to go to I was there much of the time, although I was supposed to study some old school books at home. Once, when I had been too much of a nuisance, Dad asked, "Where are you in arithmetic young man?" I answered, "I have finished it," only to hear him say, "Go home and go through it again.". . .

I had a fine assortment of friends in that camp. We had school for only a month or so, when a traveling school master taught a few of us long enough to get money to move on with.

One of these friends was "Black Billie," an ex-slave, who was a hostler for the mill company. Mother had a large print New Testament and Billie delighted to come down to our house and read aloud from it, for his own and our benefit. He was allowed to take out a small team of mean mules hitched to a wagon without a bed. . . . Those mules loved to run away with him, and when they did his remarks were not those that he had found in Holy Writ. . . .

The carpenter, though old enough to be my father, was my special chum. When I saw him come down the street, trailed by a Chinese, carrying some long iron rods, I beat it to him. His first question was, "Did you ever read *Robinson Carusoe*, Jim?" Of course I admitted it, and he replied that he was Carusoe, and that his rear guard was Friday. From that hour, the man answered to that name. On the Chinese New Years, which came in the spring, he deluged us with presents. My brother and I got firecrackers, and the girls Chinese candy, while Dad, who never used tobacco, got a box of what in China must correspond to "Wheeling Stogies." I tried one once and quit for life.

Bill Green, the teamster hauling ore from the mine, was a good man and an especial friend. He and his wheeler, "Old Beck," saved my life once [while riding on a wagon coming down from the mine]. . . . The engineer and Green were on the wagon seat coming down the mountain with a load of ore, and I was precariously seated on the seat-back with my back to theirs when we jolted over a stone and I was thrown under the hind wheel. In a mule team of that day the best animal is the wheeler to the left of the pole, known as the "near wheeler." This place was filled by Beck, a monster black [mule], and when Green yelled to her, she froze in her breaching and held the team from moving. The wagon and load likely totaled five tons. In my fall, I had struck on the backs of both hands and sprained my wrists and lay in the track against the mountain slope helpless. There was a much used liniment for sale in the camp, for man and animals. The only kind they had on hand was for animals only, and was a dark brown, so I was as brown as a Malay for a while.

One of my friends of those days on the Mexican border was the Negro cook at the mine. He certainly knew his stuff and I have never eaten better meals. When the shaft whistle on the mine hoist blew, he was ready and his welcome cry of "come and get it" was always answered by a rush of hungry miners. One thing that endeared him to my boyish heart was that he was not fussy about clean hands and combed hair. . . . I enjoyed teasing him and I early found that he had a horror of the deep shafts in the mine and so I would wheedle him to go down in the shaft with me. His stock answer was, "No sah, Mister Jimmie, I can go out the doah and dig a hole six inches deep and get into that and it is deep enough for me.". . .

Our camp was the first town in that day from the Mexican border (before the railroad came), perhaps a hundred miles away and we had a custom house. Mexican horsemen who came past our house direct from their country with a bunch of skinny fowls dangling from their saddles, asked us two reals or twenty-five cents each for them, plus the customs tax. We often wondered if the custom house ever saw that tax. The regular freighters used ordinary wagons, but there were a few of the monster ox drawn two-wheeled carts with wooden wheels that were used in smuggling. In ordinary use the spindles were never greased and made a wail to be heard for miles, so when grease was applied to stop the noise it was almost prima facie evidence that smuggling was going on. . . .

There was one story of those wild days on the border that always thrilled me. The Apaches had crawled up and surprised the family in a Mexican jacal or hogan and killed everyone present. But they did not wipe out the family by so doing, for there was a slip of a twelve-year-old girl out herding the sheep. Those runty specimens, having a pound or two of wool on them, were little kin to our Merinos or Shrops of today, and it took one both young and fleet of foot to manage them and the small shepherdess was just that. The Indians knew of her being in the hills and wanted both her and the sheep and so started after her. Though desert bred and fast on their feet,. . . they simply were not in her class, as they found, when she [ran] off and left them, never to be caught. . . .

One of the danger spots of that day was Cook's Canyon. We came down through it one [day. Tired,] I crawled back into the rear of the wagon and went to sleep. When I awoke, the wagon was standing still and I heard gunfire. I could see nothing from where I lay and suspected Indians, so did not move or raise up until I heard our colored teamster Dan say, "I got two of them." Then I looked to see that it was rabbits instead of Indians that he meant. Two friendly Apache scouts. . . came along and cooked their rabbit over our fire. They did this without an atom of cleaning and then ate it. . . . They had red handkerchiefs about their heads or necks to distinguish them from warriors. They were armed with Winchesters. . . .

My daily routine when I was a boy in the mining camp was hardly routine, for few days were alike, but I did keep the water pails full. To do that I had to go to the St. Vincent spring where most of the women of the nearby Mexican village were gossiping and filling their pails and helping hoist them to the other's head. It was the stories that we had from Bible and pictures of that time over again. I do not remember ever seeing a man come for water. It was beneath them. If you had learned border Spanish you would have gotten an ear full. I used two discarded black powder cans with bails in them for my water pails. They held three or four gallons each and were pretty heavy when full. . . .

The Mexicans brought in wood (stove length) on burros. It was packed in a great circle over the beast's back, and when it was sold the muleteer pulled one thong from the raw hide rope holding it on and it all fell to the ground leaving the burros to walk out of the pile. We had a fireplace and so occasionally Father would get a cord or two of four-foot wood. . . . When it was dumped at our kitchen door, I knew it was my job to fit it for fireplace or kitchen stove. . . . Seeing that wood cut and neatly piled comes under the head of the "glory of achievement" that some educators tell of. When that wood was neatly ricked near the kitchen door I was again free to go afield. . . .

[On one memorable trip in the Mogollon mountains] we met men who, with the hospitality of the West, shared a deer with us that they had just killed. They had never seen us before, or would again likely. That night we toasted those tender steaks of venison over our camp fire while our biscuits baked in the embers beside the fire. It was the finest food ever. Then to bed on the ground with a buffalo robe over us on top of the blankets while my engineer friend taught me astronomy from the skies above, till sleep came. It was on that trip that a magnificent black tail buck came near to camp and stood and watched us, with those great antlers raised in the air. I will never again deride a man for having "buck fever." It would be a crime to shoot that majestic creature.

As this draws to a close I must say in defense of the Indians that most of the white men of that day and area were as fine as one could ask for, but some to my knowledge were just scum and they by their actions caused the Indians to hate the whites and that hatred was often taken out on defenseless people.

To illustrate the above let me give an example. The forts of that day. . . were not walled or stockaded, but were simply posts on an open field. They had to be to permit the cavalry troops to maneuver in drill. My father told me [about] an incident at one such post that used a log cabin for a guard house and in it was an Apache Indian confined for some misdemeanor. There was a bed in one corner of the room and the Indian was asleep on the bed next to the wall. Some of the soldiers had a camp fire near the cabin and one of the less desirable ones heated a steel rifle cleaning rod in the fire and then stuck it in between the logs and burned the sleeper. In his pain and fright he dashed out the door and was promptly shot and killed by the guard, who naturally believed that the prisoner was attempting an escape. When Chief Cochise. . . heard of it he swore that he would make the "trail run red from Taos to Tucson," and figuratively speaking he did just that.

I can remember one day when seated on a mountain top I, a thirteen-year-old. . . , saw below me the valley of the Rio Grande, and the river winding through it showed like a white thread on the floor. From the same lofty perch I could see through the clear air the smoke of the construction trains of both the Santa Fe and the Southern Pacific [railroads]. They were building the lines that when they met would span the continent. As a boy I was permitted to see the nation growing. No one dreamed in that faraway day of the stature it would attain today.

ORAL HISTORIES
COAL TOWN CHILDHOOD[1]

Dawson, New Mexico, was one of many company towns established in the Southwest in the early twentieth century. Like other company towns of that era, Dawson was relatively small (population 4,000 in 1920), isolated (twenty-five miles from the nearest large town, Raton), and with a single dominant industry (coal mining in this case). As in similar communities, its company (here the Phelps Dodge Corporation) owned practically all property in town, from the coal mining operations to all stores and housing, while controlling nearly every aspect of life in a type of benevolent dictatorship.

Dawson's labor force and population were likewise typical of company towns: a "salad bowl" of ethnicities and races, including immigrants from southern and eastern Europe, refugees from the Mexican Revolution, Hispanics from old New Mexico families, blacks originally from the South, and whites from seemingly every part of the country. These diverse groups and cultures got along remarkably well in a community where "everyone was in the same boat" and there was little "keeping up with the Joneses." What was true of adults was even truer of their offspring, as reflected in the following description of what it was like to grow up in this small mining community of northeastern New Mexico.

"Hey, Mookie!" "Mookie!" "MOO-OOO-KEEEE!"

There was "Brains" and "Birdseed" and "Weasel" and "Coomy" and "Snake" and, of course, "Mookie." Growing up in Dawson so often meant acquiring a nickname. Some of the handles were obvious, such as "Lefty" or "Red" or "Skinny" or "Chubby." But others had a story of their own.

For instance, if your Dawson friends saw you holding a baby, you might wind up being called "Doc," as Earnest Bergamo did. And not just Doc for a few months; you were Doc forever. If you were Earnest Mares, and your given name was Neto, but an eight-year-old pal mispronounced it, you were "Nebs." And what of Mookie? Poor little Henry Peppin. The kid clears his throat one day, brings up a bit of mucus, and he's branded for life. . . .

Being given a nickname—"Chango" or "Puso" or Growlo"—and having it stick reveals the extraordinary fondness that people in the town had and still have for one another. Dawson may be gone, but the nicknames are one strong way the place endures. The nicknames, even the ones that describe physical characteristics, have nothing to do with ridicule. Rather, the sobriquets should be interpreted as badges of membership, to be used only by those who lived in Dawson. The names then are signs of respect and to be understood in this fashion: listen, I spent my childhood in a carefree place where everyone liked me and where we had a great time and where we frequently called each other silly things. But listen, it was all done with genuine affection.

Maybe it was because Dawson was a company town, but if you were a kid there was always plenty to do in the community. Not necessarily organized things, for it is really the unorganized, the free things, that are remembered most. Every neighborhood in town, from Capitan to Five Hill, had a favored spot, a level and smooth patch of dirt, where kids would lay down a small piece of stretched-out rabbit skin, put their knuckles on the rug, and shoot marbles. . . .

There were games of hopscotch and capture-the-flag, and everybody in Dawson had a tire. If you went to visit somebody's house, you took your tire with you, rolling it alongside you as you walked. The brave children—and girls usually were the bravest—would climb inside a tire and have somebody send them down the hill from Capitan, spinning so hard and bumping so much they felt like their insides had been taken out, stirred about, and then stuffed back.

Tire-rolling, sad to say, is a lost pastime. So is storytelling. In the evenings, after dinner, Dawson families would gather on their front porches and tell stories. . . . Grandparents would sit there and, in halting English, tell about the old country. And their grandchildren would *listen.* Children in Dawson weren't afraid to play outside in the dark because adults were right there—on that porch. Oh, once in a while an elderly Hispanic woman in Dawson might get upset with her kids out after dark because *La Llorona*, the Weeping Woman of Mexican folklore who is lamenting the loss of her children who were drowned in a river, was said to be out and about, even though the crying sounded just like the wind coming down the canyon. In fact, when rumors spread that *La Llorona* might possibly be in town, the company store sold out of flashlights.

From the very earliest days in the town, growing up in Dawson was almost wondrous. For a newcomer entering Dawson seventy-five years ago, the town must have appeared absolutely entrancing, what with the coke ovens burning night and day, and the *clankety-clank* sound of coal cars feeding those ovens, and the mule-drawn wagons pulling loads, and the kids playing in the dirt streets. Phelps Dodge did much to organize activities for kids, starting with the Scout House, which went up in 1923 atop Gobbler's Roost. Built of coke breeze blocks, inside was a kitchen, locker room, and stone fireplace, and the house was always busy. Indeed, during the 1920s Dawson had *two* Boy Scout troops. The Scouts had a basketball team, a band, a summer camp, and even held first-aid competitions. President Warren Harding was so impressed by the enthusiasm of the town's Scouts that he sent a letter saluting Dawson. Maybe the high point of those years for the scouts came in June 1923, when a Dawson Boy Scout named David Hardin jumped into the Cimarron River and rescued a small girl being swept downstream.

As Scouts discovered, along with just about every other young person, the wide-open spaces around Dawson offered the greatest playground imaginable. Sitting in the middle of a giant canyon, Dawson was surrounded by visually stunning hills teeming with wildlife. The hunt was on: some kids had traplines, but many owned an old, single-shot .22, so beat up it took a penknife to remove the spent shells. There were plenty of jackrabbits to aim those .22's at, and adults, such as George Fenlon, the school superintendent, loved to lead expeditions. Some hunting parties went out unchaperoned, of course, such as when Bill Saul and Carlyle Vickers went hunting one afternoon, and, thinking a giant bird was going to swoop down and pick them up, opened fire on a golden eagle. . . .

Was there anything better than a Dawson summer? July and August meant going to Cimarron Canyon to fish in the shade of the palisades, or over to the irrigation canals near Maxwell to get crawdads, filling up a gunnysack with them, and later at home boiling them in water and finally eating the lobster-like things. Summer meant going to the town swimming pool, or if you could not afford the dime it cost kids to get in, or even a pair of swimming trunks—and during the Great Depression, not that many people in Dawson could—it meant heading up to the Vermejo River, a couple of miles or so to where the river curved, and making a dam out of sand and rocks to construct your own swimming hole. Summer meant hiking out to the mile sign on the railroad tracks, where there stood a large grove of plums and choke-cherries to pick—or searching for gooseberries and *quelities*, or wild spinach. Summer meant going to the circus that would come to town bringing a Ferris wheel that would be set down in the baseball park, along with such sideshow oddities as "The Big Snake," a huge reptile that died during one performance in Dawson and whose owners blamed the town because the air was said to be too cold and the altitude too high.

Fall meant the arrival of the grapes, by truck or by train car, and that meant kids could help in the pressing and crushing of those grapes, which were used to make homemade wine. In many Dawson homes, especially during Prohibition, make-shift stills gave miners a chance to augment their wages. Fall meant Halloween, and that meant removing the furniture from Mr. Fenlon's front porch and putting it up on the church steeple and then waiting to hear him say, resignedly, the next day, "OK, you better get it down now." Halloween was also a time for tipping over outhouses, the standard-issue bathroom in Dawson for many years and having the town marshal, the all-knowing L. O. Mace, nicknamed "Dick Tracy," or Mace's successor, Jack "The Shadow" Randall, take you to P. K. Carson, who was wiser than a treeful of owls. In Dawson, you didn't only get in trouble with the law, you got in trouble with the town, which was worse because most fathers worked for the company, which, of course, owned the town. "*State attenti!*" Italian mothers warned their children, "Be careful." It was said less out of worry about possible injury than concern for getting in trouble with the company, which could cause a father to lose his job. . . .

Winter's arrival—and the moderate snow that Dawson usually received—signaled closing off Church Row and using pieces of tin as sleds to slide down the little incline on that street. Or checking out the toboggans that Phelps Dodge owned, and trudging up Capitan with those boards. Winter, of course, also meant Christmas and that meant going to Tip-Top, the hilly area between Loreta and Capitan, and cutting down your family's tree. . . . For a Dawson child, Christmas meant going to the Opera House and walking onstage past the big Christmas tree to receive from a P.D. official a bag of candy and a small toy. For a brief period later, when that child was older, Christmas meant getting from P.D. a necktie or a pair of stockings. New Year's Eve meant a town dance at the gym, then midnight Mass at the Catholic church, then back to the gym for more dancing.

In spring, when rains came and the streets turned muddy, Dawson kids pulled out their homemade stilts and traversed the town. Spring meant catching rabbits and raising them as pets. Spring also meant creating kites out of newspaper and wooden box frames, gluing them together with flour and water, and then flying the craft in the alfalfa field that lay between the filling station and the Vermejo.

In any season, Dawson kids would, in the tradition of Andy Hardy, put on plays or shows in their garage, shed, or basement. All one needed was a sheet for a curtain and some stick matches for the price of admission. Having a good time might mean crossing the swinging bridge to Loreta or begging for a ride on the Polly, the El Paso & Southwestern Railroad's little passenger train that followed the coal cars' route to Tucumcari. A round-trip to Roy was a great way to kill a day; you could sit on the train's wooden seats and stare at the initials "EP&SW" on the door and imagine they stood for "Eat Plenty and Sleep Well." Fun for Dawson kids was simply where you found it. Jess "Chuy" Ponce and his buddy, Tony Arellano, used to go down to the cemetery and while away hours there at night. Jess would sit on his sister's grave, and Tony on his father's marker, and they'd spend the night talking. About what? About how brave they were. Henry Reza and his friends liked to go to the White Rocks, the sandstone outcropping on Capitan. There, at night, they would build a bonfire and roast marshmallows or potatoes, look at the northern lights, sing, and tell ghost stories. When the food was gone and faces were charred, everybody went home, happy as ticks in a dog's ear.

Dawson girls did most of the things that the boys did. . . . Little Mary Calderone was the best marbles shooter in Capitan, maybe in all of the town. Dawson girls did things that boys weren't expected to do, too, such as help out when a baby brother or sister was being born in the home, which happened frequently in the camps that were far from the hospital or where the parents simply didn't trust doctors. For girls, too, there were dances in the gym after the basketball game. "Everybody went," says Lena Colaizzi Forte. "Adults and little kids, three, four years old. The young kids would dance on the side of the gym, and the others in the middle of the floor." Dawson girls also had parties. . . .

Food and drink play prominent roles in almost every Dawson childhood memory. For Paul Brozovich, whose parents were Slavic, growing up meant watching his mother, Katarina, owner of a boardinghouse, cook up huge plates of *kielbasa* and sauerkraut, *potica*, and apple strudel. Fred Becchetti can still smell slices of warm bread and slabs of cheese on his kitchen table. Often there was homemade wine on those tables as well. Alice DiLorenzo used to watch her father, Domenic, brew what everyone called "Dago red" in the family cellar, and then keep small glasses filled with it at mealtime. . . .

Part of the fun of being a kid in Dawson was seeing what you could get away with. For George Dale, that meant sneaking into the Opera House to see a movie: "This was around 1930, and here's what we'd do. Somebody younger, maybe my brother Bill, or Coomy Jackovich, who lived up the street, would pay the dime to get in and then go up in the balcony and open the fire escape door, and then a bunch of us would follow."

At any time of the year there was bound to be a shivaree. When someone got married in Dawson—say Matt Scanlon and Mary Lou Covert—the couple usually couldn't afford much of a honeymoon. Indeed, the wedding night often was spent in town at a friend's house. Every kid knew what house that was. At 3:00 A.M. after the wedding, the youthful Dawsonites would go to that address, stand outside, and bang on pots and pans until the newlyweds came out and told the rabble-rousers to pipe down. If that didn't do the trick, and it usually didn't, the groom would reach down into his pockets for a bribe, usually a few coins or a candy bar. . . .

For many young men, growing up meant thinking about your father coming home dog-tired and soot-covered from the mine. Would you follow him? You certainly wanted to work, for that was the Dawson way. For many in town, work became a chief means of coming of age. For

Harmon Black, work meant delivering the *Denver Post*, a day late, around town for a nickel. On his route, Black usually would stop at the Snake, which at the time had a big painting of a nude woman hanging behind the bar. Wearing knickers and a newsboy cap, Black would walk in and try not to stare at that startling piece of art. At some point a miner usually would say to him,. "Hey, Harmon, you can come in, but I don't want you to look at that girl," which, of course, only made him look harder.

Paul Brozovich found work in a place just as entertaining as the Snake. Brozovich's parents ran a boardinghouse up by Number One Camp. It was a hostelry filled with single miners, one of whom eventually ran off with Brozovich's teenage sister and the boardinghouse profits. Brozovich's first job was delivery boy. Pulling a red, Radio Flyer wagon, he would take wine and beer and bread and eggs from the boardinghouse up to nearby Coontown, the unfortunately named black community at the north end of Dawson. To Camp Number Three, where the shot firers and foreman lived, he'd take chickens and rabbits. And a couple of times a day Brozovich did something numerous Dawson kids did: he went looking for coal. "I got scrap coal and the other stuff that fell off the cars on the way to the tipple, and hauled it home. We didn't have to pay to heat our house that way. I used to put about two gunnysacks worth of coal in that wagon a day. Only trouble was, every year or so we'd have to get a new wagon.". . .

Steve Schulte also assisted his father, who was a baker in the Mercantile. Every morning at about 5:00 A. M., starting when he was eight or nine, Schulte would go to the third floor of the company store and help the old man fry and frost doughnuts and wrap bread, on a big workbench. Schulte would stay there until 8:00 A.M. when school started. Schulte was the envy of his crowd—who didn't like glazed doughnuts? As for pay, Schulte never told his friends how much he earned. "Every other Saturday," he says, "I would get a bottle of pop for my work."

The Toe Ticklers. That was the name of the Dawson dance band to which Bob McClary belonged. "We'd tie a bass drum on the baggage rack of a '34 sedan and play roadhouses—the Club Luna in Raton, and at Colfax, and weddings at Maxwell and dances up on Johnson Mesa, northeast of Raton. We got $120 a night, which for a six-piece band was pretty darn good. I played trumpet. I was seventeen, and I don't know how I got into some of those clubs. Maybe we played that wedding at Maxwell for free. But we got all you could drink."

Surely one of the most industrious kids in Dawson was Pete Trujillo. . . . First, he delivered milk for a dairy south of town. The driver drove a horse-drawn hearse, while Trujillo followed on foot. Ran is more like it. Then he had a shoeshine job. He'd go to the Snake on payday, when money was sure to be tossed around by miners as well as local cowboys, who would tie their horses up out front and, on occasion, even ride those horses through the saloon's swinging front doors. When Trujillo was about ten, he started selling chewing gum door-to-door in Dawson. An outfit in Cincinnati would send him two or three boxes of gum on consignment, and little Pete would walk around town and try to hawk it. Then he sold shoes and clothes door-to-door from a mail-order catalog. He sold women's dresses and panties even. If he sold five suits, he'd get one free. "I was the best-dressed kid in town," he remarks.

Not everything was idyllic for a Dawson child, of course. Sickness, particularly the 1918 influenza epidemic, left scars on the impressionable. "People were dying so fast," says Amelia Lopez García. "We had several bachelors in our neighborhood, and Mother would cook pots of soup and have us go and feed them. I think she saved quite a few people because they got a little nourishment." The bodies were taken to the cemetery by mule-drawn wagons, and García says that, even today, she can remember seeing them go by. Across the river from town, near the ranch, stood a pesthouse, a brick building where many kids were sentenced to recuperate during the days of scarlet fever and other scourges.

And, of course, the miners were always there, threatening to disrupt the innocence of youth. "The greatest fear I ever had growing up," says Albert Rivera, "was hearing the whistle blow." The power plant whistle would set off whenever there was a mine explosion, accident, or fatality. We knew when the whistle went off that it spelled disaster. It scared me."

The sight of the old Dodge ambulance, every Dawsonite knew, [meant trouble]. . . Paul Brozovich was playing outside one day when he saw the ambulance rumble by a creek near his house. . . . When the vehicle got closer, Brozovich looked inside and saw his father, a miner also named Paul Brozovich, in the front seat. Young Paul ran down and jumped on the running board to get a better look. His father, he learned, had been cutting coal when a piece of cable had come down and stuck him in the right eye. He would lose the eye, but not his life.

The whistle could mean a fire, too—one blow for each number of the camp where the fire was located. "I was in the fourth grade and looked out of Douglas School and heard the whistle at the same time," says Albert Rivera. "It was our house burning down! My brother Pantaleon had been playing with matches. The company gave us food and clothing, and people gave us things. That was one thing about Dawson: when there was a disaster, the entire town rallied around."

Some childhood memories hurt even now. Livia Montepara Mora was ten years old when her mother died. As the eldest of three children, Livia then had to take care of her two younger sisters and her father, Pietro Montepara, a timberman. . . . "I had to cook and clean, and I only got to go to the fourth grade. I taught myself to read and write. It was hard. Then when I was twelve, my father married again. I thought we had it made, but I was so wrong. This was a woman twenty years older than my father, and it didn't work out at all. She resented the three of us, my sisters and me. She started hitting us kids, and once she beat me so bad I had to go to the hospital. They took us kids away from my father, and I went to Raton to live. Finally, my father divorced her, and we went back to live with him.". . .

A lack of money, as the Monteparas and others would readily admit, did hurt Dawsonites, particularly during the Great Depression. "The times were hard, no question," says Henry Reza. "There were strikes in the mines, and families went without. But the Depression also gave us Dawson kids a better appreciation for the value of something simple. . . ." "There *were* pay cuts and layoffs," says Alberta McClary. "But I think children in other towns felt the Depression more. We got by in Dawson; the words we always used were 'make do.'"

Language for a Dawson immigrant presented problems, but many newly arrived children seemed to look upon speaking as an adventure. "I couldn't speak English when I got there in 1918," says Amelia García. "But I didn't mind because most of the children were having the same trouble. We were so many nationalities. Our neighbors were Louis Massaroni and his wife, Emma. Their children said "hurley" for *hurry*, so I figured I had learned one word."

Thirteen stands out as a memorable age, a bench mark age when the recollection of childhood and its attendant nicknames were sealed, when the responsibility of adulthood and its disappointments were only vaguely suggested. . . . For Roger Scanlon, some good memories of being age thirteen in Dawson surfaced at a crucial time in his life, as a healing force. Scanlon was in the navy in 1951, serving off the coast of Korea, on the U.S.S. *Partridge*, a minesweeper. On February 3, the *Partridge* got hit by a mine. It was a wooden ship, and the explosion ripped through the vessel. The blast killed about half of the twenty-eight men on board, and Scanlon lost his right leg. "I was hospitalized on Oakland for about nine months," he says. "I remember lying there, knowing I was one hundred percent disabled, and feeling sorry for myself. Then I start thinking about Dawson and growing up there. All the good times. That's what started making me better. . . . It was a wonderful life then, and it kept me alive."

As a result of adverse economic conditions in the post-World War II era, the Phelps Dodge Corporation closed its coal mining operation in Dawson by mid-1950. Its closing was sad, but hardly unique in an era when nearly every company town in New Mexico (and most in the nation) buckled under similar economic strains.

But Dawson's impact lived on. As with Roger Scanlon, memories of happy childhoods in Dawson helped many an adult face life's troubles with strength. Hundreds still attend regular town reunions, said to be the occasion for the most hugging among old friends in all of New Mexico. They come back, says Nick Gonzales, in search of the lost security they enjoyed in Dawson. But Nick admits they "really don't find it. See, there'll never be a place. . . without discrimination, with great friendliness, with everybody helping each other. There'll never be a [Dawson] again, but you can still remember."[2]

9

NATIVE AMERICAN CHILDHOODS

TALL WOMAN
HARD TIMES AND GOOD ON THE NAVAJO RESERVATION[1]

Rose Mitchell, whose adult Indian name was Tall Woman, was born into a highly traditional Navajo family in the mid-1870s. She spent her entire life on or near the Navajo Reservation, an enormous area stretching into three states: Arizona, Utah, and New Mexico. As a nomadic family, her parents and siblings moved with the seasons to herd their livestock and live off the plants and countless resources of their sacred earth.

Navajo girl, looking much as Tall Woman probably looked while growing up on the Navajo Reservation. Calla Eylar Wolfe Collection, Neg. No. RG84-103. Courtesy of the Rio Grande Historical Collections, New Mexico State University Library, New Mexico State University, Las Cruces, New Mexico.

W hen I was very small, we went through lots of hardships. My brothers and sisters and I barely had enough to eat and we had very little to live by. We were even barefoot most of the time. But we managed to get by. . . .

In my childhood there were no trading posts near here; all I remember is my parents talking about the ones that had started at Ganado, Fort Defiance, and Round Rock. None of those places were close to where we ever lived. . . . So it took several days to go to those far, distant places and my father did not do that very often. The women in our family would weave rugs to be taken to Ganado and traded for the provisions we needed. That's where we got the white muslin cloth[,]. . . the only kind of cloth we could get from those trading posts. Most of the time my mother, my sisters, and I would make our own skirts from that cloth; we used it just the way it was. . . .

[I]f we had any footwear at all, it was out of buckskin with a rawhide sole. That's all we wore, if we were lucky enough to have any. . . . As far back as I can remember, my older sisters and my mother had two pairs of moccasins each, which my father had made for them. To do that, he had to go hunting. . . . They went [hunting] on horseback, but I never knew where they went. . . .

I remember we all suffered from hunger. When my mother used to tell us about her childhood days and how they suffered from hunger, I used to think it was just the same with us. . . .

In those early times, we moved back and forth with our sheep; it was all open range then and there were no fences anywhere. The land was there for everyone's use and the People moved around, sharing the land. No one was permanently settled and no one thought any family owned any particular place. . . .

In those days, we gathered a lot of what we ate. My mother and father told us those things had been put there for our use, and that we should learn how to use them for our food. . . . They also said to always look for tracks of different kinds of animals that might be around, here and there, because we could eat them, too.

When I was small, we ate rabbits a lot. . . . When I was herding with my older sister, lots of times rabbits would get in among the sheep. Then one of us would come up behind them and kill them with a stick. . . . We also hunted prairie dogs. . . . The easiest way to catch them is to use water if you have that available. One person pours some water into their hole while the other stands there, ready to kill them with a stick when they come out. . . .

Sometimes we also killed squirrels and chipmunks while we were herding. . . . And every now and then. . . a dog might corner something like a badger, or even a porcupine. If that thing ended up dead, either because of the dogs or because we clubbed it, then we'd bring it home to use for food. . . . I don't know how many times I ate that when I was little, but it was very good. The meat under their spines is really good!. . .

Whenever they were available, all of us used to gather [piñón] nuts. We all liked to eat them and my mother liked to cook meat with those nuts. She would shell them first; then she'd take a backbone from a sheep or some other animal, cut it up, and cook it with the [piñón] nuts [as a stew]. . . .

We made cheese from goat's milk. . . .

When I was a little girl, there were no wells anywhere, no windmills. So everyone had to dig to get water for their own use and for the animals. . . . One of the things we carried water in was the skin of a young goat. My mother taught us how to prepare the skin for making one of those bags. You have to be very careful when you butcher, if you're going to make that. You cut the neck and then close it on that side. . . . When you fill it with water and close the neck opening, you have a big bag for carrying water. You can carry it on your back or lay it across the horse's neck and bring it home that way. . . .

We drank any kind of water, and never paid any attention to whether it was good or bad. I imagine we swallowed lots of bad things with that water. When you get water from near the surface, digging shallow holes like that, no doubt other things, like dogs, coyotes, and wild animals drink it, too. . . .; that's the way we were in those days. . . .

[M]y mother and father used both the goats and sheep for meat. . . . My mother made blood sausage after we butchered, and used everything else from those animals, too. We kept those skins, and after drying them out, we used those to sleep on; those were our beds. . . .

My mother told me that right after I started walking and running, before I was really old enough, I started trying to run after my older sister and brother who were herding. I just wanted to go with them. . . .

In spite of all kinds of weather, we had to herd. Even in the winter, when the snow was deep, we had to herd. . . . The [children who did not] herd stayed home and helped my mother with the weaving while my older sister and I were out herding. The two of us were the only ones in the family responsible for that. . . .; all we ever did when I was small was herd sheep [and goats].

What I learned right away was that once those goats got out in the open, they took off like jackrabbits or deer. And once they did that, the sheep would start following them, spreading out in all directions. When that happened, my older sister and I would have to chase around after them, just like we were chasing a deer. . . . It was so hard to get them back together. . . . But when you're herding, that's your job. . . so they aren't running all over the place and getting lost.

Water was very scarce in the summer when it didn't rain. Then we'd have to move the sheep;. . . sometimes we'd take them toward the mountains; sometimes, we just went toward Canyon del Muerto. . . . If you go far enough, you come to where there are some natural springs in the rocks. . . . But sometimes the only water we could find would be inside one of the caves in the Canyon. It'd be too hard to try and get the sheep in there, so my sister or I would go, get the water out, and haul it back down to where the sheep waited.

Sometimes when we herded, my parents let us use a donkey. They always tried to have two of them around, and sometimes if one of those was not needed for some other purpose, they told us we could ride it. When I was small, I never rode alone; I always sat behind my sister, riding double with her. When I got older, if both donkeys were available, each of us would ride one. . . .

One time when the two of us were herding, the dogs we had that helped us herd had followed us. They were big dogs and. . . started barking and howling, and carrying on when they were near us. I guess they smelled a bear. . . .

So when we got home that day, my older sister told my father about the way the dogs were carrying on while we were herding. She told him where we had gone and that even though we had looked all around, we didn't see signs of anything. But despite that, the dogs kept barking and barking. . . . [M]y father said that besides bears, there were other things up there in those mountains, like coyotes, wolves, mountain lions, and other animals. But he told us that as long as we didn't bother them, and as long as they weren't hungry, they wouldn't attack or do anything like that. He also said we should never use the word *shash* [bear]. . . .when we were out herding because the bears would hear us and be offended. He said we shouldn't be scared of them. . . . But, who wouldn't be scared when they were told about all those things roaming around up there in the mountains?. . .

Sometimes in the summer, when my father came back up to where we were living in the mountains, he'd tell us he had seen a *Bilagaana* [white person] coming through the [valley] while he was checking on his crops. Every now than then, one or two of them would come along on horseback, leading a pack horse. These people would stop at the little ramada he had built there near the fields for his own use, and try and talk with him. Then they'd go on. My father never said what their purpose was. . . .

It was a few years after my father started seeing white people that my older sisters and I saw them for the first time. We were out herding. . . .[and] we were afraid of them. A few men were coming through the valley; each of them was riding one horse and leading another with lots of things packed on it. We didn't know what they were doing. They were just all full of hair, and their beards were *big*. That scared us and we told our parents about it when we brought the sheep in. . . . Maybe they were trading, but I don't think so. Some of the People said those white people were spies or something like that.

The others who traveled through the valley in those days were Indians who came to trade with us. . . . [My mother] told us to get to know those people and learn how to exchange things with them because that would be important to us in the future. . . .

In those days, food was scarce. But after we started growing corn, we always had that around; it became our main food. . . . My mother showed all of us how to fix the corn in many different ways; we had different colored corn and there's different things you make from each. . . . Pretty soon all of us, even my younger sister, learned how to fix things for the whole family to eat. Some of the corn we made into cornmeal mush and then fixed that in different ways. Some of it we used for making different kinds of bread, like [*tortillas*], fry bread, the gig and small *tamales*, dumplings, paperbread, the corn cake we baked in the ground,. . . and other kinds. . . .

There are also some special foods that must be made when you have certain ceremonies, because they go with those. My mother started to show us how to do all those things. . . .

After we fixed something to eat, we got out the wool my mother kept in sacks in our hogan. The wool had been sheared from our sheep. Every night, all of us would sit and work on the wool, carding and spinning it for the rugs my mother and older sisters were making. And so, in that way, we kept going along while I was growing up as a young girl.

Tall Woman became a well-known weaver, an expert on the uses of wild plants, and a much-requested midwife. She married Frank Mitchell, a respected political leader, a judge, and a traditional singer on the Navajo Reservation. The couple had twelve children and led an unassuming life, following the Blessingway of Navajo culture and urging their children to do the same. "Let the Blessingway be their guide," said Tall Woman. "I believe in that very, very strongly and I know it will see all of [my children] through whatever hardships they have to face, just as it did for Frank and me all the way along."[2]

LORI ARVISO ALVORD
FULL CIRCLE[1]

In contrast to Tall Woman, who grew up on the Navajo Reserva-tion, Lori Arviso Alvord spent her Navajo childhood in Crownpoint, New Mexico, on the outskirts of the vast reservation. By living in a white-domi-nated community so near the reservation, she found herself caught be-tween two cultural worlds with few Native American role models to emu-late and admire. She also explains that she felt caught between two worlds because she was half Navajo and half white. Her childhood story describes how she coped with these dilemmas and many others, especially her father's problems with alcohol, caused largely by his inability to deal with similar dilemmas in his own life.

"**D**r. Alvord, Dr. Alvord, please call the hospital," my beeper goes off with a voice message. I am sitting at the kitchen table in my home in Gallup, New Mexico, just fifty miles from my childhood home of Crownpoint, a tiny town on the eastern border of the Navajo reservation. I am a surgeon. . . at the Gallup Indian Medical Center. Three decades ago, I played on the mesas surrounding Crownpoint, never dreaming that my life path would turn down the most unexpected of "canyons," leading me back full circle to my home and my people.

As a child, I never dreamed of becoming a doctor, much less a sur-geon. We didn't have Navajo doctors, lawyers, or other professionals. I grew up in a poor community of working-class families. Even poorer fami-lies, who lacked running water and electricity, lived nearby on the [Na-vajo] reservation. . . . My own family had a precarious existence; my fa-ther was Navajo—charming, intelligent, and handsome—but subject to alcoholic binges. My mother was blonde, blue-eyed, and very attractive, but she married my father before she finished high school. He brought her to the reservation to work with him at a trading post when she was two weeks shy of her sixteenth birthday. She had been raised in Belen, a little town along the Rio Grande. They began married life in a remote part of the reservation, a little settlement called Whitehorse Lake.

My two younger sisters and I grew up in a fragile world. I remember childhood as a succession of never-ending worries: Would my dad lose his job? Freeze from exposure during one of his binges? Get involved in a car accident that hurt him or someone else? Fear and uncertainty were a part of my everyday life, but our family seemed to respond with an abundance of love for one another, as though that would shelter us if everything else collapsed.

During the times when Dad was drinking, though, all bets were off. As a young child, I listened many nights to my parents fighting—the shouting, slurred words, doors slamming, and cars roaring off into the darkness. I remember the craziness of those nights, the despair, the rides in the backseat of an erratic, fast-moving car. When I grew older, Dad woke me up at night to discuss things far too philosophical for a child. I would listen quietly, and talk with him, hoping he would fall asleep, hoping he wouldn't get up and walk out the door into the night. . . .

I sought refuge deep in the pages of books, escaping to Russia with Dr. Zhivago, or to Alaska with Jack London's characters. My mother and grandfather had taught me to read before I entered school, and I preferred reading to almost any other pastime. In grade school, I did so well academically that I was accelerated from third to fifth grade, a move which pleased me, but which almost led to my social downfall. Younger and smaller than the other children in my class, I found it hard to fit in, and I began to retreat into solitude. . . .

Crownpoint was a very small town on the western side of New Mexico. Though there was a significant Native population, all the merchants, teachers, doctors, and engineers were white. I found myself between two worlds: living inside the Navajo world, but sometimes feeling very distant from it; being half-white, but never referring to myself as white.

My father and grandmother had been punished for speaking Navajo in school. Navajos were told that, in order to be successful, they would need to forget their language and culture and adopt American ways. They were warned that if they taught their children Navajo, the children would have a harder time learning in school, and would therefore be at a disadvantage. This pressure to assimilate—along with the complete subjugation of the tribes following the Indian wars of the 1800's, the poverty due to poor grazing lands, forced stock reduction, and lack of jobs—all combined to bring the Navajo people to their knees, and a sense of deep shame prevailed.

My father suffered terribly from this; he had been a straight-A student, sent away to one of the best prep schools in the state. My father wanted to be like the rich, white children who surrounded him, but the differences were too apparent. At home on the reservation, he enjoyed his Navajo lifestyle—hunting deer, fishing, and cherishing the outdoor world. Later, he would bring these loves to our family life; we spent many happy times camping and fishing on mountain lakes in the summer, and hunting deer in the winter. We learned how to track animals, and how to appreciate and respect wildlife. Though hunting is usually a "male" activity, he seemed not to notice that his three children lacked a Y chromosome.

Outside the reservation, however, the world was not so friendly. In his mind, my father rebelled against the limitations of being Navajo in the 1940's and '50's. He went to the University of New Mexico, majoring in pre-med and Latin, until he married my mother and took a job to support her. He began to hate himself for not being able to fit into the white world and for not fulfilling his dreams. He flooded his grief with alcohol. Later in his life, his drinking episodes became much less frequent as he sought to control the disease, but he didn't escape its ultimate outcome. My father's life ended in 1993 in an alcohol-related automobile accident.

As a child, I saw the darkness of this subjugation over our lives, but I did not understand the roots of his anguish until I was a teenager, when I began to read Native American history and absorbed the reality that the all-American hero, Kit Carson, was in fact an arsonist who waged his campaign against the Navajo by burning settlements of men, women, and children to the ground. I read the history of tribe after tribe: the broken treaties, the massacres, the battles that were won not by wits and skill, but by superior weapons technology. I was heartbroken and very angry. With like-minded friends, I watched the takeover of Wounded Knee, South Dakota, and the rise of the American Indian movement. Although I didn't agree with all the principles of the movement, I too wanted to strike out against the America that had done this to my people. It took me years before I understood that this kind of anger was more destructive than beneficial.

Meanwhile, I added courses in Navajo language to my studies. The struggle to become fluent in Navajo began as a teenager and continues to this day, for Navajo is a very complex language, described by linguists as one of the hardest in the world to master. Though I cherished both sides of my heritage, I often felt that I didn't completely belong in either world. I would find, in the non-Indian world, that respect for elders was not present: people talked too much, laughed too loud, asked too many questions, had no respect for privacy, were overly competitive, and put a higher value on material wealth. Navajos, on the other hand, place much more emphasis on a person's relations to family, clan, tribe, and the other inhabitants of the earth, human and nonhuman. In the Navajo world, there are also codes of behavior that were sometimes hard for me to follow as a child. We were taught to be humble and not to draw attention to ourselves, to favor cooperation over competition (so as not to make ourselves "look better" at another's expense, or hurt the feelings of someone else), to avoid prolonged eye contact, to be quiet and reserved, to respect those who were older than us, and to reserve opinions until they were asked for.

This was the hardest for me in the classroom, where peer pressure against attracting attention to oneself prevents Navajo children from raising their hands to answer a question in class even though they might know the answer. I enjoyed school and loved learning, so I felt like a racehorse locked in a barn. . . .

Despite serious obstacles, Lori Arviso Alvord graduated from Crownpoint High School and earned her college degree at Dartmouth College in New Hampshire. She earned her M.D. from Stanford Medical School in 1985. She returned to New Mexico to serve the needs of the Navajo people at the Gallup Indian Medical Center. She is married to Jonathan Alvord and has one son. As suggested in the title of her autobiographical chapter, her life has been a triumphant full circle.

10

SCHOOL LIVES

TOMÁS WESLEY BROWN
MISCHIEF AT A HOMESTEADERS' SCHOOL[1]

Tomás Wesley Brown was one of five children born to a Quay County homesteading family in eastern New Mexico. The Browns were among the more fortunate homesteaders, thanks largely to their determination, hard work, and many blessings. Their life seems primitive by modern standards: they lived in a small house, relied on mesquite brush and cow chips for fuel, and used a doorless outhouse (claiming that having no door improved ventilation).

Despite their hard living conditions, the Browns wanted their children to have an education that might lead to new opportunities and better lives than their own. Tomás and his siblings therefore attended a small rural school where all pupils in the elementary grades met in a single classroom. Tomás eventually adjusted to his school environment, but not before he engaged in his share of mischief.

During my entire first year of school I can't recall getting any unsatisfactory grade in deportment. My academic grades in most subjects were not quite as high as those obtained by [my brother] Eldon, but I always made a better grade in penmanship than he made, and pointed out to my parents that one couldn't be good in everything. A prize and special recognition was given at the end of the school year for the student being judged best in penmanship. Erma Bell received first prize and I received second prize. Mama thought I should have been number one. She was probably a little prejudiced: Besides being her son, my writing looked very much like hers.

Although not personally participating in the indoor sport throughout that first year of school, I did see how much fun some of the students had shooting paper wads when the teacher was busy with another class, or was at the blackboard unable to see everything that was going on. One student seemed to enjoy taking potshots at me. It was difficult to refrain from shooting back, but I resisted doing so. Papa was president of the school board and had let us know that he expected nothing less than good behavior in the classroom. If we did something which called for a whipping in school, we could expect to get another one from him at home. No one had explained to him that it is unlawful to punish one twice for the same crime. His warning, along with the fact that I was quite sure Eldon would inform him of any misconduct on my part, pretty well kept me in line.

The second year of school Ruth Stanfield was our teacher, and many of the students continued to shoot paper wads. She even had a list known as the "paper wad family." Perhaps it was a desire on my part to be part of the family which influenced me to take some action one day which assured my entry into that exclusive club. Miss Stanfield was at the blackboard, unable to see what was going on behind her back. Students were informed back in those days that teachers had eyes in the backs of their heads, but it didn't take me long to learn that this wasn't true, so I took advantage of that opportunity to shoot back at Louie Ritter, something I had really wanted to do for a long time. Being very inexperienced at the time in the art of shooting paper wads, I can now understand how things seemed to go all wrong. I had never studied ballistics and was not aware of all that went into the proper preparation of the wad prior to firing in order for it to be as accurate as a stone fired from a P-shooter.

When I nervously fired that very poorly constructed missile, it functioned as though it were a guided missile that had been fired in the wrong direction and quickly given the signal to home in on the desired target. Although I was looking straight at Louie when firing that paper wad, it made an amazingly steep climbing turn to the left, and. . . even appeared to pick up speed prior to hitting the teacher in the back of the head. Even with all his practice, I don't believe Louie could have done any better. It seemed to me that every student in the room was looking directly at me as the teacher turned around to see who the culprit was who would dare do such a thing as shoot her in the back of the head. During recess I received some much-needed instruction from the paper wad armament section on how to construct a paper wad that would go in the direction aimed by the shooter. Louie soon discovered that my marksmanship improved quite rapidly.

[Years later I learned that my teacher, Ruth Stanfield was still alive. I felt compelled to write her a letter in which] I told her I was sorry about shooting her in the head with a paper wad, and promised not to do it again.

As I look back now to the classroom activity I enjoyed most, I believe it was probably the spelling matches. It was a real challenge to learn to correctly spell the list of words that would be used in these matches. We also had ciphering matches. In these I recall Loyd Dennis being able to complete the problems so much faster than I that it was rather embarrassing to even go to the blackboard while everyone in the room watched to see who would finish the math problem first. . . .

While on our way to school Eldon and I occasionally saw coyotes, badgers, wildcats, and other animals that I decided I would like to try my hand at trapping. We had a couple of single-spring traps that Papa finally allowed me to set. He first gave me some instruction on how to set the trap and also had the jaws wrapped with a rag so that they would be less likely to break the bones of the captured animal. At the time one could send off the cured furs to Trinidad, Colorado, and get paid a small amount for each fur, the price paid naturally dependent on the quality.

After the traps were set, we checked them every morning on our way to school and again on the way home. One morning I found we had caught an animal in one of the traps. Instead of the beautiful coyote pelt I had wanted, however, we found a skunk in the trap. Eldon preferred to not even get close to the animal so I was left with the stinky job myself. There was no possible way of just turning the creature loose. I shot him with my P-shooter, took him out of the trap, tossed him in a hole, and went on to school.

School had hardly started when the teacher wanted to know who had been close to a skunk. When I held up my hand she immediately suggested I take the rest of the day off. I was glad to get out and took my time going home. When I arrived home it wasn't even necessary to explain why I had been dismissed early that day. I still think Mama had something to do with persuading Papa that it wasn't practical for us to run a trap line on our way to school [anymore].

Encounters with skunks were not the only way one could be released early from class. Most of us boys at school had tried smoking cedar bark or mesquite roots, and had taken at least one puff on a Duke's Mixture or Bull Durham cigarette. One day one of the older boys told me I should try chewing on the remains of a cigar he had found. Thinking it might taste a little like the tobacco that Grandpa seemed to enjoy so much, I put it in my mouth.

The bell rang for classes to start again, and I had no chance to get rid of the wad now inside my mouth because the teacher was only a few feet away and, I imagined, was somewhat suspicious of my actions. One must remember that this was not an electrically operated bell. It was a bell that usually sat on the teacher's desk. The enclosed hollow cuplike portion of the bell was an ideal place to put either a small lizard or a horned toad. A few female teachers, upon lifting the bell, screamed louder than the sound of the bell itself as the liberated reptile raced across her desktop.

The inkwell of my desk was only about half full of ink, and I soon had it full of a combination of saliva and cigar juice. I had never seen an inkwell filled with such odd-looking liquid before. The problem now, however, was more serious than the unusual appearance of the tobacco-colored ink. I was beginning to swallow a considerable amount of the juice. I also was beginning to feel quite ill. When the teacher wished to know if I had a headache, I assured her that I felt awful. She said if I wished to do so I could go home.

Papa was going to Tucumcari the following day and decided that my headache might be due to my eyes. He took me to an optometrist who naturally fitted me with a set of glasses. I was about the only kid in school with glasses, and really felt quite distinguished with them until the new wore off. A few weeks later my eyes had returned to normal and the glasses were not used again. Haven't tried eating any cigars since then. . . .

Tomás clearly enjoyed and appreciated his childhood on a New Mexico homestead. At nineteen, during the Great Depression, he joined a federally-funded youth program called the Civilian Conservation Corps (CCC) and was assigned to a camp near Santa Fe.² A year later, in 1936, he began college atNew Mexico Normal University (now New Mexico Highlands University) in Las Vegas, New Mexico. He also joined the National Guard and learned to fly aircraft. During World War he proudly served in the army as a flight engineer and aerial gunner. He married his wife, Darline, at the war's end in 1945. After a career in the Air Force, he served with the U.S. Information Agency in Latin America before teaching at the University of Colorado and the Defense Language Institute at Lackland Air Force Base in San Antonio, Texas.

Later in life, Tomás returned to his family's homestead to find that it had changed drastically. "One can now travel across. . . large cattle ranches without even being able to note where homesteaders once lived and raised their families." Sounding much like Lula and Ruth Collins (chapter 5), Tomás added that it was almost as though the old homesteads had never existed except in the minds of the happy children Tomás grew up with many years ago.³

ORAL HISTORIES
PUEBLO CHILDREN AT THE SANTA FE INDIAN SCHOOL[1]

*The Santa Fe Indian School was one of twenty-five Indian board-
ing schools established by the federal government by 1900. Their common
missionwas clear: to strip Indian children of their native cultures by removing them from their tribes and villages and imposing "modern" Anglo
values and ways. Founded in 1890, the school in Santa Fe belittled Indian customs and taught skills and subjects of little use to children once
they returned to their families and home communities. Through valuable
oral histories, Sally Hyer has captured the essence of this cultural imperi-
alism and its tragic impact on Indian youth. Tellingly, the following excerpt is from a chapter of Hyer's history of the boarding school entitled,
"We Little Ones Suffered a Lot at Santa Fe."[2]*

During the harvest season in 1915, a Pueblo girl, her mother, and
grandparents were tying *chile* peppers into long strings to dry
for the winter. The girl's father had died of tuberculosis, and she
was living with her relatives at San Juan. She was startled when a Pueblo
man from the Santa Fe Indian School appeared at the house with a white
woman. They were looking for her older brother, who was out herding
cows. The Indian school people had come to take him away to boarding
school. But the young boy was badly needed at home, protested the grandfather. [Years later the little girl later recalled her grandfather saying,]
"'If you'll excuse him this year at least until next year, then he'll go.' And
so this lady told in English to Mr. Cata, 'Well, we have to take somebody.
What about her (pointing to the five-year-old girl)?'. . . Then right away
my grandma and my mother started to cry, 'Her? She's just a little girl!
She's just a little girl; you can't take her.'

"'But we have to take somebody. We can't take your grandson, so we have to take your granddaughter. So you have her ready.' In those days, you had to obey the government. 'You have her ready tomorrow morning and we'll come with the mailman and pick her up around nine o'clock.'

"The next day my mother sent me to the ditch to bathe. It was still warm, and in those days we used to bathe in the canal. She sent me there and then she sent me to the relatives' houses to be blessed, where they always send us when we are leaving our village. . . .so that the Creator can take care of us while we are away from our families.

"Here comes the mailman. He had a buggy. There was a front seat there and he was sitting there with this woman, white lady. I was all ready and my grandmother and mother were crying. I can still see my mother and my grandmother just crying their hearts out, wiping with their sleeves. They used to have full sleeves on their dresses that they made, and they were crying.

"My mother put her best shawl on me. It was getting a little chilly. It was late. Pretty soon the train whistled around the bend near the Rio Grande, and it came. I was already five years old, but my grandpa was holding me on his lap, loving me. So when the train came, I got in. I saw the tears coming out of that brave man, my grandpa, who was so brave and strong.

"I still picture my folks to this day, just standing there crying, and I was missing them. . . . I got on the train and I don't even know who was in the train because my mind was so full of unhappiness and sadness. . . ."

On the train to Santa Fe, the girl wrapped herself tightly in her mother's shawl. But then, "that [Indian school] lady said she was taking my shawl off. She didn't want me to wear a shawl. You know, they didn't want us Indians to be Indians in those days. They wanted us to be something else than that. *No!* I held it to me because that shawl touched my mother and I loved it. I wanted it to touch me."

As she approached the imposing red brick school rising out of the desert, the girl was struck by how different it looked from her own village. Still clinging to the shawl, she was placed in the care of another girl from San Juan, Cresencia, an "adjutant" in the school's military hierarchy. Cresencia took her through all the steps needed to become a proper school girl. . . .

"The first day, the adjutant took me downstairs. We had breakfast first. There were two restrooms with showers on one side, and then a long row of sinks. There were faucets. . . . She put me in the shower and told me to take a shower. She told me to wash my hair good. As she put me outside in the sun, she rubbed kerosene in my hair because I had nits and black bugs in my hair. In those days, there was hardly any water. We had to go far to get our water. Like I said, we go to the canal to bathe.

"After my hair dried, they took me to the sewing room to be measured for my clothes. For nightgowns, two of everything. We had what they call bloomers. They were made of denim. Thick denim, like you use for mattress covers. We had two dresses, and two everyday dresses, and one [olive-green] uniform made out of serge, and a cape. They measured me for that.

"From there she took me to the principal's office. I still had my shawl on because they could not make me take my shawl off. I kept holding it. . . . "The principal pointed to a clock up there and he asked me if I could tell time. I just looked at it and I didn't know what to say. I didn't know how to tell time, so I just covered my face [with my shawl] and the students laughed."

[That night the San Juan girl missed her grandfather] so much. . . that she could not sleep until dawn, when she heard the sound of a bugle playing reveille. She recalled, "Just as I was falling asleep, I heard nice music down below. I peeped out the window and there was this little boy all dressed in khaki clothes. . . .blowing the horn to wake us up. The music sounded pretty to me, because my grandpa always sang songs. He made songs about nature as we were in the wagon together. . . ."

[She and other children] suffered greatly from homesickness. . . . "I was very sickly, unhappy because I would stand at the window. Cerrillos Road was the unpaved road to Albuquerque at that time. I used to stand there and look that way and just wish that my grandfather could come. I'd just stand there, just so sad. I don't know how to explain that lonesomeness that I had at that time."

Administrators used a relentless schedule to isolate students from each other and to impose a never-ending load of work on them. The school's guiding assumption was that this discipline would eventually transform the inner life of the [students. The government's goal was to strip the Indian children of every reminder of home and family. The rooms they lived in, their language, meals, and daily routines were drastically changed.]

One of the school's main goals was to produce English speakers from Indian children who knew their native language and perhaps Spanish. "When they got us to the Indian school, we all had to line up for roll call. It was just pitiful. You see, some of us hardly knew how to talk English!" said a [former student from Taos Pueblo]. "It's hard. English has been a very hard subject for all of us."

As another Taos student remembered, "I moved here from Taos Pueblo Day School. My first year, of course, I was scared. I didn't know English enough. It was a strange place. We were very shy because we didn't know how to talk to each other, with all the kids with different languages.". . . [Children] learned to accept the situation and make the best of it. A San Juan woman said, "I guess in our days we just accept things. [We] never question, we just accept.". . .

An imaginary line down the middle of the dining hall divided the school in half. Boys and girls ate on opposite sides of the room. They formed separate battalions, different vocational classes and details, and could not even walk or talk together. Strict control was intended to prevent romances from occurring. . . . A Taos woman remembered that she could not sit next to her brother at weekend assemblies. "Even my own brother! I had to have permission to talk to my own brother.". . .

[Students, especially those who were related, found ingenious ways to communicate secretly. When a Taos boy was not permitted to go home for the summer, he pretended to sing a Tiwa song from his dormitory window. His sister said, "I remember my half-brother. . . .singing to me from his room window, 'You tell my mother I'm not coming home, but tell her I love her anyway.'"]

Marching. . . made an indelible impression on the students. They mention it with far more frequency than academics. . . . [A former student from Sandia Pueblo remembered,] "We marched to meals, we marched to school, we paraded on Sundays. . . . " [Another student said,] "We were just like prisoners, marching every place. . . ."

The school administration used military drilling to break down tribal values of group solidarity and to encourage competitiveness among the students. Students were chosen to be officers as a reward for good school work or approved behavior. In the pueblos, however, leaders did not actively promote themselves. The school's attempt to create a hierarchy among the students often meant more to the staff than it did to the reluctant students. . . .

Cultural differences were dramatically contrasted in the school's dining hall. Not only the food, but the utensils, the table manners, the way of serving, and the attitudes towards food were different from home. In the pueblos, food was sacred and brought people together. Families shared everything, often eating from the same bowl. At the school, each child had their own dish and spoon. Meals were timed by a series of bells. Students could not laugh or joke. . . .

Pueblo children had grown up eating corn, beans, squash, and chile stews. At school they had strange, unsatisfying food like gruel and hardtack. They longed for their familiar Indian food. . . . Former students almost always mentioned being hungry. Meager meals of unfamiliar food left them feeling empty. The only way to have enough to eat, many said, was to work in the kitchen or secretly dig up vegetables from the garden. . . .

Students tried desperately to create their own Indian food. A woman from Taos described eating dry pinto beans, while another cooked red chile on the dormitory radiator. . . . [One student remembered that] "They used to feed the horses. Besides alfalfa they fed them corn and bran. They shelled corn. We used to go in there and take that corn and go back there by the arroyo and find a piece of roofing tin, build a fire under it and parch corn. . . . Some of the kids who were smart, they'd take the bran and mix it with water. . . .and make little patties, little tortillas of bran.". . .

Diseases spread quickly at Indian schools because of the barracks-like dormitories. A highly contagious eye infection called trachoma was virtually endemic at Santa Fe. . . . Children's inner eyelids became rough, grainy, and irritated. The disease led to blindness if it was left untreated. "I had trachoma," recalled an Apache man. "I was treated. They had brown stuff. They used a medicine dropper. They'd hold your eyes open, squirt it in there. Then the people who had it real bad,. . . they had a blue stone. They'd have to get in there and scrape their eyelids from the inside. . . . It was very contagious. We all used the same towels. I mean, we'd wash and then we'd just pass the towel around and as long as it was still dry, we'd use it. There were never enough towels. So we all got trachoma."

In general, students were quiet and well behaved. Their most common offenses were speaking their own language, running away, and breaking the school's rigid schedule. "If you didn't obey any rules in the school, we were punished," explained a Taos woman. "They used to give us demerits. And we were kept away from social life, like going to dances or shows. . . . Then in the girls' building, when we were taught doing something we weren't supposed to do, they'd make us kneel in the hallway all night." [Other p]unishments ranged from assigning extra work details to whipping repeat offenders and putting them in chains.

The worst punishments were reserved for the "deserters," those who ran away from school. They left, said a former student from Taos, "because either they didn't like the school or they were lonesome. . . . But they used to bring them back.". . . Indian school officials punished runaways by publicly embarrassing them and giving them extra work details. A group of girls walked two days before they were caught by boys on horseback and returned to the school. "Then we were punished. We had to wear a gunny sack for two days. Just wear it, like a shawl. They made us walk around the grass [in front of the dorm]. I wore it for two days. It was a long punishment." Ridicule of the traditional shawl reinforced the school's rejection of Indian values. . . .

The most exciting school event was a visit from home. [Parents relied on burros or horses and wagons for transportation. When they came, former students remembered joyfully, relatives stayed at the back of the campus in a humble structure called the "Indian house." A Taos student remembered,] "When we see smoke coming out of that Indian house, everybody would be happy because somebody is there from home!"

Happily, as a result of an educational reform movement begun in the 1920s, Indian boarding schools across the nation radically changed their missions. A new respect for Indian culture replaced former attitudes. Indian arts and crafts were increasingly valued, largely replacing the inappropriate training earlier students had received. The Santa Fe Indian School was at the forefront of these changes, becoming a showcase for the reforms implemented under government officials led by Indian Commissioner John Collier.

The Santa Fe school has gone through additional stages since the 1920s, but the majority have been positive and helpful to the Indian youth of New Mexico. As the best proof of this progress, most students since 1928 have fond memories of their time at the school, and many have encouraged their own children to attend the institution when it is time to begin their non-tribal education.

ORAL HISTORIES
HISPANIC BOYS AT THE MENAUL SCHOOL IN ALBUQUERQUE

"I am Mexican, born and brought up in New Mexico, but much of my life was spent in the [Menaul] School where we had different training, so that the Mexican way of living now seems strange to me."
Polito Padilla, 1905[2]

The Menaul Training School, founded in Albuquerque in 1896, was named after the Reverend James A. Menaul, sixteen years a Protestant missionary in New Mexico and the founder of Albuquerque's First Presbyterian Church. Operated by the Presbyterian Church, the Menaul School (as it became known) was established as a boarding school to educate male Protestant Hispanic students, who often felt discriminated against in their largely Catholic villages and local schools.[3] In sharp contrast to the Indian children who were often forced to attend distant boarding schools, Hispanics attended Menaul voluntarily, knowing full well that the school's religious focus and cultural ways were far different from those of their native villages. Satisfied with their decisions and educational choices, most Menaul students remember their years at the Albuquerque institution fondly and with few regrets. In fact, many, including the three former students interviewed here, contend that their school years at Menaul represented the turning point of their lives.

Hispanic students in school uniforms, Pierson Hall, Menaul School, Albuquerque, New Mexico, 1908. Courtesy of the Menaul Historical Library, Albuquerque, New Mexico.

Tell us about your earliest days in the Southwest.

JULIÁN DÚRAN:

I was born on January 4, 1888, in Dixon, New Mexico. My father and mother were Leonides Dúran and Cruzita Martínez Dúran. There were ten of us in the family [although] two little girls in the family died while they were still children. . . . My father and mother were very, very poor people. We had a small farm. . . , but a lot of it was not good for planting. It was hilly. But we managed for many years. . . . My father and mother were both hard workers, and as soon as we children were able. . . we had to work on the farm. And then for us boys, we had a small flock of goats that we took care of, especially in the summertime. It meant that most of the food that we ate we grew ourselves.

ABEL SANDOVAL:

I was born in December 1902. And at that time my grandpa was a minister in Chacon. . . . [My father was also interested in religion and] became what they called at the time an evangelist. . . . My dad came and settled in Chamisal and started a church there.

MANUEL GALLEGOS:

I was born on September 14, 1923, in Center, Colorado, to Manuel A. Gallegos, Sr., and Lily Ortega Gallegos. I spent my early childhood years in Capulin, Colorado.

How did your family convert to Protestantism?[4]

ABEL SANDOVAL:

[My grandfather, Manuel Sandoval,] and some other men from Chacon went to take some freight to Trinidad, Colorado. It happened that they [arrived] there on a Saturday and they had to stay over Sunday before they could finish their business. . . . Somehow or other on Sunday they heard some singing and it happened to be a church. . . . They decided to go and listen to the singing. And from all accounts that I've heard, that was the first time that they ever had contact with a Protestant church. So they came back [home] and became interested in reading the Bible and eventually my grandfather was converted into the Protestant faith and became a minister.

JULIÁN DÚRAN:

My dad had a very good friend in Rinconada. . . on the Rio Grande. . . . There was a lady [there] that came from Kansas City by the name of Susana Thresher. We called her Tía Susana. And she came and bought herself a place and planted some first class fruit trees—apples, peaches, pears. . . and almost any kind of fruit that would grow in the valley. And my dad, especially in summertime, used to walk over there. . . to work for Tía Susana. He used to get one dollar a day for his work and worked from seven in the morning to six at night. . . . But of course Tía Susana became a very strong influence in his life. And I think because of her my father decided to look into Protestantism. . . . [When] the first missionaries that came [to Dixon], my father went to the meetings and became converted. My mother became a Protestant at the time that my dad and mother were married.

Where did you start school?

JULIÁN DÚRAN:

I remember very little about the first school that I went to. All the schools that I ever went to were Presbyterian mission schools. . . . All of us in the family. . . .never went a single day to a public school. We used to have the school in the church building. We didn't have a school building at the time. And we were so crowded that three of us would sit on one bench. . . . I remember the year that I was going into the fourth grade. There was a rumor that there was not enough room in our building for all who would be in the fourth grade, and I was afraid I would have to go to the public school. But somehow the teachers made room for all of us and I was saved from having to go to the public school.

ABEL SANDOVAL:

[I started at the mission school in Chamisal in] a building which served a dual purpose: it was a school on the weekdays, and it was a church on Sundays. The teacher that came to Chamisal was a young fellow [named Cosme García] that had graduated from Menaul. . . . He was one of the first Menaul graduates [and later married my aunt Leonor]. . . . I went through the first four grades with Tío Cosme. . . . [O]ccasionally after school had started, some priest would come and advise the [local Catholic] people that they were doing wrong by sending their kids to a Presbyterian school. So a lot of them withdrew their kids [and] sent them to public school. But not all. . . .Even with this pressure, maybe the next year they'd change their minds and send their kids again to the mission schools.

MANUEL GALLEGOS:

In Capulin, Colorado. [I went to high school in Alamosa, Colorado,] except for my senior year. My senior year I graduated from Menaul School in Albuquerque, New Mexico.

What led you to attend Menual School?

JULIÁN DÚRAN:

After the sixth grade I came to Menaul. And I happened to come to Menaul because several of my friends had been at Menaul before. And when they went back I really wanted to do anything I possibly could to go to Menaul.

ABEL SANDOVAL:

In 1914, Superintendent John C. Ross of the Menaul School] offered Uncle Cosme a chance to send five boys from his school on scholarships. But they had to start in the sixth grade, and I was just finishing the fourth grade. Out of the five boys that he selected. . . , three of them did come. But two. . . notified Tío Cosme. . . that they wouldn't be able to come to Menaul. So he decided to send me and another boy [Benito Arellano] that was finishing the fourth grade. He gave us a little bit of [tutoring] during the summer months. We were scared to stay at Menaul [because] you know Menaul was a very reputable school by that time and we thought it would be very strict and we might not like it. But with the tutoring [Tío Cosme] gave us we made it alright. Not only did we make it, but we were always at the top of the class.

MANUEL GALLEGOS:

The main reason I attended Menual School was the fact that Alamosa, Colorado, was a very prejudiced town. They were very prejudiced towards Spanish-speaking people, and they didn't give you much of a chance to play in sports unless you were ten times better than the Anglos competing for your sport. [In] the summer of 1941 there was a fellow from Albuquerque attending a Presbyterian convention in Alamosa. He was Carlos Candelaria [who] was attending the Menaul School. He got me interested in coming to Menaul School [by telling me] that there was no prejudice at Menaul School and that if I wanted the opportunity to play in sports to come to Menaul School.

What were your earliest memories of Menaul School?

JULIÁN DÚRAN:

When I came to Menaul it was an entirely new world to me. Of course I never had been out of Dixon. Menaul was four miles out of [Albuquerque], but even then I knew that we were near a city, and I never had had that experience. And [that] was all very thrilling to me.

MANUEL GALLEGOS:

What impressed me mostly was that it was a boarding school. I never had seen or been to a boarding school. I was impressed by the students living on campus, that they did not go home at night, but stayed there at the school all year long. . . . Another thing that impressed me was that Menaul School was made up mostly of Spanish boys and girls from the state of New Mexico and some. . . from southern Colorado.

Did you like your fellow students at Menaul?

MANUEL GALLEGOS:

I found the students at Menaul, a big percentage of them, who were very nice, very friendly, because they were first year students like myself, and we pulled [for] each other. The ones who had been there for quite some time. . . were kind of cliquey and were not very friendly to the new students. But as we got to know them, we found that all the students were very nice [and] got along very well together.

Did you play in any sports?

MANUEL GALLEGOS:

I played football, basketball, and went out for track. I think I did quite well. We took the state championship in track. We had an undefeated season in football. We were only tied once. We were not beaten in football. In basketball we did not do that great. . . .

ABEL SANDOVAL:

I was always interested in that sort of thing, by golly. I had to be doing something all the time, so I went out for everything. Basketball, everything. Whatever there was to do, you know.

What were your favorite courses and who where your favorite teachers?

JULIÁN DÚRAN:

At Menaul I found that I could learn (chuckles). In Dixon I didn't think that I was too good at learning anything. Perhaps I didn't have enough interest in school. I repeated the sixth grade because I was afraid that if I went to the seventh grade that I probably wouldn't make it. But Miss [S.B.] Sutherland, who was [my] teacher, insisted that instead of entering the seventh grade that I take up the work of the seventh and eighth grades [at the same time]. . . .and I was of course ready for high school. . . . But when I went to Menaul I discovered that I could do school work. And I fell in love with it. . . . I began to make good grades. Of course I had learned to study, and I dedicated myself to study. Several of the boys in my class were much smarter than I was, but they didn't *dedicate* themselves to study. And from the ninth grade through high school I was able to go to the head of the class. Every year, even the year I graduated.

ABEL SANDOVAL:

[Let me tell you about our typical student's day.] After we ate break-fast we came back to the dormitory, made our beds, and then we had a little time to study before classes started. After classes started they were. . . . through the whole [day until about] 3:30 p.m. . . . I remember one [teacher] in particular, Miss Cora Moore. She was the most wonderful teacher I ever had. . . . It just came naturally to her, I guess. She didn't waste any time. She was always teaching us something. [After classes] of course you were taking part in athletics and the rest of the time was for practice. . . .

Menaul was reputedly a very good school, you know, and they kept up with the requirements of the state. . . . We were pretty much like any public school, except that of course Menaul had a little extra to offer: the teaching of the Bible and attending chapels and a few other things that compensated for being away from home and under somebody else's care. We were getting good care. . . . There was no pressure, but I would say that a fairly good percentage [of the Catholic students] of their own free will would become Presbyterians. . . . The ones that came to Menaul and didn't want to become Protestants went back to [their] communities and kept on going to the Catholic church as before. [But] any Catholic boy [who] came to Menaul received exactly the same treatment as a Protestant.

MANUEL GALLEGOS:

My favorite courses were always mathematics, and I think my favorite teacher was Mr. Bauer. And I also liked history with Miss Hart.

What was your job on campus?

MANUEL GALLEGOS:

I was assigned to work in the mess hall and also assigned to work at the barn and on the farm.

ABEL SANDOVAL:

We all had jobs. Especially the ones that had scholarships. Now a scholarship didn't mean that you were just coming and everything was paid for. We all had to do a little bit of work if you were on scholarship. You had special assignments. Most of the years I paid part of my expenses by being a monitor at Old Brick. . . . Mr. [Harper Collins] Donaldson must have thought that I was sufficiently responsible to take care of Old Brikc at night. And even if there were a lot of boys older than myself, I could control them. Of course there was a. . . housemother, and I was accountable to her, but she hardly ever had to do anything. [I also] worked on the farm. Eventually I worked in the bakery and. . . in the kitchen. . . . One year I worked in the laundry.

Did you ever get in trouble at Menaul? If so, how were you punished?

JULIÁN DÚRAN:

We had as a superintendent at Menaul a Mr. [John] C. Ross. He was a wonderful person, but his method of dealing with us boys was kind of rough. I don't know if he had been an Army man before he came to Menaul, but he used to beat us up if we broke rules or did anything that showed that we were disobeying. . . . I think most of us were afraid of him. That was when I came to Menaul in 1914. But in 1916, two years after I came, Mr. Harper Donaldson came [to serve as the superintendent], and Mr. Donaldson was such a wonderful friend of all of us (becomes emotional) that we all wanted to do whatever he asked us to do. You wanted to do it because we loved him.

ABEL SANDOVAL:

I was at Menaul two years under Mr. Ross and five years under Mr. Donaldson. But Mr. Ross had been there a very, very long time. He was there when my dad came to school there. . . .and he was getting a little tired, I suppose, and he was a bit impatient, you know,. . . .and he was a little too quick on discipline, and sometimes that wasn't too good.

He was. . . a very strict disciplinarian in a sort of a militaristic [way]. He'd slap somebody every day for little things that did not harm [anyone]. Whereas Mr. Donaldson earned the respect and love of the students. . . . He didn't need to use physical force. He used psychology and example by the way he lived his life, and he was a far more successful superintendent, in my opinion.

[If you got] twenty-five demerits you had to work on Saturday afternoon and it was my hard luck to work most of the time. I had a friend [named Isaac], and we were always running into mischief. . . . They had calves [on the Menaul School farm], and we were both raised on farms. So one day [Isaac] said, "Why don't we go and ride some of those calves. They're old enough for us to ride them." So we were riding those calves and [Mr. Thurber,] who was in charge of the farm,. . . came and found us doing that. He got awfully mad about it [and said,] "You guys should know better than that. I'm going to make it twenty-five demerits." And Isaac said, "Why don't you make it fifty." [So Mr. Thurber] said, "I'll make it fifty, and I'll give each one [of you] fifty demerits." "Oh, make it seventy-five," [said Isaac]. And then I said, "Isaac, don't say anything [more] for goodness sakes. Seventy-five is enough. You're getting me in trouble as well as yourself." But [Mr. Thurber] said, "I'll make it seventy-five." And that's tough at that particular time. But that made three Saturdays [we had to work].

[In 1916, while I was in the eighth grade,] there was a little bit of a revolution at Menaul. . . . [Early in that year] somebody read an article in one of those church magazines that had been written by Mr. Ross. And he made some very derogatory remarks about the Spanish people and the kids that came to Menaul. Things that were perhaps exaggerated. And some of the high school boys. . . .got this article and passed it out. They didn't like it, and they decided to have a meeting with the faculty and with Mr. Ross. . . to air it out. [They met] the whole morning, and they didn't come to terms. The high school boys came out of the meeting at noon for lunch. They said, "Well, it's gonna go. The school's gonna close. You'd better get ready to go home. Everybody's going to go home." So there I was. I didn't have any money. I didn't know what I'd do. . . . But anyway, they went back after lunch and discussed it some more. And the agreement that came out of it was that Mr. Ross and all his teachers had to leave. [That's when Mr. Donaldson came and major changes were made at Menaul before my high school graduation in 1921.][5]

MANUEL GALLEGOS:

Yes. [T]hey were very strict. I didn't like that about Menaul. They never let you go to town, never let you go out on a Sunday afternoon or a Saturday afternoon to go to a movie or something like that [unless it was your turn to go]. You were confined to the campus. . . . [I'll] give you an example of what would happen if you went to town without permission. One Sunday afternoon I took the afternoon off because I wanted to see a movie so I stayed [in town on the way home from church] to see a movie and I missed Christian Endeavor, which we had on Sunday afternoons, and I just about got expelled. But one of the things that saved me was that Mr. Bauer asked me, "Where were you during Christian Endeavor, and I told him truthfully, "Sir, I wasn't there [because I went to a movie instead]," and he appreciated the fact that I was honest with him and he went to bat for me, and therefore I was not expelled from school. I never did it again.

How important was your experience at Menaul in your life?

ABEL SANDOVAL:

I would say it's the most important thing that ever happened to me in my whole life. Especially coming in contact with a teacher like Miss Moore. She was an inspirational person. Some way or another she inspired you to do your very best. And I think that carried over for me throughout my life in whatever I attempted to do. I tried to do my very best.

Most Menaul School graduates, including Julian Dúran, Manuel Gallegos, and Abel Sandoval, led happy, productive lives. Many, in fact, grew up to become ministers in the Presbyterian Church. Hundreds of former students, like Julian, Manuel, and Abel, remain active alumni, interested in the school and its ongoing success.

CHARLES S. PEARCE
ROUGHING IT AT THE ELITE
LOS ALAMOS BOYS RANCH SCHOOL[1]

For twenty-seven years before Los Alamos became the center of scientific research for the development of the atomic bomb, it served as the remote location of the elite Los Alamos Ranch School campus. The school had been founded in 1916 by Ashley Pond, a wealthy Detroit business-man. A sickly child, Pond had recovered his health when his parents had sent him to live a rugged, mostly outdoors existence in New Mexico. The cure worked so well for Pond that he hoped to provide a similar opportu-nity for other youths. The school he established in Los Alamos was expen-sive (among the highest in the country) and small (its peak enrollment equaled forty-five), but no one could argue with its success. In addition to Charles S. Pearce (class of 1938), who shares his memories in the follow-ing excerpt, other successful graduates of the Ranch School included au-thor Gore Vidal, former Sears, Roebuck president Arthur Wood, former Santa Fe Railway president John S. Reed, and the founder of the Santa Fe Opera, John Crosby.[2]

New Boy at School

Standing in the Chicago [railroad] station, I was scared. There is no other way to put it. Several months earlier, a representative of [the Los Alamos Ranch School] had stopped by to look me over. I had put in a dutiful appearance and tried to say all the right things. As a result, I had been accepted for the school's fall term. Now, a summer later, it was time to leave. The confidence I had felt earlier had disappeared, and in its place was uncertainty.

217

Close by me stood my parents. God knows I needed their support, but for all that, I felt ashamed. After all, a boy of fifteen supposedly can take care of himself. To be sure, I had been away at summer camp, but that was different. Camp lasted but a few weeks and wasn't all that far from home. Now I was going halfway across a continent to country and customs different from any I had ever known. The last thing I wanted was for other boys to know my fears.

Kids were everywhere! Big kids, little kids, old-timers, first-timers! It wasn't hard to tell new from old. The veterans stood around in smug little groups, laughing too loudly and bragging of their summer exploits. Most were cutting their eyes around at the new boys as if to say, "Look at those little twerps. We'll set them straight in a hurry!" I felt their eyes ooze slowly toward me, pause briefly to make a judgment, and then drift on to further surmises. Yes, I was scared. After all, I was one of the "little twerps," and I did not look forward to being "set straight."

An authoritative voice ordered all [Los Alamos Ranch School] boys to assemble under the school banner. It was time to board the train. Good-byes were hard—not so much my father's firm handshake as my mother's loving kiss. That kiss nearly paralyzed me with embarrassment. A second announcement sent me hurrying to stand under the school banner! I was on my own! The last thing I saw was my mother's face, wet with tears. Under the pretext of blowing my nose, I wiped away my own tears and followed the school banner to the Santa Fe Chief. . . .

The trip west went smoothly enough. I had traveled on trains before and in general knew what to expect. We new boys pretty much stuck to ourselves, debating what might lie before us. From time to time, we were able to corner some condescending old-timer who would tell us a little of what we might expect at school. Life there sounded pretty rugged—a prospect that did not particularly alarm me, since for the most part I had recovered my health. Some of the kids, however, seemed frail, and the idea of a spartan life did frighten them. We were led to believe that we would be living high in the Jemez Mountains and that, except for mornings in class, we would spend long hours on horseback—up to twenty miles a week. . . .

[Los Alamos Ranch School] was indeed in high country, on a remote mesa tucked tight against the Jemez Mountains. . . . When the buses rolled to a stop, the old boys scattered to well-remembered places.

We new kids, however, were shown into a large three-story log building called "The Big House." There we were ordered into a kind of dispensary and told to strip. Now I was not an unduly modest kid. Summer camp had taught me the glories of nakedness. Still, coming to a new place and being told first thing to strip, that was a little unsettling.

In the dispensary I saw a nurse and several men—one an older man, who I later learned was the head of the school.[3] I was weighed and measured and then ordered to stand in front of the older man. I was told to turn around and around and was scrutinized from every angle. The whole process gave me a very strange feeling. . . . I later found out what it was all about. I had assumed that kids in the same grade roomed together. . . . At [Los Alamos Ranch School] that was not the case. Every boy was classified according to physical maturity. Boys roughly equal roomed together. A mature freshman, for instance, might room with a slow-maturing sophomore. At first I thought the system stupid, but later came to realize that it had some advantages, particularly in sports and other extracurricular activities. It also helped by mixing old boys with new, to the advantage of both. Even though I was a freshman, I guess I was hairy enough in the right places to be declared a "Juniper" and placed with sophomores. . . .

A New Day

Notice on [the] bulletin board:

Get up bell will ring promptly at 7:00 a.m. Bed covers must be pulled all the way back so beds can air. Students will wash, dress, and report to exercise field at 7:30. Breakfast is served at 8:00. Time immediately following breakfast is reserved for making beds, cleaning rooms, and personal chores. Classes begin promptly at 9:00. Excuses are not welcome.

It all sounded sort of rugged, but after all, I thought, school is school. . . . A guy can get used to most anything. . . .

Students, I was told, did not sleep in their rooms. That was obvious since there were no beds there. There beds were on sleeping porches, open to the elements except for screens and heavy canvas curtains, the kind that could be rolled down in case of rain or, in winter, snow. The older boys said it really wasn't all that bad, that there were flannel sheet-blankets and canvas bed covers. It worked best, they said, if you just pulled the covers over your head. That way you kept warm and shut out the noise of the curtains that popped and banged in the wind. Sure it was tough jumping out of bed on a cold morning, but then it wasn't always all that cold. . . . You got used to it or else!

My first morning I will never forget. . . . We boys rushed to our rooms, pulled on our brittle new uniforms, splashed water on our faces, gave our hair a lick and a promise, and rushed outside to the exercise field. There, we were told to line up, younger boys in front, older kids behind. A teacher stood ready to lead the exercise and count cadence. Then came the bombshell!

"All boys strip. Place your clothes in a neat pile to your right."

My God, I thought, this is weird! Forty-three boys all jumping around stark naked! Still, the older boys didn't seem to mind. They shucked their clothes and stood unconcernedly waiting for exercises to begin.

Exercises lasted about fifteen minutes. There were stretching exercises, twisting exercises, [and] jumping exercises. . . . Whatever else, the exercises set one's blood to coursing and made one's breakfast of fresh fruit, cereal, bacon, eggs, toast, and milk taste especially good. So [that was how] every day began in [Los Alamos Ranch School]. . . .

The only school I had known before [Los Alamos Ranch School] was the Latin School in Chicago. It was a large brick building with spacious rectangular classrooms all lined with small desks at which students sat [with a teacher]. . . .at the front of the class lecturing or diagramming on a huge slate blackboard. . . .

The ways at [Los Alamos Ranch School] came as quite a surprise to me. The classrooms were small. Teachers and students sat informally around a table [in] no set place, wherever convenient. . . . Most unusual was the size of the classes. A large class might be seven or eight students, a small one as few as three or four. The atmosphere was entirely informal with occasional jokes and laughter not considered out of place. For all that, studies were the main purpose of the school. Teaching was personalized, learning was easy. To me it was all quite wonderful.

Algrebra class, Los Alamos Ranch School, Los Alamos, New Mexico, 1941. Photography by T. Harmon Parkhurst. Neg. No. 1322. Courtesy of the Museum of New Mexico, Santa Fe, New Mexico.

The way students and teachers came to know one another also was a revelation. Classes met in the morning. The rest of the day we boys might spend riding, skating, skiing, playing baseball, or touch football, whatever was in season. In every case, our teachers were part of our games. On the hockey rink one might give a teacher a hard body check and send him sprawling. At dinner that night the victim would laugh about how lame he was. Of course, turn about was fair play. . . . But there was respect. . . . Relationships were comfortable and often very close.

Valle Grande

When it came time for the annual pack trip, I knew I would be going, because I was one of the boys who had been taught to pack a horse. With a good partner I could throw a solid diamond hitch—one that would hold fast over the rough mountain trails that led into Valle Grande and the camp at Rincon Bonito.

For many days—even weeks—the pack trip was looked forward to with eager anticipation, for the experience was viewed as a sort of test of one's manhood, a dropping back into the days and ways of the early pioneers. Preparations were long and many, but finally came the day when, pack saddles firmly girted, paniers hooked in place, bedrolls and other equipment balanced on top, and a tarp spread evenly over all, the diamond hitch was pulled tight. With suitable fanfare, the train of horses set out for the summit of the Jemez Mountains and down the other side into Valle Grande. . . . Cold, rain, or even an occasional late spring snowstorm made no difference. We latter-day pioneers set out, grim determination our badge of honor.

Cinching up donkeys on a camping trip, Los Alamos Ranch School, Los Alamos, New Mexico, 1941. Photograph by T. Harmon Parkhurst. Neg. No. 1282. Courtesy of the Museum of New Mexico, Santa Fe, New Mexico.

The whole trip was run along quasi-military lines. There was a vanguard to check conditions along the trail and to mark detours. Next came the main body and supply train. And finally there was a rear guard or "drag" to scoop up stragglers or repack any horse whose load had shifted. That's where Super, [my roommate,] and I came in. We were a team trained to work together. I particularly enjoyed working "drag" because it was something of an independent unit. . . . Nobody thought much of it if we straggled into camp an hour after the others.

Getting to the valley was the difficult part. The way up was often steep and always rocky. For all that, it was a wild and beautiful adventure [with] the gradual transition from the mesa land of piñons and junipers to the high peaks of fir and spruce. One often felt like the first human ever to set foot in the area until, that is, traces of an old Indian camp or a blazed tree reminded one that he was indeed a latecomer on the scene. . . . The hysterical wailing of coyotes was friendly music, the occasional yowl of a mountain lion less friendly, particularly to our horses, who would begin flicking their ears and shying at shadows. . . .

Coming over the crest of the mountains and looking into Valle Grande was always a thrill. After the giant trees of the mountains, one looked abruptly into a vast valley, an endless sea of grass stretching for miles before the eye. The Valle, we had been told, was the crater of the largest extinct volcano in the world, one that, when it exploded, had sent dust flying as far as Kansas and California. From rim to rim, the crater stretched for some fifteen miles. . . .

Super was not as romantic as I about volcanoes, but he did enjoy adventure and found something to laugh at in all that happened. To him, life was one big gamble, to be played with all the skill and bluff of a professional gambler. He was the perfect counter to my own more conservative nature. . . .

About halfway across the Valle was a spot Super and I kept as our special secret. It was on an especially cold, sleeting day when we first discovered it. We. . . were really suffering from the cold. I was the one who spotted it—a strange cloud of steam rising not far from the stream that dissects the valley. At first I was puzzled, but as we rode closer, it was obvious that it definitely was steam we were looking at.

"Do you suppose this thing is about to blow again?" Super said, not entirely joking.

"I'd hate to end up in Kansas," I laughed. "My mother would never forgive me!"

Together, Super and I set out in a high lope toward the steam. Curiosity is built into boys. Besides, steam theoretically meant heat, and we were "hurtin' cold."

The steam was real enough, coming from a small vent in the earth. Close alongside was a wooden trough through which flowed piping hot water. It was a long-abandoned sheep dip. I looked at Super, and Super looked at me.

"What do you think?" he said.

"I think I'm cold," I replied. "I'm game if you are."

"Last one in is a horse's ass!" Super shouted, pulling off his chaps and jacket.

I don't know how long the two of us lay luxuriating in the steaming water. I do know that if there were any ticks on us when we climbed in, we were clear and clean when we got out!

An hour later, we rode into Rincon Bonitio Camp. Everyone had thought we were lost in the storm. They had really worried. Our tent was pitched and ditched, our bedrolls neatly laid out inside. At the camp kitchen, hot meals were waiting for us.

Mr. Big came bustling up, concern showing on his face. "You boys must have had a bad time of it," he said. "We've been very worried."

"Nothing a couple of good drag men couldn't handle," I said importantly.

"Yeah, but we sure thought we were in hot water for a while," Super added as he held out his plate for a second helping of beans.

He had a very sheepish grin on his face.

Graduation

Our parents sat on the portal of Fuller Lodge. With just forty-five boys in school and a senior class of only ten graduating, there was more than ample room for all.

We boys, graduates leading, came riding two by two from the corrals. We rode straight and tall, proud as only boys can be. We passed in review in front of the school staff and parents and rode on to the hitch rails in front of the Big House. There we dismounted and reformed on foot for the march back to graduation ceremonies in front of the lodge.

I don't suppose there was ever a graduation ceremony quite like ours. Again two by two we slow marched to the beat of an Indian drum: Dum-de-de-de-de-de, dum-de-de-de-de-de. The beat was steady. The beat was solemn. Every boy marched in perfect unison. Halfway to the lodge, we began our school song—a rhythmic chant such as Indians sing.

> Hi-o, we sing of the mountains,
> Hi-o, we sing of the school we love.
> Far away and high on the mesa's crest,
> Here's the life that all of us love the best,
> Los Al-a-mos!

There were two other stanzas, after which we arrived at the lodge. There we struck a new formation facing our parents and visitors. Piñons. . . stood up front. Back of them stood the Junipers. Next came Firs and finally the graduating Spruce.

Mr. Big came to stand in front of us. He made a brief speech explaining what the school had done for us and how proud he was. Then, one by one, he called out the graduating seniors and with a solemn handshake gave each of us our diploma. It didn't take long. . . .; there were only ten of us.

Super stood next to me in line. I looked at him and with a wink gave him the finger. I don't think anyone saw me. Super made a wry face and gave me the finger back. After four long, adventurous years, we were graduates of [Los Alamos Ranch School].

The Los Alamos Ranch School suddenly closed in late 1942 when it received official notice from the federal government that its land and property were needed for a special wartime "installation." Saddened, but willing to sacrifice in the nation's wartime interests, school officials compressed a year's study into six months before the school's doors were closed. With many young faculty members joining the military, it had been difficult to operate the school for some time. After an attempt to reopen the school in Taos, Ashley Pond's dream of a rugged school for privileged boys finally died a quiet death, an institutional casualty of World War II.

After graduating from the Los Alamos Ranch School, Charles S. Pearce received his B.A. degree from Cornell University in 1942. He served in army intelligence during World War II before moving to Texas, becoming a rancher, and writing six books. He has visited Los Alamos only once since leaving the Ranch School in 1938. Startled by the vast changes he found, he concluded that he would much prefer to remember his school as it was in his happy teenage years.

HAROLDIE KENT SPRIGGS AND SAMMIE J. KENT INTEGRATING A WHITE HIGH SCHOOL IN THE 1950s[1]

Black Americans have suffered extreme prejudice in the United States, from their earliest days as English colonial slaves to, in many ways, this very day. During much of our history they suffered unjust racial prejudice from cradle (birth) to grave (death), facing segregated institutions at every stage of life until the dramatic changes brought by the civil rights movement of the 1950s and 1960s.[2] Segregation was most strictly enforced in the South, but it was also prevalent in other regions of the nation, including New Mexico in the Southwest. Although New Mexico had only a small black population, black families and their children encountered unfair treatment in various ways, not the least of which was in segregated schools in towns on the eastern plains bordering Texas.

The Kent family of Tucumcari, New Mexico, suffered in this manner until desegregation led to their admission to previously white and Hispanic schools in the 1950s. In oral histories recorded in the summer of 2001, Haroldie Kent Spriggs and her brother, Sammie J. Kent, described their educational experiences first in segregated schools and then, when desegregation began, in the integrated public schools of their town. As star athletes, they also related their experiences on high school athletic teams and when traveling to play other schools in New Mexico and Texas. Their collective story is one of perseverance and great human courage.

(l. to r.) 4- or 5-year old Sammie, 3- or 4-year old Frances, and 6- or 7-year old Haroldie Kent. Courtesy of Haroldie Kent Spriggs, Albuquerque, New Mexico.

Parents

HAROLDIE KENT SPRIGGS:

I was born in Tucumcari, New Mexico, on May 26, 1938. I am the oldest of four children (in birth order: Haroldie, Alice, Sammie, and Frances) born to Harold and Bessie Mae Kent.

My dad was from Texas, as was my mother. My dad left home when he was about thirteen years old with a guitar on his back and nothing else. He was a migrant worker for years and that's how he got to Hollis, Oklahoma, where he met my mother, who had also moved there from Texas. My parents worked in the oil mill quarters, pressing oil out of cotton seed. In about 1935 they heard there were jobs in Tucumcari so they borrowed five dollars from my mother's father to buy gas for their Model T or Model A Ford and traveled to Tucumcari. My dad first worked at the Pelzer Motor Company. Later, he worked as a porter on the Southern Pacific Railroad. His route was from Tucumcari to El Paso, Texas, and back. He did that until he felt the need to be home with his family. That's when he built the family grocery store, which he and my mother operated for about thirteen years. The store was closed after a small fire. My dad also worked as a custodian at the First National Bank until his retirement. My mother worked in our store and was also employed as a housekeeper and cook. My parents loved Tucumcari.

My dad was really a self-made man. He only went through the third or fourth grade, but he was extremely brilliant. He was an excellent blues guitarist, had two or three patents to his credit, built his own home, operated his grocery store, and owned several rental units. My parents worked hard all of their lives and firmly believed in working to get what they wanted. They were just common people, but they were very well thought of in the whole community because of what they were able to accomplish with so very little.

When they arrived in Tucumcari, they were just looking for a niche, someplace where they could be successful despite their meager means. They made it. It was important to my father that we always had plenty of food to eat because he remembered the days when he had to do without. He didn't want that for us. My mother was the same way. And she wanted us to have certain advantages, like piano lessons and tickets to various performances and concerts by traveling groups that came to town each year.

When "poor" black people came to Tucumcari, their living conditions were a shock to me. I remember a poor black woman arrived with several children. I became friends with one of the girls and one day went home with her to their one-room hovel. When she served her brothers and sisters cereal for supper, she poured water on it and didn't use any sugar. I had never experienced such poverty before. We were pretty well off for blacks. We always had plenty of everything that my parents could afford to give us.

Values

HAROLDIE KENT SPRIGGS:

My parents were never ones to talk about issues of racism or poverty or being black. They just lived the experience, and of course we absorbed some of their beliefs. We got a sense of the work ethic from both of my parents. They were never on welfare; in fact my father would turn over in his grave if he thought any of us were on welfare because he believed that as long as there was a dish to be washed, a ditch to be dug, cotton to be picked, no matter how menial the job you could work and didn't have to go on welfare. He drilled that into us. I got my first job as a domestic worker cleaning the houses of the white families in the area. I was eleven years old, making thirty-five cents an hour. I did that through college. I also worked in our grocery store. My dad taught us to save, to be frugal, and to support ourselves. I started buying my own clothes and other teenage things at a very early age.

Those were the days when a lot of people were hopping on freight cars on the railroad—hobos we called them. Both black and white hobos would come through and somehow the word got out that my parents would feed them. So they'd come by the store and my folks always had some loose ends of balogna and some bread to feed them. He'd always tell us, "You never know when you're going to need someone to feed you." Most of the time these people would offer to work. Sometimes my dad accepted their offer, but most of the time he simply gave the needy some food. My dad was frugal with his money, but he was generous about feeding people when they needed it.

My dad used to say that if you didn't want menial jobs then you need to get an education. We had to be home by sundown. That was the law. You had better have at least one foot on the property or you were in for it—you were in trouble. We sat around the table every evening to do our homework. Although my parents couldn't help us with our studies, they encouraged us to figure out a way to learn and do well in school. They could never have checked any of our school papers, but they did know the difference between an A and F on our report cards. D's and F's were not acceptable. My parents tried very hard to give us what we needed to succeed in school.

My father had an expression that we all grew up with and knew very well. He said it every time we faced a problem or wanted to quit. He'd say, "They killed old can't and they whipped old couldn't till he could." He drilled that into us day after day.

Racial Groups in Tucumcari

HAROLDIE KENT SPRIGGS:

We had three different racial groups in Tucumcari. There were the whites, the Hispanics (or Spanish as we called them), and a small community of blacks or coloreds or Negroes. At that time we were typically known as colored people. We lived on the north side of Tucumcari along with most of the Hispanics. Across the tracks on the south side lived the white people and some Hispanics. The stable community of black people included my parents, the Joneses, Richards, Dillards, Mitchells, and about five or six other families. We had a lot of people who'd come for a while and then leave, but the stable families were there to stay.

The racial pecking order in Tucumcari included the whites at the top, the Spanish people next (because they were able to go to school with the whites), and then, at the bottom, were the "colored" people. We were the low people on the totem pole. If there were any problems between the racial groups, it was between the Spanish and the blacks, not because one group felt any better or worse than the other, but because they primarily lived on the same side of the tracks. If we got into a real fight they'd call us "nigger" and we'd call them "Mexicans" which was as bad as calling a black "nigger." However, there weren't too many fights that I recall.

At our grocery store the customers were of all races. We owned the only grocery store on the north side of town. My dad was generous and would allow credit for many of the customers. The store was serviced by white people. The milk man, bread man, and all the other delivery men were white. We were never worried about being robbed, and to my knowledge we never were.

Segregation and Racism

HAROLDIE KENT SPRIGGS:

We clearly understood our position in Tucumcari. We did not have the same privileges as the white or Hispanic people. My parents and other black adults understood their status, whether they liked it or not.

We never questioned why. We just accepted it until the civil rights movement when we said we would not accept it any more.

We were only allowed to sit in the balcony in the two movie theaters in Tucumcari (Odium and Princess). This area included the noisy projector room. I never gave it a thought. The one who had real problems with it—it just cut to her bone—was my sister Alice. That's why she became so involved in the civil rights movement and the NAACP [the National Association for the Advancement of Colored People]. My attitude was: you are who you are, and I am who I am. Don't bother me, and I won't bother you. At that time, I was a loner and just accepted things as they were.

SAMMIE J. KENT:

I never went to the town swimming pool on the south side of town where the whites lived because blacks were not allowed in the swimming pool. As a matter of fact, I never even looked at the pool. It never concerned me because I knew I couldn't go there.

HAROLDIE KENT SPRIGGS:

There was a black motel owned by Mr. and Mrs. Nolan Jones on old Route 66. Mr. and Mrs. Joseph Mitchell also owned a hotel in which the black railroad porters would stay when they had to lay over in Tucumcari. Blacks could not stay in the two big hotels in town. We could clean them, but we couldn't stay in them.

We had a section allocated to black people in the Tucumcari cemetery. That's where my parents and my uncle are buried.

My dad belonged to a black Masonic lodge, and my mom belonged to the black Eastern Star. Of course, these groups were separate from the white groups.

We seldom went to restaurants other than the malt shop near the high school where we could sit at the counter or anywhere after the schools were integrated. We never went to other restaurants because my mother was too good a cook for us to want to go out to dine.

SAMMIE J. KENT:

Tucumcari was a great little town, but I can remember when we had to go in the back doors of the restaurants. We could not eat in the front areas. So we went in the back doors and we ate and talked and had good times.

I remember my friend, Paul "Wagon" Zucerias, and I went to a hamburger restaurant once, and even though they knew me, they wouldn't serve me. So "Wagon" said, "If Sammie can't eat here, then I'm not going to either." We left, but "Wagon" took a box of hamburgers on the way out.

HAROLDIE KENT SPRIGGS:

I knew about segregation, but I had never experienced being looked down on or talked to in a demeaning manner until I cleaned the house of a woman who had come from the South and had brought racist attitudes with her. She was extremely mean. She would not allow me to eat on her table. If I had lunch, I had to eat it off to the side. She also wanted me to do work that she was not willing to pay me for. My dad did not allow us to talk back to blacks, whites, or anyone else, so I couldn't "sass" her. I stopped working for her after a few weeks.

When I was seventeen, I went to Chama to work for a wealthy white family which included five kids I looked after. The lady of the house had been reared in the South and had been taught to treat blacks in a demeaning manner. I never will forget that she told me to eat on a bread drawer and she would not allow me to use the silverware that the rest of the family used. When I was asked to return the following summer I refused.

SAMMIE J. KENT:

Growing up in Tucumcari I knew all the kids five or six years order or younger than me. There was not really that much of a problem because we all knew each other from birth through high school. But there was a lot of name calling. A lot of the kids used the word "nigger" when we fought.

One time I was put in jail. My younger sister Frances had had a fight with some other black girls, and one of the girls pulled a knife on my sister and cut her hand. Well, I took the knife from the girl. "Tootsie" Velasquez, the chief of police and my Golden Gloves boxing coach, arrived at the confrontation just off the school grounds. For some reason they apprehended me even though I wasn't involved in the fight other than taking the knife from the girl who had cut my sister. When I was brought to court, I was the one blamed for everything. For some reason, the chief of police and several teachers lied in court. I have a gut feeling that the chief lied due to pressure from other whites. He feared losing his job. The judge sentenced me to jail.[3] I didn't get to finish my junior year, but my grades were high enough that they went ahead and passed me to my senior year. I got out of jail after ten days. If I remember correctly, all the teachers who lied were reprimanded in some way. I went on to my senior year and, because I was popular with all the kids, I was elected the vice president of my senior class. But I wanted to get out of Tucumcari after high school because I knew that if I stayed I would have probably ended up back in jail or would have gone to the penitentiary because of all the prejudice in town.

HAROLDIE KENT SPRIGGS:

We could shop anywhere in Tucumcari. A dollar talks, no matter what color the skin. We could try on clothes and shoes. But when I moved to the Washington, D.C., area, a black woman could not try on a hat or some of the clothes in the stores. Racism and prejudice was even more prevalent in our nation's capital than in Tucumcari.

SAMMIE J. KENT:

I always had my own clothing accounts in town. Bonhem was a men's store, and Mr. Bonhem told me, "Sure, Sammie, you can buy clothes and just pay it out." I tried to buy all my own clothes and not be a burden on my parents. That's why I worked when I was a kid.

HAROLDIE KENT SPRIGGS:

My parents didn't have any trouble voting. In fact, my mother was a die-hard Republican and worked at the polls every time there was an election. She strongly believed in the party of Lincoln, which is credited with ending slavery.

Black Culture

HAROLDIE KENT SPRIGGS:

The black community in Tucumcari was close-knit. We had social gatherings that were well attended and a lot of fun. We also put on plays to which the white and Hispanic people were invited. We often had picnics for just the black community.

We celebrated Juneteenth.[4] The black community would get together and have a very good time. We'd have a big cook-out, and often white and Spanish people would join us.

My mother was a very religious woman and was a charter member of the Mount Calvary Baptist Church in Tucumcari which was established in 1943. The church was like the community center for blacks at the time. It was the center of our religious and social life.

I never knew there was a black world out there. I had never seen anything like an *Ebony* magazine or anything like that. My parents were astute enough to realize that in Tucumcari we would not have an opportunity to experience life in a large black community. So they subscribed to the *Pittsburgh Courier* and the *Black Dispatch*. Through these newspapers we'd got information about what was happening with the NAACP, the Colored Womens Club, and other social and political news about black America. We missed that sense of an extended black community that provided a social environment in which to grow and thrive. I had never seen a black doctor or any black professionals except for Celoa Hollis Ray Sutton, my black elementary school teacher. Growing up, I had a very narrow view of what I could be. I never thought that I could be a lawyer or a doctor or go into the military or do any number of things. I am eternally grateful to the Morgans, a white family that took me out of Tucumcari, out of New Mexico, and into a whole world of possibilities in the East. I really believe it had to be divine intervention. I was treated like part of the family, not as a maid, which is what I went there to be. When I got on a street car in Washington, D.C., I saw more blacks than I had ever seen at any one time in my life. I was totally overwhelmed and fascinated by a whole new environment of people who looked like me.

Conditions in the Segregated Schools[5]

HAROLDIE KENT SPRIGGS:

When I started school I was in what was called the primary grade. We went to school on the north side in a one-room building two or three blocks from where we lived. I clearly remember this school building because of the large wood burning stove that was used to heat our small classroom. We had one teacher who taught all of the grades. She was brought in from a normal [teachers'] school somewhere in Oklahoma. There were maybe twenty students in all the grades combined. I had the same teacher from the primary grade through the second grade. Then Mrs. Ray Sutton was my teacher from the third through the eighth grades. As I grew older I was asked to listen to the younger children read. I liked the idea of being able to work with the younger children and help them with their lessons. That's where I first experienced my love for teaching.

We received our cast-off books from the white school. Instead of discarding them, they brought them to us, and we thought it was the greatest thing in the world. The desks, slides, and swings were also hand-me-downs from white schools. However, we had a strong black parent-teacher organization which provided or supplemented the things we needed in order to get a well-rounded education.

The whites and Hispanics always had nicer school buildings. They had big brick buildings with shades and curtains on the windows. The high school had a modern gym, a science lab, and a cafeteria. We had none of these facilities. Even the "new" black school was really just an old barracks. We moved to this "new" facility when I was in the fourth or fifth grade. We had to walk home for lunch everyday. We even had to clean our school since support services of any kind were not available.

Integrating the Schools

HAROLDIE KENT SPRIGGS:

Sam Ingram was a black student who attended our segregated schools through the eighth grade. He is about six years older than me. When he was ready to go to high school, he had to go to Clovis, New Mexico, because it was the closest segregated high school available. There was no high school for black students in Tucumcari.

When I was ready to go to high school a few years later my father did not want to send me to Clovis. We didn't have friends or family there, and he was just not going to send me away to school. So my parents and some well-meaning white families, like Dr. Thomas "Archie" Gordon and his wife, Helen, successfully petitioned the state to integrate the schools in Tucumcari. When I entered the ninth grade in 1952, I was able to attend an integrated high school in Tucumcari.[6]

Although one might perceive our early education as inferior, the opposite was true. Our education was comparable to that of the white and Hispanic students. I had a most overwhelming experience that confirmed my ability and my sense of self and affirmed that I had nothing to be ashamed of in being black. During our first month of school, my Social Studies teacher asked if anyone could name a country that was shaped very much like the United States. My classmates suggested several different countries they thought might be shaped like the United States. I recalled a lesson in our segregated school where Mrs. Sutton taught this very lesson. If Australia is turned upside-down, it looks very much like the United States. I was the only black student in a class of about thirty students. I was very shy and unsure of my place or of how I was being received, and felt terrified, absolutely terrified. Finally, I very quietly raised my hand and said, "Australia." You could have heard a pin drop in that room because no one expected me to know the correct answer. That experience had a profound impact on my life. I realized that I was bright, I was capable, and I could learn as well as the white and Hispanic students. There was no stopping me. That affirmation motivated me to go from one day to the next with confidence.

Attending a newly integrated high school was quite an experience. We were never physically or verbally attacked. I never heard the term "nigger," but I had some experiences that let me know that a lot of people didn't approve of the newly integrated schools. Some teachers commented that, "There are places for people like you," and they'd mention black schools in the South that I had never heard of. And then there were instances when some of the boys would say things that I thought were inappropriate. But as I grew up I discovered that it was typical stuff that boys said to girls of any color.

While in high school, I became as much a part of the school as I could, being a black person. However, I did not socialize or visit white girls in their homes nor did they ever come to my house.

SAMMIE J. KENT:

Even after integration began, a lot of white teachers in the Tucumcari schools were very prejudiced. My Algebra teacher was so prejudiced that he would actually use the word "nigger" in the classroom. He would also send me to football practice during class time. Some of the coaches were also prejudiced, but not to the extent that they would use the word "nigger." I've hated the "n" word all my life. I would do whatever was necessary to keep anyone from using that word around me.

Most of the blacks were pretty good in school. I think it was because we grew up under so much pressure that we wanted to be better than the whites and the Spanish. I loved to read, and my older sisters helped me. Because I was liked by all of my schoolmates, they'd also help me. Most of my teachers were good if you wanted to learn. So I received a lot of my education because I wanted to learn, not because I had to as an athlete. I learned a lot more after high school when I joined the Navy. I always say, "Too soon we get old, too late we get smart."

Most whites were very, very helpful. I had the feeling it was because I had known them all of my life. They knew that I wasn't a thief, and I didn't get into a lot of trouble. They knew I respected other people's property. They trusted me and didn't show prejudice. From the heart, most of the whites were good people.

Dating

HAROLDIE KENT SPRIGGS:

I couldn't date much because there weren't enough black youths my age to date. And there was no inter-racial dating. It was unheard of and would not have been condoned. Some white boys were interested in me and I was interested in them. But it never, ever developed into anything more than a casual look. Neither I nor a black classmate, Jayne Richard, had dates for the prom so we went together. We didn't dance with anyone. We just sat off to the side with the white and Hispanic girls who didn't have dates either. We got dressed up, and I thought we were just gorgeous in our gowns. I still have the picture of me in my beautiful prom gown that my mother kept on the piano for years.

It was a little different by the time my brother came along three years later.

SAMMIE J. KENT:

I went to my prom. I didn't take a date because I was dating the girl that I eventually married and she was only a sophomore and couldn't go to the prom. I had no problems at the prom. I danced with the white and Spanish girls. There were only three blacks in my graduating class of about a hundred.

I was very popular with the white and Spanish girls in school. Many of them wanted to date me, but they were afraid to because their parents would disapprove. Their parents didn't mind my dancing with their daughters at school dances, but dating was not allowed.

I used to shine shoes at John Jennings' Barber Shop (for twenty-five cents a shine) and sometimes I'd hear white customers say, "We don't want that damned nigger dating our girls." But I don't recall anyone directly threatening me. I did have Spanish guys tell me not to date their sisters, but that was trivial as far as I was concerned because I was going to date them whether their brothers liked it or not. I married a Spanish girl after I graduated from high school. Her brothers disliked my dating their sister, although as individuals we got along fine.

HAROLDIE KENT SPRIGGS:

I was very involved in sports in high school. I made all-state in girls basketball and field hockey. We played against schools that were already integrated so we had no problems. There were very few blacks, though. There just weren't many blacks in New Mexico at that time.

SAMMIE J. KENT:

I played football, basketball, baseball, and I ran track. I played on the varsity teams throughout high school. I was best at baseball. Once I pitched both games of a doubleheader, and we won both games. I set the state high school record for strikeouts: nineteen in one game. To my knowledge, I still hold that record.

Some of the coaches were very prejudiced. I remember one coach in particular who was so prejudiced that he would instruct the white football players, "Don't block for Sammie. We don't want him to score more touchdowns than our white stars." He said that at a state championship game in my senior year, and we lost the game. I scored the only touchdown for our team. On the bus home the coach finally made a public apology. He said, "Sammie, had I not been so prejudiced" (or whatever word he used), "we could have won the game." He really felt badly about how he had treated me during the three years he had coached me.

Another time I scored forty-four points in a basketball game, but it never showed on the score sheet.

I sometimes encountered prejudice in towns in which we played. East Las Vegas, New Mexico, and Dehart, Texas, were probably the worst. The prejudice was not so much with the players as with their parents sitting in the stands. They'd yell, "Don't let that nigger do that!" When I heard things like that it would really anger me, but I tried to hold my anger inside. The more I held it inside, the better athlete I became. I'd push myself harder and play much better. I'm sure such incidents affected the other black athletes as well.

But I had some good coaches, too. Bob Hart was a great man. He tried to do the best thing by me and another black athlete named Charles

Richard. We also had a coach named Bill Litchfield. Of all the coaches I had, he was probably number one. He encouraged me to be the best athlete I could be. At my thirtieth high school reunion, Coach Litchfield told my wife that if Tucumcari hadn't been so prejudiced in those days, I could have received a scholarship to almost any college in the country. But his hands were tied.

Dr. G. Morris Benson, a dentist, was another great man. In football practice we had a drill we called the bull ring. The players would gather in a circle and they'd call out a number and that player would go into the ring and the other players would block you or tackle you or whatever the coach wanted them to do. One coach would have me in the bull ring probably half an hour longer than any other player on the team. I can remember distinctly this one time when Dr. Benson and his wife were in the stands watching practice—their son was on the team—and Dr. Benson came out on the field and really got on the coach's tail about the way he was treating me differently from the other players.

I played American Legion baseball one summer under a coach named Clemens who'd been a professional wrestler. We called him "Big Train" Clemens. After playing a game in Amarillo, Texas, we went to a restaurant to eat. But the restaurant manager said, "Well, we're not going to serve that nigger in here." "Big Train" responded, "If Sammie doesn't eat in here, then none of us eat." We also sensed prejudice in many other restaurants and motels. But after integration began we weren't turned away anymore. George Carman, a white player, and I usually roomed together on road trips. The black athletes were not forced to room only with other blacks when we were out-of-town.

I know I was exploited as an athlete. All that really mattered to many whites was that I won games for our team. In fact, other towns, like Clayton, wanted me to move there so I could play for their teams and help them win.

Final Thoughts

HAROLDIE KENT SPRIGGS:

I have found that in life there are well-meaning people in every racial group. I don't care where you come from. I don't care what your station in life is—whether you're rich or poor or black or white or brown or red—there are good people. The few rotten apples in the whole barrel are just that: a few. If you pluck out those few, you have a country that is multi-racial, multi-ethnic, multi-cultural, and multi-lingual. This mix of people is full of diversity, beauty, and good will. I tend to see the world that way. I see beautiful people everywhere I go.

Haroldie Kent Spriggs, Tucumcari High School graduation picture, Tucumcari, New Mexico, 1956. Courtesy of Haroldie Kent Spriggs, Albuquerque, New Mexico.

After graduating from Tucumcari High School in 1956, Haroldie Kent Spriggs earned her Bachelor and Masters degrees at Howard University. Her masters thesis was entitled, "Minority Group Education in New Mexico Prior to 1954." She earned her doctorate from the University of Maryland in 1974. After starting her career as an elementary school teacher, she became a school counselor. After graduate school, she worked in a prototype program that trained teachers how to teach in the inner city. She later worked for the U.S. Department of Education in Washing-

ton, D.C., retiring after thirty-two years of service. She has traveled around the world, including to the Holy Land and to Africa. Haroldie and her husband are retired and now reside in Albuquerque.

After graduating from Tucumcari High School in 1959, Sammie J. Kent joined the Navy and married his high school sweetheart. He served in the Navy for over twenty years, facing far greater prejudice in the military than he ever encountered in Tucumcari, but rising to the rank of Chief Petty Officer. Sammie and his second wife reside in Albuquerque where he attended the University of Albuquerque and taught welding at the Albuquerque Technical-Vocational Institute.

Haroldie's and Sammie's sisters, Alice and Francis, also live in Albuquerque. Alice served as the president of the Albuquerque branch of the NAACP for twelve years.

11

WARTIME CHILDHOODS

MARGARITA GRACIELLA ARMIJO
WORLD WAR II IN ALBUQUERQUE[1]

Margarita Graciella (Marge) Armijo was only five years old when the United States entered World War II in December 1941. Her story of growing up in Albuquerque's north valley is noteworthy for two main reasons. First, her childhood was clearly full of family love and traditional customs passed on from one generation to the next. But, second, while Marge grew up in a closed world of serenity and love, the rest of the world seemed full of war and hate. Somehow, Marge and her world were insulated from the larger world, almost as if the war was not going on at all. In fact, in remembering these years, Marge recalled only two war-related incidents: an accidentally dropped bomb and her older sister's frustrated desire to date soldiers stationed in town. Otherwise, the innocence of childhood and the blanket of family love, religious faith, and strong traditions made Marge's world secure when the rest of the world had seemingly gone insane.

My name is. . . Margarita Graciella Armijo and I was born on April 16, 1936. My mother says that was the happiest day of her life. My dad was Epimenio John or Juan Armijo. My mother was Pauline Salazar, but her mother was an Armijo. She was born in Villanueva, up in northern New Mexico. My dad was born in Albuquerque. He went to San Felipe School, and so did my nieces and I.

I was brought up in northwest Albuquerque [in]. . . Los Tomases, and it was its own little barrio. They had their own little chapel over near Menaul, east of 12th [Street]. They used to have fiestas—I remember, I was four years old, my grandfather took me to the fiestas in Los Tomases. They had a man playing a base fiddle, a guitar, and I remember my grandfather carrying me and dancing with me. . . .

I felt really loved in my life. I felt so lucky. My grandfather Jorge, George Armijo, absolutely adored me. He had a fantastic sense of humor, but he was very much the patron. He ruled the roost. He had a truck and used to grow all kinds of vegetables. He had a truck garden, and he'd go along 12th Street where all those big homes were and he'd sell vegetables, and that's how they lived. They had goats, they had horses, they had all kinds of animals. . . .

We were very family-oriented. My mother and dad worked outside the home, but they worked in a way that we didn't have baby sitters. They managed their time so they could be with us, one or the other. And my dad really helped with us. He took care of us almost as much as my mother. My dad worked in Parks and Recreation for the City of Albuquerque, and my mother worked for TWA for thirty years; it was then Transcontinental and Western. . . . She had a fantastic sense of humor. She brought us up to worry about our neighbor, and to worry about earning our space. God put us on this earth for a reason, and we were to relate to each other as human beings and help each other any way we could. She did a lot of volunteer work; she was very involved with the community. She found time. My dad, of course, helped. He felt he wanted to support all her activities. . . .

I remember having a library card really young, and I became interested in books and in music. My mother said I would hang onto the radio and dance, and my diaper would fall off!. . .

My grandfather adored me. . . . My grandfather always used to bring me little presents; my grandmother used to bring me little wrapped-up things in her apron. She was a beautiful woman, fair, with beautiful green eyes. And she wore little hats on Sundays. I used to go to church with them, because I liked going to the Mass at San Felipe—my parents would go to St. Anthony's, to the orphanage. My grandparents would go to the same pew every Sunday. [We rode to church in my grandfather's truck] and he used to put a board across [the bed of the truck] for me to sit on.

And I had. . . one of these big Breton sailor hats with sashes. . . .[that] would fly off and my grandfather would stop and pick it up and put it back on my head, and then he'd go a little further, and the same thing would happen. It seemed like it was forever to go to church; it's really not that far. . . . [M]y grandmother—she was very patient—would finally take the hat and put it on her lap.

I went to San Felipe School because that was the school that all of the family had always gone to—my aunts and uncles, my mother and father. I spoke Spanish at home and English at school. I remember making my first communion. . . . And I was very much involved with San Felipe. We all grew up together, the same group [of kids], all the way up to ninth grade. And some of us are distantly related. I remember belonging to the Ignacitas. . . . We were like Girl Scouts. We used to wear veils and have prayer services. In the month of May we went to church every day carrying little flowers, like baby's breath. We'd take our little bouquets from our yards and say prayers. The month of May is Mary's month, and we were very much involved with Mary. I remember my mother saying, "The Blessed Mother wouldn't like it, if you did that." And I remember growing up with this [warning]. It would make us really stop and really look at things. And October was another month we did this. It's also Mary's month, the month of the Rosary. And for the May crowning, we'd carry our little flowers and somebody would get chosen to crown the Blessed Mother, and put a crown of flowers on her head and we had this beautiful ceremony.

And at that time we had *Matachines. Matachines* were. . . spirits, I felt. They dressed differently and they used to dance and come in ahead of us. We had processions—our big processions were during Lent. We'd march not only around the plaza, but we would go beyond that, all around Old Town and down Central [Avenue]. One of the things we did on Holy Thursday—my grandmother Armijo would take us all, she'd get the cousins, the *primos*, and say, "Cousins that are that close, they are like brothers and sisters, they do not fight, they do not argue." And this is how we were brought up, like we were all brothers and sisters. My grandfather would gather us around and tell us *cuentos* (stories). This was our story time. Stories of things that happened, legends, sometimes religious things—a combination.

Summers were fantastic, we did so many things. I remember on the twenty-fourth of June, my grandmother used to take us down to the ditch. The property was huge, and they had this apple tree that had special little apples, they were called "manzanitas de San Juan," you know, for San Juan's day, his feast day. So we would all go down to the ditch, the one that used to feed off into the others. . . . She'd take us all like little ducks, she'd go up to the ditch, and she'd say, "Today is the day of San Juan, and this is the first day you can swim." And she would put water on our *moiera*, the crown, just a little bit, and that way she'd make everything well, so we would not have problems with drowning, and then we'd swim. . . .

During the day we had chores. We fed the animals. We had pigs and goats and geese and chickens. Of course, we had chicken every Sunday. And we had huge gardens and a big orchard. We used to pick fruit. They kept us busy.

My favorite animals were always the pigs. My mother would say prayers with me at night, and she'd see all these lumps underneath the blanket and she'd lift up [my covers] and here she'd have to gather up all the piglets and take them out. . . . I used to have a pet pig, Gus-Gus, and I used to take him out on a walk, with a stick. But Dixie, my Dalmatian, was so loyal, she followed me everywhere I went. You always knew that wherever Dixie was, that's where I was.

My grandfather used to finish his work about 3 or 4 o'clock and my grandmother used to fix a big meal for him. He used to count his money, and I used to help him. I was the only one he would allow in the kitchen.

I lived with my maternal grandmother, Josefita Salazar, for a while. She lived in Martineztown, on Edith [Street], across from Mt. Calvary Cemetery. I lived there for the school year I was in second grade. That was all I could take, being away from my mom and dad and my brothers. So my mother came by every day and my dad came by twice a day to visit me. My grandmother was alone, and I was the one chosen to stay with her. They had *velorios*—wakes—where they would carry statues of saints to different houses, mostly in the spring. It was more urban than I was used to.

My grandmother canned her own things, and she did a lot of praying. She made me kneel down and pray long prayers. I mean, for a child in second grade it was really hard on me. She gave me little pinches when I didn't settle down. All I had at my grandmother's was a dog named Lobo and a cat. And I remember the cat, and the cat, all of a sudden, just swung up, flew off, and landed on the stove with all fours! Yeoow! And just hit the ceiling. And my grandmother came in, and, boy, did I get a spanking. And I didn't do a thing!

During the war something funny happened. It was my mother's day to water, and she had the three of us [with her]. And it was an open field beyond us where the horses and cows grazed and there was a plane coming over on a maneuver, and a bomb came out! My mother threw herself on us. It killed several horses.

My mother and dad told my sister, who was about eighteen or so, [to] forget it, you're not dating. They just didn't let her go out with any of the people from the Air Force, from the base. She didn't take it well. Katherine was really rebellious. . . .

I took piano and *folklorico* dancing in Old Town. At that time, there was a post office on the side of the church. There was a grocery store where the basket shop is now. There was a *chile* parlor on the other side. There weren't so many shops. You socialized mostly at church, after church. Where the fairgrounds are now, that was really out of town. . . .

I did a lot of the same things other children did growing up, but I still think our times were special.

Marge Armijo graduated from UCLA and remained in California during most of her professional career as a teacher and businesswoman. She returned to her roots in Albuquerque in the early 1970s to do volunteer work and to work in community cultural affairs at the KiMo Theater and the South Broadway Cultural Center. She is now retired in the city she grew up in, the city she loved.

ORAL HISTORIES
TEENAGE YEARS AT LOS ALAMOS,
THE MOST SECRETIVE TOWN OF WORLD WAR II[1]

The Manhattan Project, code name for the U.S. effort to develop an atomic bomb, was supposedly the most secretive research operation of the Second World War. Site Y of the project, located at Los Alamos, New Mexico, enjoyed the highest security of the entire operation because it was the center of atomic research and the home of many of the scientists engaged in this sensitive work. In the interest of top security, the scientists faced many rules and restrictions involving communication, travel, and other peacetime freedoms.

In one such move to ensure security, the scientists' families were brought to live on The Hill, as Los Alamos was known to its newly-arrived residents. How did these often-urban, often-urbane family members react to their isolated, regulation-filled environment? Now retired, the scientists and their wives have answered this question in many written memoirs and oral histories. The children reared in Los Alamos from 1943 to 1945 have had less opportunity to describe their reactions and coping skills. Katrina R. Mason's oral histories with former children of The Hill helps to fill the void in our knowledge of childhood during this important era of New Mexico state history.[2]

While the elementary-school-age children recall the freedom to wander and explore a fascinating natural world, those who came to Los Alamos as teenagers between 1943 and 1945 were more aware of the upheaval in their lives and the restrictions placed upon them. Most of the teenagers in the early years were children of machinists, technicians, and support personnel. Many had come from Texas; others came from the Midwest, and still others were from the neighboring towns of New Mexico. Those whose parents had construction jobs were accustomed to living in a town a short time and then moving on. Others had lived all their lives in one town and felt wrenched away from familiar surroundings and expectations and plunked down in a strange land.

As they recall those early years, they say they noticed right off that Los Alamos was different, but were so caught up in teenage concerns that they gave little thought to the particulars. They missed the activities available in most towns—the high school was too small and too secret to offer activities like team sports, cheerleading, a band, or a yearbook club. They. . . took advantage of the recreational facilities left over from the Ranch School—the skating rink, tennis courts, and stables. Boys were fascinated by the military trucks and machines but disliked the military drill that passed as physical education. Girls similarly disliked the drills that "their" WAC [member of the Women's Army Corps] put them through but enjoyed opportunities to explore classical music records and such magazines as the *New Yorker* while baby-sitting in the homes of the scientists. Several who baby-sat for the [Edward] Tellers remember Mici Teller with fondness—for broadening their horizons and reinforcing their ambitions.

Some felt the town was repressive, too strict; others delighted in finding ways to get around the rules and, often, sneaking out of the town. As they look back on the intensity of war years, they remember a close community where everyone was pulling together and there were few class distinctions—a town where "everyone was in the same boat." Bill Fox, who came at age twelve in 1943 when his father took a job as a fireman at Los Alamos, recalls, "One of the big things that was different about this town is that there has never been a distinction. As I understand it. . . if you lived in a university town, it's 'My daddy is Dr. So and So.' Here they might be a Ph.D. in physics but they were 'Jim' [to everyone]."

Betty Marchi, who also arrived in 1943 when her father, a chef, ran the dining room at Fuller Lodge, remembers, "We were on the basis, 'We're one people up here at Los Alamos, trying to get a thing done.' It didn't matter if you were the janitor, or the street worker, or the scientist. We all got along." The class song that Betty Marchi remembers succinctly conveys the plight of teenagers. Sung to the tune of "You Are My Sunshine," it goes:

> The other day, dear, as I lay dreaming,
> My dreams were full of thoughts of home.
> The gates surround me, and peace confound[s] me,
> And I fear I cannot roam.
>
> Los Alamos, Los Alamos,
> We find its comforts all too plain.
> In spite of sunshine, our favorite pastime
> Is complain, complain, complain.

BILL FOX:

In March 1943 a young widower from Santa Fe sold off his furniture and brought his twelve-year-old son and fourteen-year-old daughter to a new life in a new community. He had taken a job as fireman in the secret town that was going up on the mesa. The family was given a three-bedroom home in a Sundt apartment building, furnished with army cots and tables. To make ends meet the father worked two jobs—adding an evening job at a snack bar. His long hours left the children on their own, but they were taken care of. The son, Bill Fox, who loved sports, learned, to his delight, that he could go to the movie theater that also served as the gymnasium and shoot baskets whenever it wasn't being used by the GIs [soldiers].

In the summer, at least for a time, there were swimming and canoeing at Ashley Pond (named for the Ranch School's founder); in winter every afternoon after school, Bill rushed to the outdoor rink in the canyon where you could shovel off an area and skate. There were tennis courts, too, and he got good enough that one summer he was asked to teach younger children. After an afternoon's sports Bill could meet his father at one of the cafeterias around the town. For a motherless boy from a poor family, it was not a bad place to be. . . .

"[That first spring, 1943,] we went to school in a log building from the Boys Ranch," Bill recalls. "There were probably thirty to forty people in there from the first grade to the twelfth. As I recall, there was one teacher, and most of the time was recess. We did read a few books, but seems like it was a passing thing till they could get Central School built. I don't know if they graduated them or not. . . but three or four boys who were old enough left to go in the army. . . .

"We'd go to the skating pond in the winter. You didn't pay anything. You just went. You took the shovel, cleaned the ice and went skating. I myself did that about every day in the winter, as well as probably ten other kids. We did swim a little bit in Ashley Pond. One of the boys got killed, drowned, and that took care of anybody swimming there. We had canoes. There was a canoe rack out there [from] the Boys Ranch. . . . You could just go get one, put it on the water and use it. [But then this] kid got killed. . . .

"They [had] put a fence around the place and were patrolling it on horseback. As kids, if you wanted to ride a horse, you'd go down there, go get you a horse in the corral, throw a saddle on it and go riding. Some of these boys. . . knew how to ride well. . . .

"It seems like the time we came there were a lot of Sundts [apartments] under construction, but. . . I don't believe there were over about thirteen that were up at the time I came. . . . It was amazing how many workers were working on every building. You would have maybe fifty or sixty. . . people working on a fourplex. They were like ants, so the buildings went up in a hurry. Two- and three-bedroom apartments [went up] with hardwood floors and fireplaces. . . .[3]

"During those early times the mud was awful. One of my first jobs [was at] a barbershop, and I shined shoes for a little while. Not too many people wanted their shoes shined. Things were so dirty you'd walk outside and get dirty again. It was dusty in summer, mud in winter. . . .

"I remember one year. . . they had to put in a big water tank. The population must have been growing a little bit more than [the water supply could handle]. They put in a big tank in the middle of town. They dug some pits on this side of the Rio Grande. . . . They had big trucks go up and get the water and bring it here, and they put it in that tank. I remember they had so much chlorine in it, that you took a silver spoon and it turned black."

BETTE PETERS BROUSSEAU:

In the fall of 1943 the Peters family arrived from Amarillo, Texas. As Rex Peters, who would head up a large machine shop, maneuvered the hairpin turns, his wife noticed the gloom surrounding their older daughter, Betty At fifteen, Betty had anticipated attending Amarillo High School and cheerleading for the football games. To boost her spirits, her mother suggested, "Why not look at this as a new adventure? Do something different. Change the way you spell your name or the way you wear your hair." Betty thought about that and decided that from now on she would spell her name like her favorite movie star, Bette Davis. So as the car chugged up the final incline, it was Bette Peters who stared at the mountains, the guard gates, and all the military machines and wondered if this new place would ever feel like home the way Amarillo did. . . .

"The way I felt, and a lot of other kids felt in those days, you lived and died in the same town," Bette recalls. "I had gone through grade school, through junior high with the same group of students. . . so it was a little traumatic. . . . [But] coming here changed my whole life. . . . Lots of times you don't realize it at the moment. But as time goes by,. . . you realize the opportunities you had. . . . Just meeting people from all over the. . . world and the country. And seeing different backgrounds and cultures."

She remembers sensing that the community was different: "I think most of us who came here knew off the bat that this was not a normal community we were in. Because of the war. . . . [But] nobody really gave it an awful lot of thought." And she clearly remembers instructions not to talk about where she lived, especially on excursions to Santa Fe: "When somebody told you, 'You don't talk about this. Keep your mouth shut,' people did. . . . They did not talk. Every time you went off The Hill you were cautioned by your parents. One time I was in Santa Fe, and my father happened to come down. He was going to go hunting. And he was in this hardware store. . . . He says, 'I'm getting a license.'. . . And he says, 'Now I'm putting down that I live on a ranch out here. If anybody says anything, that's what you say.'. . .

"For a while, the big thing was to see if you could sneak off The Hill. . . . [You] would get somebody's daddy's car, wait till real late at night and sneak out of the house. . . . Not everybody had their passes. Some parents would hold the teenagers' passes just [to be] on the safe side. So if you didn't have a pass to get out, what [your friends would] do is put you on the floor of the car and cover you up. . . . The main thing was the challenge. . . .

"There was a record store in Santa Fe, and we'd go down there and play all these records and maybe buy one or two. . . . There was a drugstore and we'd go over there and have something to drink and just kind of kill time, and then we'd come back [to Los Alamos] on the [military] bus. And we'd sit on the bus and we'd sing. Some [adults] used to get upset about that. We'd sing 'Ninety-nine Bottles of Beer on the Wall.'"

BETTY ANN WILLIAMSON:

Betty Ann Williamson arrived in Los Alamos—over her protests—when she was fifteen, in 1945. She had lived most of her life in a small Texas town, where the family had roots. Her father left his pharmacist job to sign on as an electrician [in Los Alamos]. . . . While observing that "this place was different," Betty was primarily caught up in the business of being a teenager—seeking out amusements and ways to get off The Hill. . . .

"We followed a couple of cousins up here [in 1945]," she recalls. "They said, 'You'll love it. It's a lovely town on a hillside.'. . . I didn't really want to come up here. [It was] one more place where I didn't know anybody. . . .

"There were all sorts of wild rumors [about what was going on here]; I'm not sure it made any difference [to me]. I was here under protest. And, if we were not getting into mischief of some sort, I had a horse that I could go out and ride. In these early stages I was riding military horses and later Mounted Patrol horses. [We lived in] I think they were called the National Huts, a square box. You had a boardwalk to go down to the one big restroom. The clothes lines were all in the middle. . . in the mud. [Later] we did move to a Sundt [apartment]. We lived over [my friend] Mary Alice. Mary Alice's mother was very, very strict. She kept her pass. The only time she could get off The Hill was when she was with her parents.

"My mother worked so I had the car [and I'd drive off The Hill]. There were usually several kids in the car. We'd put [Mary Alice] in the trunk when we got near the guard gate. We'd go plowing through. When we got far enough away, we'd stop and take her out of the trunk, let her back in the car again. At night we'd frequently put her on the floor, put a blanket over her and just go out that way. So her mother had no idea how many times she was in Española or Santa Fe. Or just off. It was nice to get away. Because there wasn't a lot to do. And it was very confining. . . .

"Our [physical education] teacher was a WAC. . . . She didn't really want us or anything to do with us but she had to, so we marched. We marched from Central School to the Big House. We were really quite good. [But] we were tired of marching. Some of us got together and decided we didn't want any more of it, and the next time she did this to us, we were going to refuse. So we [went] down to the field with our books. And when she said, 'Fall out and in,' one by one we just dropped our books. She turned livid. She couldn't punish the whole school, so, I think, we got away with that. . . .

"Lots of our mail was censored. And that was not something that I was certainly used to. . . . So much of our stuff was Trans-shipped. We'd get candy bars in here, chocolate candy bars. You know how they get white when they get too old? A lot of ours were that way. They had been overseas and back [before getting] to us [in the commissary]. . . . We were pretty aware that we were in a different place."

The United States successfully detonated its first atomic bomb at Trinity Site in southern New Mexico on July 16, 1945. Within a month, two additional bombs were dropped on targets in Japan, bringing the war to an end on August 15, 1945. Reaction by the scientists and their families—including their teenage children—was mixed. Some were proud to have been part of a project that contributed so much to end the terrible war overseas. Others had grave misgivings about what had been invented and its impact on the world's post-war future. Their personal reaction to the explosions of the atomic bombs, combined with their coping with a life of rules and security, helped shape the children who came of age in Los Alamos during World War II.[4]

12

ATHLETIC CHILDHOODS

ROY A. STAMM
SPORTS—FROM FOOTBALL TO BICYCLING—IN THE 1890s[1]

    The Stamm family Bible records Roy A. Stamm's birth in Janesville, Kansas, on December 11, 1875. He was the oldest child in the Stamm farm and ranch family. Unfortunately, by the time Roy was five years old, droughthad caused much of the family's cattle to starve and the hog cholera had killed off its breeding stock. Discouraged, Roy's father sold practically everything he owned and moved to Albuquerque in 1881, just after the Santa Fe Railroad had reached that western town. With New Town Albuquerque booming, Roy's dad succeeded in the wholesale fruit and vegetable business and sent for his family to join him by 1882. Roy thus grew up in the expanding town, remembering a lynching (complete with formal invitations), wooden boardwalks (before sidewalks), an open ditch (running through backyards and under restaurants), ladies of leisure (led by madams named Lizzie, Nellie, and Minnie), and a price war among breweries (that culminated in three days of free beer).

    By the 1890s, as Roy and New Town began to slowly mature, new interests began to dominate both the boy and his city. Like many adolescents then and now, Roy devoted increasing amounts of time to a wide variety of athletic activities then popular in Albuquerque. He describes several of these activities—and his relative success or failure in each—in the pages that follow.

In my childhood [I was] rather an introvert, [but] in early adolescence, [in the 1890s, having] entered high school, I became more of an extrovert; plenty there was to see and do.

Outdoor sports strongly attracted me. Of course,. . . many of these were seasonal. Weather had a lot to do with it but the leadership of a few established the time to start and to quit. Marbles and tops were left to children; we high schoolers had more important things. Shinny and kites were for early spring; baseball and tennis for summer; and football for fall. Pom-pom-pull-away, run-sheep-run, prisoners' base and other running games were largely all seasonal, to be started whenever conditions seemed favorable.

Pelota

My horsemanship and age were not up to the melee of horses and men participating in the "sport" of rooster pulls, but in another I always took part if permitted.[2] This was shinny, [played with a] *pelota* (ball) with a puck made of buckskin or rawhide sewed around a stuffed center. The *pelota* was about two inches in diameter and those older players could loft it out of the dust or sand for long gains. If you really worked at it you had plenty of running and rough stick work. None would deliberately hit you, but you must stay on your own side and protect your own shins. We town boys played quite a bit but those villagers had behind them centuries of competition and our game was not so good as their, especially in clever stick work.

We made our own shinny sticks by cutting inch-and-a-half saplings from cottonwood thickets along the river, then trimming off their branches and leaves and building a small fire across which we placed the sapling about six to eight inches back from its heavier end. When sufficiently cooked, this end could be bent up to slightly less than right angle and wired in that position. After a few days drying, it would hold its angle; then we peeled and whittled the sapling to the shape desired.

One game in shinny we called "soup" or "scramble." A circle fifteen to twenty feet in diameter was made by holes in the ground six to seven inches wide and four to five inches deep. Another hole of the same size was dug in the center of the circle and the number of holes was determined by the number of players. Each participant had a three to four foot straight stick of not over one-and-a-half inches in diameter. A broomstick or a peeled sapling was usually used. The circle holes were spaced two or three feet apart and a goal chosen, generally a wall, fence, or tree. For the "puck" we used a medium-sized tin can.

To start the game, all players lined up and "lagged" their sticks to see who could come closest to the goal. The loser took the puck outside the circle and the others stuck their sticks into circle-holes. So long as a player had his stick in a circle-hole not yet taken, he was safe. The player with the puck then tried to work it through the circle into the center-hole while the players nearest him attempted to knock it away as far as possible. Should the puck be holed in the center, all defenders dashed to tough the goal with their sticks and ran back to place their sticks in vacant holes. The former attacker had chosen a hole and the defender, unable to find a vacant hole, became the attacker.

All defenders must be alert to see that no other defender steals his hole when he removes his stick to strike at the puck; and the thief himself risks his own hole to the attacker or another defender since the attacker and defender change places the moment the attacker's stick is stuck into a vacant circle-hole. No attacker was kept outside too long; the game is tricky and "scrambles" are frequent. . . .

Football

In 1892, when I became a [high school] Junior,. . . teams were formed to play the American game [of football]. Our canvas suits carried little padding except where towels were stuffed over shoulders and knees. Headgears, nose guards, and helmets were not yet introduced and all players cultivated heavy heads of hair for protection. Then it was a really rough game and in poor repute with those conservative [in nature]. The ball was not dead until it touched the ground, and you could hurdle "cleated shoes first" if you wished. Soon, flying wedges, revolving "turtle-back" plays and tandem line bucking became common. Eventually, these massed plays were forbidden by new rules, but they lasted for quite a while. I had my nose broken twice and my cheek bone caved in, [and] also [had] a trick knee, but escaped more serious injury probably because I was compactly built.

Football team, Albuquerque Indian School, Albuquerque, New Mexico. Neg. No. 000-119-0442. Courtesy of the Center for Southwest Research, General Library, University of New Mexico, Albuquerque, New Mexico.

As captain of the high school team, the superintendent of the [Albuquerque] Indian School asked me to coach his boys which, from time to time, I did for one season. Many of these [Indian players] were adults—not heavy, but tough and hard. This school fielded four teams with several good runners among them. Not expecting to play them, I taught those braves all our best plays and threw in our signals for good measure. We met them for a practice game one Saturday and won 12 to 0. They gave us a good game and we should have left well enough alone; we took them on publicly two weeks later and got trimmed 20 to 0! With four teams playing each other almost every day and their natural ability for speed and endurance, I decided I'd coached them enough. . . .

Tennis

In my junior year, tennis also interested me. Two U.S. Army pay-
masters were transferred to Albuquerque: Majors Baker and Towner.
The first named had two pretty daughters and two sons who were fine
tennis players. . . . We youngsters admired their tennis but their sisters
even more. The Bakers made a clay court and their younger sister was a
sophomore in the high [school]. Too juvenile to interest the older sister,
we sure converged on the younger girl. An Army daughter, soft-voiced,
modest, and graceful, she accepted the situation and handled it with skill.
We were invited to play on her brothers' court, but usually they were
using it. Mature enough to understand our position, we kept out of the
way.

Obviously, we must have a court of our own and one made by nature was ready and waiting. In the western edge of town, along the river
meadows. . . this was the level bottom of a miniature "bolson" formed by
rain and snow water draining from clay hummocks surrounding [an] open
space. In our dry climate of six to eight inches of annual rainfall probably
it [would have] taken a hundred or more years to build up the six inch
thickness of hard clay blanket covering the windblown sand on which it
was dropped.

A New Mexican rain seldom is long [or] drawn out; often it is a
brief but heavy downpour. After one of these scarce but welcome rain-
falls, that chosen area became a muddy pool which our thirsty air and
all-day sun dried to leave the bottom leveled by water and almost cement
hard. After we painted lines and built backstops, a fine but probably the
cheapest and most unusual good clay court in these United States was
ours. . . .

Hunting

Before I entered high school, our family spent two or three summer
weeks at San Lorenzo Springs a mile or two north of Whitcomb Springs
in the South Sandia. Near these was the summer camp of younger Indian boys from the [same] Indian School at Albuquerque. With these I
learned to kill rabbits with light bows and untipped but sharp pointed
arrows. Also, for several nights our camp had been raided by a big dog

belonging to a rancher somewhere in the distance. We were forced to keep our food inside the tents and were not particularly pleased to have those Indian boys point out and prove by his tracks that the raider was not a dog but a small black bear.

A week later eight of the old Indian boys laid for the bear, cornered him against a high ledge back of our tent and put several arrows into him before he broke out of their ring. At daybreak they found the bear was wounded and easily tracked him for a couple of miles to the final kill with arrows and clubs. These boys had no stone or metal pointed arrows, but only shafts hardened by fire. With their comparative light bows they could put one of these shafts clear through a rabbit, but the bear was tougher meat and before they finished him he looked like a porcupine. I followed them to the kill and only kept up because they had to track on rough and stony ground. I was twelve then and greatly thrilled. All through the affair the bear tried to escape, but those young braves—two Apaches, two Navajos, one Pueblo, two Pimas, and one Papago—were just too many for him. . . .

Bicycles

Young Seymour Lewinson and his high wheel bicycle. Cobbs Memorial Collection, Neg. No. 000-119-0297. Courtesy of the Center for Southwest Research, General Library, University of New Mexico, Albuquerque, New Mexico.

By 1890, displacing the high-wheel/low-wheel bicycle in previous use, the low, two-wheeled, pneumatic tired bicycle became increasingly popular. When I was given one of those "safeties" as these were called, I lost some interest in my horse.

Most of my riding and driving of horses and buggies was in the valley, while I bicycled largely on the mesa east of town. Valley roads too often were likely to be muddy from overflowing irrigation ditches, while the mesa roads were at least dry, even though sand, ruts, and stones made some stretches rough going. Even on these, a strong bicyclist could make his "century"—one hundred miles in a day—without too much trouble. One favored trip was southeast over the mesa to Largo Canyon, northeast up this and over the divide into Cedro Canyon, down from there to the northwest into Tijeras Canyon, and west down to its entrance; and then straight west over the mesa back to Albuquerque.

Hardy souls would ride to Santa Fe and back within a time limit of twenty-four hours. On long trips I could hold my own with the best, and in short races I was not so bad when I finished second in an amateur mile race at the Fair Grounds with thirteen entries. That was the only race I ever entered, and I decided it was too specialized and demanding more hours than I wished to spend on bicycling.

For tennis, I always had time. Of average height, but compactly built, as a younger boy I found myself a fine sprinter. Riding and bicycling slowed me by overdeveloping muscles not needed in sprinting, but my reactions were still fast and I could cover the court. Football and tennis became my specialties, [and] in both I was good.

Sports remained an important part of Roy Stamm's life as he grew to maturity, entered the business world, and enjoyed an interesting, fulfilling life. He completed his autobiography in 1954, just three years before his death. As the editors of his autobiography explain, Roy had a good reason for the title of his life's story. He called his memoirs For Me, The Sun *because he loved New Mexico's dry, sunny climate. He "was down-right uncomfortable elsewhere. New Mexico is where he belonged."[3]*

JOHN BAKER
A TRACK STAR IN ALBUQUERQUE, 1960s[1]

In 1978 William J. Buchanan wrote John Baker's biography, entitled A Shining Season. *Although Buchanan could have been referring to any single season in John Baker's career as a star runner, he was actually referring to John's short life as a brief, shining moment in the history of sports in New Mexico.*

John Baker. Courtesy of the John Baker Elementary School, Albuquerque, New Mexico.

Many residents of Albuquerque's Northeast Heights remember the day the Baker family moved into the neighborhood. It would be a hard day to forget, for the Bakers arrived "on camera."

In the 1940s Jack Baker's name was a household word in millions of homes coast-to-coast. Radio and television fans of the era will remember him as the thickset, ruddy-faced impresario of *Don McNeil's Breakfast Club*, a popular variety show broadcast from Chicago. He starred for McNeil for eight years. Then, in 1943, following his marriage to one of his most ardent fans, twenty-year-old, raven-haired Polly Willoughby, from Ben Wheeler, Texas, he switched from performing to station management in the rapidly expanding field of television.

For the next eleven years Jack and Polly traveled extensively while Jack managed TV stations in Arkansas, Missouri, Illinois, Tennessee, and Wisconsin. On June 29, 1944, in Springfield, Missouri, their first child, John, was born. For Jack it was a day for double celebration. It was his thirty-sixth birthday.

Two years later, in Nashville, on September 7, 1946, a second son, Robert, was born. Then, on January 16, 1948, in Memphis, the birth of a daughter, Jill, completed the Baker family.

In 1953, with growing children, Jack and Polly became concerned about the effect of their rootless lives on the family. That spring Jack was contracted to launch and manage a new station, KOAT-TV (ABC), in Albuquerque. He fell headlong in love with the city. The clear mountain air and unlimited elbow room were ideal for raising a family. A week later he moved the family from Wisconsin to New Mexico, settled them in a rental apartment, and started searching for a permanent home.

In June a prominent building contractor visited Jack at his office. The contractor was starting a new housing development and wanted publicity. Jack was still looking for a house, and the contractor agreed to build Jack a house at cost in exchange for Jack's personal appearances in commercials for the company. For the next eight weeks Channel 7 viewers were treated to a brick-by-brick account of the construction of "The House That Jack Built."

On August 29, 1954, while television cameras broadcast the scene live, Jack, Polly, John, Robert, and Jill walked through streaming banners into their new house at 1700 Kentucky Street, Northeast. The Bakers were home at last.

From his first days in Albuquerque, ten-year-old John learned that his past uprooting held an unexpected advantage. His knowledge of strange places and practices, coupled with his outgoing personality, made him an instant hit with his new pals. Though skinny and inches shorter than most of them, it was still John who took the lead in organizing activities, assigning roles, and settling disputes. And he knew some exciting new games. One was "Tug."

"Tug" was played at evening just after dusk, when lengthening shadows made visibility poor. On opposite sides of Kentucky Street, John and a companion would crouch behind shrubs and await an oncoming car. Just as the driver reached their hiding places both boys would leap up, pretend to grasp opposite ends of an imaginary rope, and loudly yell, "TUG."

"Seeing" the threatening barrier, motorists would screech to a jolting halt. Then, as angry curses filled the air, the culprits would flee to safety, laughing all the way. One evening John's partner was his eight-year-old brother, Robert. But this night the motorist didn't simply sit and curse. He leaped from his car and gave chase. Robert escaped, but John was caught.

Ten minutes later the irate motorist, John in tow, stood on the Bakers' porch telling Jack what had happened. Punishment was swift. After a stern lecture, John was assigned to do all the household chores—cleaning, dusting, dish washing, garbage carryout—for one week.

Robert was remorseful. "I gotta tell Dad," he whispered down from his upper bunk that night in the room he shared with John.

"No way!" John replied. "You escaped. Now keep quiet."

Reluctantly, Robert agreed. But secretly, all that week, he helped John do the chores.

At the end of the week Jack took John aside. "I hope, young man," Jack said, "that all this has taught you a lesson."

"It sure has," John agreed. "I gotta learn to run faster."

The next morning John called his friends to come over and bring rakes, hoes, and shovels. When they arrived he assembled them at the rear of his house where the mesa lay in open range. Just behind his back fence he and his friends spent the day scraping away tumbleweeds, cacti, and sagebrush, until they had cleared an area suitable for a ball diamond. That evening, in a rousing game of softball, umpired by his father, John began to train himself to run faster.

In September the Baker children entered nearby Mark Twain Elementary School. John was in the fifth grade. Unlike Robert, who approached his studies indifferently but still made high marks, John had to struggle for good grades. But determination was already one of his traits. At the first PTA meeting that year his teacher took Polly aside. "Mrs. Baker," she asked, a bit apprehensively, "do you and your husband. . . well. . . demand perfection in your children?"

Puzzled, Polly asked for an explanation.

"John is so intense," she said. "He gets upset with himself when he can't grasp a lesson right off. He sometimes works through recess."

Polly laughed. "Next year you'll get Robert in your class. You'll see then that John's doggedness is his own doing, not a Baker trait."

The following year she reminded Polly of their talk. "I see what you meant," the teacher said.

On their first day of school a gangly, handsome, tow-headed boy walked up to John on the playground and looked down on him from a two-inch advantage in height. "You John Baker?" the tow-head demanded.

"Yeah."

The tow-head nodded toward some boys who stood with him. "We hear you're supposed to have a hot-shot ball team over on Kentucky Street."

"That's twice you're right," John replied.

"My name's John Haaland. I say we've got a better team. Wanta find out this afternoon—your field?"

"We'll be waiting," Baker said.

At six-o'clock that evening, with the score tied 20-to-20 in the fourteenth inning, two bone-weary teams decided to call it a draw. Exhausted, the team captains, Baker and Haaland, dropped to the ground and sat back against the Bakers' rear fence. The aroma of the evening meal wafted toward them.

"Hungry?" Baker asked.

"You kidding!" Haaland exclaimed. "I could eat a coyote."

"All we got's chicken."

"That'll do."

That evening John Baker and John Haaland shared the first of many meals they would eat over the years at each other's homes. It was the beginning of a lasting friendship.

By the time he entered high school John had become a competent outfielder, and he made the freshman team. Then, in his sophomore year, his sports career almost came to an end. That year, with a rapidly expanding student population, the Albuquerque school districts were realigned. While his new high school was under construction, John was temporarily assigned to another district. Within weeks his morale plummeted, and his grades began to drop. One afternoon, Jack took him aside and asked for an explanation. After some hesitation, John said, "Dad, I've got a problem at school."

"Tell me about it," Jack said.

John explained. At the end of the first week, when he hadn't reported for baseball practice, he'd been called to a coach's office. The coach had demanded to know why John hadn't come out for practice.

"I was thinking about waiting for track," John had replied.

"Track?" the coach had retorted. "Are you kidding? A scrawny kid like you? You wouldn't stand a chance. Besides, on my campus you play what I say you play." He pointed a finger at John's face. "And I say you'll be at ball practice this afternoon. Hear?"

Throughout John's story, Jack's anger had mounted. "And?" he asked.

"I didn't go," John said. "And I'm not going. But now the coach is picking on me. He puts me down in class and everywhere."

Jack looked at his watch. Ball practice would still be going on at the school. Without another word he left the house, got into his car, and drove away. When he returned a half-hour later, John was sitting at the kitchen table with Polly. "There won't be any more picking on you at school, John," Jack said firmly. "I can promise you that." Though Jack never again mentioned the incident, or what he'd said to the coach, the pressure on John ceased. His pride in his father, always high, soared. Moreover, he'd learned a lesson about the negative side of coaching that he'd never forget.

He stayed away from school sports for the remainder of that year. Then, in his junior year, he initiated a turn-of-events that changed the course of his life.

In 1960, along with most of his chums, John was transferred to newly opened Manzano High School. He was sixteen. Eager to build a first-rate track team from the beginning, Manzano's coach, Bill Wolffarth, had his eye on a promising young athlete—John Haaland. But his overtures to Haaland fell on deaf ears.

One afternoon Baker went to Wolffarth's office. "Coach, I hear you've been trying to recruit Haaland?"

"Trying is about all," Wolffarth admitted.

John's brown eyes flashed merrily. "I'll make you a deal. Let me join the track team and I'll get Haaland to join too."

Wolffarth chuckled. Baker a runner? He looked at the boy fondly. He liked him, had known him ever since grade school. But Baker was too short-legged, to uncoordinated for track. Still, he *was* Haaland's best friend.

"You really think you can deliver on that deal, old buddy?"

"I know I can," John replied.

Wolffarth thought for a long moment. The kid had spunk. "Tell you what," Wolffarth said. "You have Haaland here at two-thirty tomorrow, both of you dressed out. And you've got a deal."

John flashed a winning smile. "We'll be here."

When John left, Wolffarth shook his head. He had no hopes for the boy as a runner. It was the most fortunate misjudgment of his career.

The first meet that fall was a 1.7-mile cross-country race through the foothills of the Sandia Mountains just east of Albuquerque. Under a bright sky a crowd of two hundred fans clustered around the starting line to watch twelve runners limber up. Most eyes were focused on Highland High School's reigning state champion miler, Lloyd Goff. Speculation centered on how closely Manzano's new hope, John Haaland, could trail the champion. No one paid attention to another Manzano entry: number 33; height 5 feet 6 inches; weight 135 pounds; previous entries, none; name—John Baker.

At the crack of the gun the runners kicked off, pacing themselves slowly in the mile-high mountain air. The field lined up as predicted. Goff set the pace with Haaland following closely. At the end of four minutes the runners disappeared behind a low hill just inside the far turn of the flag-marked course. The spectators switched their gaze to where the runners would emerge from behind the hill. A minute passed. Two. Then a lone figure appeared.

Kneeling near the finish line, squinting against the sun, Bill Wolffarth nudged an assistant. "Well, here comes Goff." Wolffarth raised his binoculars. With an ear-splitting yelp he jumped straight up in the air. "That's not Goff," he screamed. "That's Baker!"

Pounding toward the homestretch, John grinned and glanced back over his shoulder.

"Don't look back, boy!" Wolffarth shouted. "Run! Run!"

Leaving a field of surprised runners behind, John crossed the finish line in 8:30.5. He had not only scored an upset, he had set a new meet record. The crowed cheered wildly.

What had happened on the far side of that hill? Later that evening John told his family.

Halfway through the race, with things going as expected, he had asked himself: *Is this my best?* He didn't know. Resolutely, he fixed his eye on the back number of the front runner. He closed his mind to everything else. Only one thing mattered: catch and pass that number—that runner. A new energy surged through his body It was almost hypnotic. One by one he passed the front runners, then took a commanding lead. Forcing himself to ignore the fatigue tearing at his muscles, he maintained his furious pace until he crossed the finish line and collapsed in exhaustion. He was to repeat that pattern many times.

Elated at finding this unexpected talent, Wolffarth tried John in other events: cross-country, the mile, the medley relay. The result was always the same. On the track the modest fun-loving teenager became a relentless competitor. Doubts dispelled, Wolffarth rebuilt his team around Manzano's new star—John Baker.

One day an assistant coach criticized John's style. "His form is terrible. He tilts his face up like he's looking for rain. Look how he throws that right leg."

"True," Wolffarth replied. He fixed his assistant with a no-nonsense stare. "But you don't change feed on a winning horse."

To sportswriters who were just beginning to notice John, Wolffarth put it differently: "It doesn't come easy to Baker. He's a heart runner. A triumph of determination over style."

By the end of his first year in competitive track, John had broken six state records.

In his senior year John carried the Manzano purple-and gray to victory after victory in individual wins as records continued to fall to his free-style onslaught. By spring of 1962, sportswriters were predicting he would complete the season undefeated.

Then came the last meet of the year.

New Mexico's finest high school runners converged on Albuquerque's University Stadium that afternoon of May 12, 1962, for the fiftieth Annual State Championship Track and Field Meet. Conditions were not ideal. The temperature in the mile-high city was forty-one degrees. A steady north wind gusted at times to forty miles-per-hour. Worst of all, swirling clouds of dust and sand, whipped up from the surrounding desert, plagued the runners, clogging their throats and irritating their eyes.

Midway in the meet Bill Wolffarth pondered tactics. He knew Manzano was in trouble. The coveted first-,second- and third-place team positions had already been won on points by older schools with long-established sports programs. But to finish in the top five against such experienced competition would be a respectable prize for Manzano. To win fifth place Manzano had to take the next race—the medley relay. It was Manzano's weakest event.

The medley relay was a one-mile race between four-man teams. Each starting runner had to race 220 yards (one-half lap of a standard outdoor track), then pass a baton to the second runner on his team who would also race 220 yards. The third runner would race one full lap, 440 yards. The anchor man would lap the track twice, carrying the baton a distance equaling that covered by his teammates combined, 880 yards—one-half mile.

Wolffarth knew Manzano's first three runners were outclassed. The race depended on the anchor man—John Baker. But already that afternoon John had won the mile championship race. He was undefeated for the season. Would it be fair to risk his flawless record in a second grueling race for a questionable team win? Knowing that John would insist on staying in the race, Wolffarth resisted the impulse to make a substitution.

Within minutes after the gun Wolffarth regretted his decision. As he feared, Manzano's first two runners were no match for their opponents. Nor could the third, buffeted by a blinding sandstorm, make up the deficit. By the time the baton was passed to John the anchor men of the opposing teams were already nearing the first turn, almost a hundred yards ahead.

High in the stands one burly spectator, rooting for another team, yelled, "Looks like that prima donna Baker isn't going to win 'em all this year after all!"

But John was tearing along. On the far turn, in the midst of his second lap, he kicked into his final sprint, 220 yards from the finish line. With each stride he gained on the front runners. Could he maintain maximum effort for such distance? The spectators rose to their feet. Entering the final turn John passed one, then another of the lead runners. He was now second. The crowd roared. Ignoring the forty-mile-per-hour headwind sandblasting his face and body, John held his sprint. With less than fifty yards to go he closed fast on the front man.

In the stands, the man who had loudly predicted John's defeat felt something strike him on the shoulder. He turned to see an attractive brunette directly behind him flailing away at his back with her first while she screamed at the top of her lungs, "GO, JOHN! GO!" At that instant, on the track below, John crossed the finish line, the winner by inches.

When the crowd's frenzy abated, the brunette grasped the astonished man's hand and apologized profusely. "You see," a beaming Polly Baker explained, "I'm that prima donna's mother."

It was a fantastic finale to an improbable high school sports career. By now a prime attraction to sportswriters throughout the Southwest, John was touted as "the finest miler ever developed in New Mexico." He was not yet eighteen.

John continued to develop as a champion runner over the next six years. Eventually ranked eighth in the world among indoor milers, his goals were to break the four-minute mile and to qualify for the Olympic games to be held in Munich, Germany. But then tragedy struck: he was diagnosed with terminal cancer. Always a fighter, John struggled against his new nemesis and attempted to enjoy a productive life for as long as he could. Despite severe pain, he continued to work with children as a teacher at Albuquerque's Aspen Elementary School and to coach the Duke City Dashers, a track team for school-age girls. John fought gallantly for eighteen months, twelve months longer than his doctors had thought possible. He finally died on Thanksgiving Day, 1970. As a freshman at the University of New Mexico, he had written a poem entitled, "Race to Death."

Many thoughts race through my mind
As I step up to the starting line.
Butterflies through my stomach fly,
And as I free that last deep sigh,
I feel that death is drawing near,
But the end of the race I do not fear.
For when the string comes across my breast,
I know it's time for eternal rest.

The gun goes off, the race is run,
And only God knows if I've won.
My family and friends and many more
Can't understand what it was for.
But this "Race to Death" is a final test,
And I'm not afraid,
For [I know] I've done my best.[2]

In John's honor, he was named to the Albuquerque Sports Hall of Fame, had an athletic scholarship named after him, and was the subject of a television movie produced in 1979. Of most significance, Aspen Elementary School was renamed John Baker Elementary School. As John's biographer wrote, the school remains "a fitting monument to a courageous young man who, in his darkest hours, transformed bitter tragedy into an enduring legacy."[3]

CONCLUSION

Sometimes at the end of a journey it is well to look back at the path followed and to ask ourselves if there is not some lesson of hope or encouragement to be drawn from our record.

Marion Sloan Russell
Land of Enchantment

We have been introduced to a wide range of New Mexico children who lived and came of age over an equally wide range of New Mexico history. Diversity was clearly the children's dominant quality. Yet they were all New Mexicans with certain common characteristics. It is possible to identify ten main characteristics that most New Mexico children shared. Children everywhere and in most periods of history shared most of these characteristics. But, given their unique physical, cultural, and social surroundings, New Mexico's children often shared them in ways not often found in other states, nations, or communities of the past.[1]

Families

The strongest, most frequently expressed shared characteristic of New Mexico children was their abiding love for their families as a whole and for individual family members in particular. Families were the center of each child's universe, and family members were by far the greatest sources of affection, security, guidance, encouragement, skills, wisdom, values, and plain-and-simple fun. Having read the chapters of this book, few will forget Cleofas Jaramillo's loving mother who told her children Spanish fairy tales (chapter 3) or Marge Armijo's adoring grandparents who brought Marge little gifts wrapped neatly in her grandmother's apron (chapter 11). Who will forget Tall Woman's Navajo mother patiently teaching her daughter which wild plants were edible (chapter 9) or Marcelina Chávez's Hispanic parents telling her which herbs could be used to cure which ailments in her life (chapter 5)? *Padrinos* (Catholic godparents) were almost as important as one's own parents and grandparents. Angelica Chávez said of her *madrina* (godmother), "I remember going to spend time with her. . . and she loved me so much and I loved her so much too" (chapter 3). Cleofas, Marge, Tall Woman, Marcelina, and Angelica are but five examples. Strong sentiment and bonds prevailed in most families, regardless of race, culture, or adversity, throughout New Mexico.

Baca family, Belen, New Mexico. Neg. No. 135010. Courtesy of the Museum of New Mexico, Santa Fe, New Mexico.

Family leaders taught their children values to be used as durable internal compasses, giving direction and added meaning to their lives. Many of these values were based on whichever culture or religion a family belonged. Lori Arviso Alvord's Navajo parents taught her to respect privacy, not to be overly competitive, and not to be preoccupied with material wealth (chapter 9). Other values were more universal in what is often called the Code of the West. All children were taught to share with strangers, even if they were suspected outlaws, as Agnes Morley learned (chapter 6), or neighbors who might otherwise seem to neglect their families, as Marcelina Chávez recalled (chapter 5). Through actions more often than words, children learned that strangers were not to be questioned and that everyone was to be treated equally. From the poorest family to the most affluent, all stressed the need for every family member to pitch in and work hard for the good—indeed the survival—of the whole. In good times and in bad, the key value taught was to make do and not to complain.

New Mexico children respected their elders for their strong values and support. Children expressed their deep respect in both formal and informal ways. Agnes Morley respected her mother Ada for her strength and ability to hold her young family together on a distant ranch when "It would have been so very easy to sink under the all-but-overwhelming flood of hardships and disappointments that were hers." Agnes showed her respect for her widowed mother by obeying her wishes and helping out on their ranch whenever possible (chapter 6). More formally, one way that Marcelina Chávez and her siblings showed their respect for their father and visiting adults was by bringing them water and patiently standing with arms folded until each elder was done drinking (chapter 5).

But most children expressed their respect with simple love and admiration. Who will forget Ralph Reynolds's respect and admiration when his ranching dad went to great lengths to rescue a suffering animal, despite the hours this act of compassion consumed and the long delay it caused (chapter 6)? Aubrey Lippincott loved and respected his father for staying in a tent pitched in the backyard of their Fort Union quarters rather than expose his young son to the diphtheria he had treated as the post doctor during an outbreak of this dreaded disease in 1889 (chapter 2). Conversely, it has been argued that William Bonney (Billy the Kid) began to lose respect for most elders and the authority they represented after his much-loved mother died of tuberculosis when he was only fourteen years old in 1874 (chapter 7). Without the parent he most loved and respected to guide him, Billy was left to fend for himself on a tragic path that led to frequent violence and an early death.[2]

Traditions

A second major characteristic shared by most New Mexico children involved cultural traditions. Taught and practiced by respected family and community leaders, traditions were learned and enjoyed from an early age. Regardless of a child's culture, traditions served to unify groups and solidify each child's place in one's family, one's community, and, indeed, the world. Traditions, and the larger cultures on which they were based, reinforced the values that gave New Mexicans clear direction in their lives. Abe Peña's memories of his childhood in rural Cibola thus centered on such time-honored traditions as participating in religious plays, witnessing rooster pulls, and helping at *matanzas* (the butchering of a pig with a feast to follow) (chapter 3). Children especially remembered wonderful cultural foods and drinks, such as *chile* and beans for Hispanic children, fry bread for many Indians, *kielbasa* for Slavic kids, and homemade wine for Italians.[3]

Children dancing at fiesta, Taos Plaza. Photograph by Russell Lee. LC-USF 33, Neg. No. 12875-M1. Courtesy of the Library of Congress, Washington, D.C.

Traditional Indian and Catholic ceremonies, St. Augustine Church, Isleta Pueblo, New Mexico, 1947. Photograph by Tyler Dingee. Neg. No. 120-314. Courtesy of the Museum of New Mexico, Santa Fe, New Mexico.

Many traditions focused on the children themselves. Children always enjoyed the attention they received at storytelling time when folk tales and *dichos* (sayings) filled with subtle lessons were artfully passed from one generation to the next. Fabiola Cabeza de Baca and her siblings always looked forward to El Cuate's (the Twin's) stories when he was in the right mood, especially when it rained on their arid *llano*. Spitting out a wad of tobacco (a sure sign of his good humor), the ranch cook recalled wonderful tales of buffalo hunts, Indian raids, rodeos, and *fiestas*. As Fabiola exclaimed, "What stories he could tell!" (chapter 6) Children often heard wonderful *cuentos* (stories) and *chistes* (jokes) told by their elders during *visitas* (visits) to the homes of family friends and relatives.

Grandfather and grandson, Chimayo, New Mexico. Prudence Clark Collection, Accession No. 1975.001.011. Courtesy of the Menaul Historical Library, Albuquerque, New Mexico.

Children even appreciated scary stories, as when Cleofas Jaramillo's nursemaid, Tiodora, told terrifying witch tales featuring long hooks and terrible fates for *males hijos* (bad children) (chapter 3). Those who misbehaved were often told that *El Cucuy* (the boogeyman) or *brujas* (witches) would get them if they failed to alter their mischievous ways.

Indian children also learned through folk tales told by adults who knew their tribal histories and customs best. It was the elders' sacred duty to convey their ancient lore and, in the telling, help succeeding generations internalize each folk tale's crucial meaning. Winter, when evenings were long and the weather turned cold, was the ideal season for storytelling at nightly gatherings.

Charles F. Lummis, who lived at Isleta Pueblo from 1888 to 1892, described one such gathering led by an elder named Lorenso. Lummis claimed to have heard some gifted storytellers in his life, but declared that he had "never heard a more eloquent [one]" than Lorenso. "I can tell you the words [he uttered], but not the impressive tones, the animation of eye and accent, the eloquent gestures of this venerable Indian." No wonder the children of Isleta loved to hear Lorenso's stories and begged him to tell them over and over again. The elder told each tale as expertly as a potter formed a beautiful pot: "The Antelope Boy," "The Coyote and the Crows," "The Man Who Married the Moon," and many more. Attentive children learned these tales and their meanings well, preparing them for adulthood and for the responsibility of telling the same stories to future generations "so the legends will pass on and on."[4]

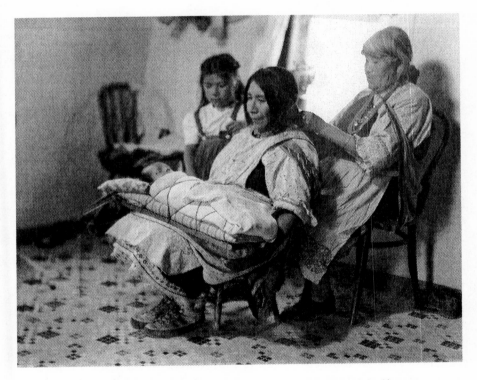

Three generations, Laguna Pueblo, New Mexico, ca. 1935. Photograph by Harmon Parkhurst. Neg. No. 2879. Courtesy of the Museum of New Mexico, Santa Fe, New Mexico.

Mescalero Apache mother and children, ca. 1890s. Blazer Family Papers, Neg. No. Ms100, 7.3.23. Courtesy of the Rio Grande Historical Collections, New Mexico State University Library, New Mexico State University, Las Cruces, New Mexico.

Children often played significant roles in cultural traditions, thus helping the young realize and accept their important roles in family and community life. Children certainly played key parts in religious plays or folk dramas like *Los Pastores* (The Shepherds) and *Los Comanches* (The Comanches) at Christmas (chapter 3).[5] Marge Armijo remembers her grandmother taking Marge and all the children in her family down to the ditch on another religious holiday, San Juan Bautista's feast day each June 24. Once gathered at the ditch, their grandmother would place a little water on each child's head and pray to San Juan for the saint's protection. Having done this, "she'd make everything well, so we would not have problems with drowning, and then we'd swim" safely through the summer months (chapter 11).[6]

Other children participated in customs clearly identified with coming of age rituals. Francis Quintana described one such ritual involving the cleaning of his community's *acequias* each spring. Helping and, in the process, becoming a trusted *péon de la acequia* was a vital part of Francis's coming of age as a proud, contributing adult in his family and his village (chapter 5). More formally, Mexican girls turning fifteen years old participated in elaborate *quinceañeras*, with serenading *mariachi* bands and large "coming out" parties, with the first dance reserved for their fathers. The young woman often threw a doll to a crowd of young girls, symbolically showing that she had left her childhood behind.[7] Indian children like Tall Woman came of age in sacred, highly traditional puberty rites of their own.[8]

Nature

Readers were undoubtedly struck by how close New Mexico children were to nature, from animals—both wild and domestic—to plants, the terrain, rivers, and the elements. Nature could be wild and unpredictable, but it could also be calming and comforting, adding to a child's sense of stability and belonging. Children who lived close to nature could feel as secure and eternal as the mountains or mesas or *bosques* that surrounded their New Mexican family homes.

Young goat herder. Accession No. 1995.153. Courtesy of the Menaul Historical Library, Albuquerque, New Mexico.

Many children helped care for and raise their family's livestock. Tall Woman wanted to help herd sheep and goats from such an early age that her older siblings scolded her and sent her home from the fields (chapter 9). Marcelina Chávez's family brought calves and lambs inside at night in the winter months (chapter 5). Marge Armijo went one step further in caring for baby animals. When Marge and her mother said their prayers by Marge's bed at night, her mother would sometimes "see all these [little] bumps underneath the blanket and she'd lift up [my covers] and. . . have to gather up all the piglets [I had hidden] and take them out" (chapter 11). Ralph Reynolds helped brand calves on his father's ranch, although he could never bring himself to do the actual branding (chapter 6).

Harris children and their pet dog, Albuquerque, New Mexico. Neg. No. 000-119-0330. Courtesy of the Southwest Research Center, General Library, University of New Mexico, Albuquerque, New Mexico.

Isleta boys and their pet dog, ca. 1900. Neg. No. 2714. Courtesy of the Museum of New Mexico, Santa Fe, New Mexico.

12-year-old Billy Jones and his horse at Ditch Camp, Circle Cross Ranch, New Mexico, 1927. Bob and Panzy Jones Collection, Neg. No. RG98-020-23. Courtesy of the Rio Grande Historical Collections, New Mexico State University Library, New Mexico State University, Las Cruces, New Mexico.

3-year-old Roy Chávez and his grandfather's horse, Las Nutrias, New Mexico, 1945. Author's collection.

Nearly every child told stories of favorite pets, usually dogs or horses. Tip, the Collins' family dog, was said to be so clever "that we thought he could almost talk to us." The Collins showed even greater love and respect for a horse named Fritz, said to be "a magnificent, spirited beauty" (chapter 5). Aubrey Lippincott rode his admired horse so much during his years at Fort Union that he later claimed that his main childhood "recollection is living on a pony" (chapter 2). Agnes Morley's horse took her everywhere, allowing her, and many children like her, tremendous mobility and endless opportunities to explore their surroundings, learn the secrets of nature, and occasionally encounter strangers, both good and bad (chapter 6). Janaloo Hill could ride on her own by the time she was four and thereafter "roamed the hills" near Shakespeare in search of adventure on a little black mare named Neysa.[9] Caring for their trusted four-legged companions instilled a respect for life and gave youngsters a sense of responsibility far beyond meeting their own personal needs.[10]

Children saw wild, sometimes exotic, animals as they explored their expansive "backyards" on horseback or by foot. Young Douglas MacArthur spotted a camel near Fort Seldon where Douglas's father served as the commanding officer from 1884 to 1886. The unusual beast was a survivor of an ill-fated Army experiment in the use of camels in the arid Southwest of the 1850s (chapter 2). Wild animals were both feared and respected. James Hastings remembered a "magnificent black tail buck" that wandered into camp in the Magollon Mountains "and watched us, with those great antlers raised in the air." James believed that "It would be a crime to shoot that majestic creature" (chapter 8). Marion Sloan Russell felt much the same way about the deer, the buffalo, and the birds—including roadrunners—she encountered on the Santa Fe Trail (chapter 1). Children stood in proper awe of the animals they raised at home or happened upon in New Mexico's vast wilderness.[11]

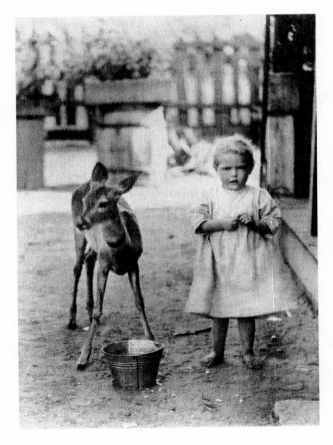

Fay Byfield with fawn. Edgar Garrett Family Collection, Neg. No. Ms0364.0071. Courtesy of the Rio Grande Historical Collections, New Mexico State University Library, New Mexico State University, Las Cruces, New Mexico.

Trujillo boy with pet bear. Audrey Alpers Collection, Neg. No. RG2001-032, Box 5. Courtesy of the Rio Grande Historical Collections, New Mexico State University Library, New Mexico State University, Las Cruces, New Mexico.

Children also stood in awe of the breathtaking landscapes they discovered at seemingly every turn in New Mexico. Traveling into New Mexico on the Santa Fe Trail, Marion Sloan Russell remembered "so clearly the beauty of the earth. . . . [T]here were miles and miles of buffalo grass, blue lagoons, and blood red sunsets" (chapter 1). Agnes Morley and her brother Ray climbed a nearby mountain shortly after their arrival in their new home on the frontier. Once at the top, Ray declared in amazement, "It's an awful big country." Agnes, who seldom lacked for words in her life, "had no words at all. I was taking that scene into my heart and soul as *my country* for so long as I should live" (chapter 6). James Hastings fondly recalled lying awake at night in a camp in the mountains, watching the wide sky above, and learning the location of countless stars till a peaceful sleep finally overtook him (chapter 8).

But while children often stood in awe of the beauty of nature in the Southwest, they were frequently reminded of the potential problems nature could cause for themselves, their families, and whole communities. What New Mexican (past or present) could think of spring without remembering the region's powerful dust storms? In eastern New Mexico, Tomás Brown vividly recalled that "Dark clouds would appear to look like rain clouds but would turn out to be dirt whipped up by the wind and by its centrifugal force became a whirling mass of soil to be deposited in drifts around every object: barns, houses, fence posts, rocks, shrubs" (chapter 10).

Farmers and ranchers disliked strong winds, but dreaded droughts even more. Rain was essential to good grass and ample grazing on the open range, as Fabiola Cabeza de Baca, the daughter of a cattle rancher on the eastern *llano*, explained. "In years of drought," she later wrote, "Papa's blue eyes were sad, but when the rains poured down, his eyes danced like the stars in the heavens on a cloudless night." Fabiola, who seldom asked for "favors from heaven,. . . always pleaded with every saint and the Blessed Mother" for the life-sustaining blessing of abundant rain. Without rain, emotionally strained ranchers only half kiddingly claimed they would have to feed their livestock cactus, suggesting the title of Fabiola's celebrated childhood memoirs, *We Fed Them Cactus* (chapter 6).

Chores

Boys drawing well water at a gasoline station. Photograph by Russell Lee. LC-USF 33, Neg. No. 12829-M3. Courtesy of the Library of Congress, Washington, D.C.

The young were well aware of their physical surroundings and weather conditions largely because children were essential workers in their families' many outdoor activities. Outdoor labor knew few limits in gender, task, or age. As historian Elliott West reminds us, "Most families could not afford idle children."[12]

When old enough, Tall Woman herded sheep and goats, Ralph Reynolds helped round up cattle, and Sammie Kent worked in their father's grocery store, and Francis Quintana assisted in the annual spring cleaning of his farming community's *acqueia* (chapters 5, 6, 9, and 10). Ruth and Lula Collins hauled water from a neighbor's well (two miles distance), weeded their family garden, helped harvest crops, and milked often-cantankerous cows, both morning and night (chapter 5). Some children joined their parents as migrant farm workers in neighboring or distant Western states (chapter 5). Menaul School and Indian boarding school students labored throughout their institutions, on campus grounds, and in well-kept gardens (chapter 10).

Students doing laundry chores, Menaul School. Accession No. 1995.174. Courtesy of the Menaul Historical Library, Albuquerque, New Mexico.

The variety of children's jobs seems endless. Some were self-employed, offering an array of inexpensive goods, like newspapers, and services, such as house cleaning (for thirty-five cents an hour in the case of Haroldie Kent) or shoe shining (for twenty-five cents a shine in the case of Sammie Kent) (chapters 8 and 10). Most children were simply assistants to older siblings, their parents, or other adult workers. Angelica Chávez in Belen and several youngsters in Dawson even assisted in their dads' small-scale bootlegging operations during Prohibition (chapters 5 and 8). James Hastings assisted his father in the silver mining camp he grew up in by standing on the roof of a cupola to hose down any stray sparks that might have started a fire and endangered some, if not all, of their camp (chapter 8).

Other children could be classified as hunters and gatherers. Ruth and Lula Collins gathered cow chips from the prairie for fuel. Kids in Dawson gathered pieces of coal that fell off of coal cars, also as a source of family fuel. Angelica Chávez picked up cantaloupes that dropped off of over-loaded trucks as they crossed bumpy railroad tracks (chapter 5). Many children hunted or trapped small game (especially rabbits) or gathered edible plants to help feed their often large families (chapter 9). Regardless of the nature of their chores, all children learned the essential lesson that "without common effort, common failure was assured."[13]

Girl caring for baby, Zuni Pueblo, New Mexico, ca. 1900. Keystone View Company, Neg. No. 89326. Courtesy of the Museum of New Mexico, Santa Fe, New Mexico.

Girl carrying a pot on her head, Isleta Pueblo, New Mexico. Neg. No. 27371.
Courtesy of the Museum of New Mexico, Santa Fe, New Mexico.

Indoor household chores occupied much of the balance of each child's day, especially for young girls. Girls learned to prepare traditional foods, wash and mend clothes, care for younger siblings, and help clean and maintain family homes. Marcelina Chávez sprinkled water on the dirt floors of her family's house before sweeping them with a home-made broom. Too short to reach the table where her family's dirty dishes waited to be washed, she had to stand on a wooden box to complete this nightly task (chapter 5). Navajo children often carded wool in the evening after long hours of herding sheep and other forms of outdoor labor in the day (chapter 9). Many Hispanic and Indian children assisted their mothers in the task of replastering the mud walls of their adobe homes each spring. Particularly responsible children were sent to live with their aging grandmothers not only to help them out, but also to learn traditional ways, including the healing skills of a *curandera* (healer) in some cases. Short of becoming a *curandera*, children learned that the bitter tasting roots of *yerba de manzo* healed stomach disorders, while the awful smelling *hediondilla* (grease or stink weed) healed rheumatism and arthritis, to name just two popular *remedios* (remedies) of the Southwest.[14]

Rather than complain or bend under the weight of their responsibilities, most children completed their chores (with the knack of making much of their work into play) and took great pride in the vital roles they played in their family's survival and success. As hard workers, children enjoyed heightened self-esteem and were usually appreciated for their efforts, winning the respect of their elders much as their elders had won the respect of their offspring: with actions and not simply words.

Ingenuity

At work or in daily circumstances, New Mexico children displayed a penchant for solving problems in ingenious ways. Often living and working in isolated locales far from ready assistance, the young dealt with problems with a degree of independence far beyond their years. As with values, traditions, and work, they usually learned their problem solving skills and fierce independence from the examples of pragmatic Western adults in their lives.

Little Aubrey Lippincott, for example, devised a way to mount tall horses without the assistance of soldiers stationed at Fort Union where his father served as the post surgeon. After placing a treat on the ground before his horse, Aubrey would wait for the animal to lower his head to take the offering. With the horse's head down, the boy would quickly "put my leg over his head and he'd lift his head and I'd [slide] back and turn around" ready to ride. Aubrey simply reversed the procedure to dismount from his high perch (chapter 2).

Stricken with spinal meningitis when only six months old, Wilbur Coe was left partially paralyzed, but was never pampered by his parents and never let his condition get in his way as a child. To travel to the local one-room school house a mile from his ranch home, Wilbur experimented for hours to build just the right wagon pulled by just the right beast (first dogs, then goats, and finally a single burro). His finished vehicle met his needs and worked so well that other kids hitched rides to school on their friend's highly efficient mode of transportation (chapter 6).

Indian children were equally ingenious in solving dire problems. Deprived of their native foods and often hungry, students at the Santa Fe Indian boarding school secretly gathered corn and bran feed from the school's horse stables. Constructing a small stove from a piece of roofing tin, they parched the corn and, mixing the bran with water, made little *tortillas*. The improvised results were never as good as their mothers' cooking, but they helped to temporarily satisfy the children's hunger and serve their cultural needs while far from home and family (chapter 9).

Friendship

Whether at home, at work, at school, or in other social environments (like church meetings and *fiestas*), children often established firm and lasting friendships. As historian Stephen E. Ambrose put it in expressing the importance of friendships, "Many things, such as what you know or do or experience make life better, but nothing compares to who you have as friends."[15]

Agnes and Ray Morley, sibling friends, sharing a cart. Cleaveland Family Papers, Neg. No. RG94-046. Courtesy of the Rio Grande Historical Collections, New Mexico State University Library, New Mexico State University, Las Cruces, New Mexico.

Sibling friends, Zuni Pueblo,
New Mexico. Neg. No. 145-951.
Courtesy of the Museum of New
Mexico, Santa Fe, New Mexico.

Siblings frequently made the best friends, especially in isolated areas, as with Agnes and Ray Morley on their ranch home (chapter 6), or when far from home, as with John and Howe Watts in Santa Fe (chapter 4). In some places, like Dawson, children expressed their fondness for each other by giving each friend a nickname based on an obvious physical characteristic (like Lefty and Red) or because of some unusual experience in their young lives (hence, Birdseed and Snake) (chapter 8). However or wherever friends were made, they served an essential social and psychological need: they allowed children to share their perceptions, most intimate knowledge, and personal experiences with others of their same age and generation. Friends helped one another understand and master the often-complex path of childhood.

Lydia Peña with adult friend, Dionel Mirabal, at a sheep camp near San Mateo, New Mexico, ca. 1940. Abe Peña Family Collection, RG90-006. Courtesy of the Rio Grande Historical Collections, New Mexico State University Library, New Mexico State University, Las Cruces, New Mexico.

When far from others their own age, children often formed close friendships with kind adults. Francis Xavier Aubry may or may not have had a romantic interest in Marion Sloan Russell's mother as he led the wagon train that brought the Russells and other pioneers down the Santa Fe Trail, but Aubry became Marion and her brother's closest, most respected friend en route (chapter 1). James Hastings befriended an assortment of older residents in his isolated silver mining camp, including Friday, a Chinese worker who "deluged" James with gifts each Chinese New Year, and the camp's black cook, who good-naturedly tolerated the youngster's boyish pranks (chapter 8). Of course, not every adult had a positive influence on young companions. George Shaffer, also known as "Sombrero Jack," befriended Billy the Kid while the Kid was still young and impressionable in Silver City. Unfortunately, George liked to drink and was said to have a "mania to steal." Lacking his mother's guidance (following her death in 1874), Billy turned to George and "took his first big step toward a life of crime," in the opinion of Robert M. Utley, Billy the Kid's foremost biographer (chapter 7).

But most childhood friendships were positive, and many were long lasting. When Douglas MacArthur and William Hughes became "inseparable comrades" while their fathers served as officers at Fort Seldon, they hardly imagined that they would still be friends and fellow soldiers years later when Hughes served as Douglas's chief of staff during World War I (chapter 2). And when John Baker met John Haaland on the playgrounds of Albuquerque's Mark Twain Elementary School, neither boy could have imagined how close their friendship would grow as John became a champion track runner and, most importantly, as he battled the cancer that ended his athletic career and, eventually, his life (chapter 12).

As boys and girls entered their teenage years, some male-female friendships blossomed into romance. When John Watts came to live in Santa Fe to recover his health in 1859, he could not forget the girl he left behind in Indiana. John dreamed of Bettie Ruter, imagining himself sitting on a familiar rocking chair with Bettie at his side until he held her in his arms and "gave her three sweet kisses which. . . made me feel better all day. . . when I thought about it." To his disappointment, John later learned that Bettie could not wait for his return; she had become engaged to another young beau in Indiana (chapter 4).

But other youths enjoyed far happier love lives. Always traditional, Cleofas Martínez was properly courted by Venceslao Jaramillo after "Ven" received permission from Cleofas's protective father. Ven showered Cleofas with gifts "at every feast day" and sent letters regularly. After receiving one such correspondence, Cleofas later wrote of having "lost my appetite for my supper and sat dreaming, pressing the letter to my heart. This genteel young man had become my ideal suitor and had [forever] changed my mind from my becoming a nun or remaining an old spinster." Ven and Cleofas were soon planning their wedding. (Apparently, Ven was never served *calabaza* [squash] when he dined at the Martínez home. Every young suitor knew that his offer of marriage had been subtly rejected if he was served *calabaza*.) The happy couple's 1898 marriage ceremony in Taos became the defining moment of Cleofas's life and of her famous memoir, *Romance of a Little Village Girl* (chapter 3).[16]

Fun

Boys playing marbles, Chimayo, New Mexico. Prudence Clark Collection, Accession No. 11975.001.019. Courtesy of the Menaul Historical Library, Albuquerque, New Mexico.

As with children in any part of the world and in any period of history, youngsters in New Mexico thrived on moments of fun alone or with family members and friends. Having fun was a natural, wholesome part of childhood that allowed many children relief from the hard work and harsh reality of their daily lives.

Childhood playgrounds varied from the space between camped wagons on the Santa Fe Trail to the parade grounds of frontier military forts, but the results were much the same: good, clean fun was as essential to healthy growth as a good diet and a loving home environment. Some forms of entertainment, such as *bailes* (Hispanic dances) and square dances, were organized and semi-formal, but most were informal and spur-of-the-moment. Games like leap frog, marbles, blind man's bluff, tire-rolling (often with a playmate spinning inside the tire), town ball (an early form of baseball), pool (for older boys), and bicycle riding (especially in the 1890s) were popular in towns and villages alike (chapters 4 and 12). In more rural settings, fishing, hunting, and simply exploring on foot or, preferably, by horseback were also fun excursions that led to children knowing their wilderness landscape as well as, if not better than, most adults.

Boy fishing. Cobbs Memorial Collection, Neg. No. 000-179-0665. Courtesy of the Center for Southwest Research, General Library, University of New Mexico, Albuquerque, New Mexico.

Square dancing at 4-H camp, Scott Abel Canyon, New Mexico, ca. 1950s. Charles Family Papers, Ms0018.0503. Courtesy of the Rio Grande Historical Collections, New Mexico State Univesity Library, New Mexico State University, Las Cruces, New Mexico.

Traveling or seasonal shows were especially popular among rural children. For brief moments their often-isolated worlds were expanded with new sights and sounds and general fun. Hispanic children remember small traveling troupes of *maromeros*, featuring acrobats, magicians, clowns, and singers. Accepting products like eggs or chickens or skins as payment for admission, these performers visited one village after another in rural sections of the state (chapter 5).[17] *Los Titeres* (puppet shows) were equally popular, with master puppeteers performing dramas and comedies to the delight of audiences, young and old.[18] Chautauquas, more typical of Anglo-dominated communities like Mountainair and Cloudcroft, offered special musical and cultural programs for young patrons.[19] Passenger trains with celebrities on board could also be called traveling shows for children in railroad towns who waited for hours to see stars like Tom Mix and the Little Rascals appear at their local train depot.[20] Circuses came to larger towns like Belen, as Marcelina Chávez recalled years later. Marcelina went to at least one circus and enjoyed it immensely until a riot broke out, the circus tents collapsed, and show animals ran in all directions (chapter 5). Annual *fiestas* drew crowds from miles around to attend church services, eat good food, hear Spanish music, dance under *carpas* (tents), and see pretty girls in colorful *fiesta* dresses. It was also an opportunity to visit relatives, renew old acquaintances, and make many new friends (chapter 3). Indian ceremonials served much the same spiritual and social purpose. As Elliott West has asserted, "The greatest public display of children's bond to [their] community came in holiday celebrations."[21]

Merry-go-round at the Belen Fiesta, c. 1920. Valencia County Historical Collection. Courtesy of the Rio Grande Historical Collections, New Mexico State Univesity Library, New Mexico State University, Las Cruces, New Mexico.

The Territorial Fair (forerunner of the New Mexico State Fair) drew the largest urban crowds. Kenneth Balcomb fondly recalled the exhibits, races, and daily baseball games at the fairgrounds west of Old Town in Albuquerque. But Kenneth's fondest memories were of early balloon ascensions. Daring balloonists rose into the air "amid cheers [and] a tune from the band" before reaching "what seemed like a terrible height" and jumping out in parachutes, "maneuvering. . . so as to land in front of the grandstand" to thunderous applause (chapter 4). What greater excitement could stir an urban child's sense of daring adventure?

While children clearly enjoyed the spectacles and fun of circuses, fiestas, and fairs, they were usually left to their own devices in creating their own toys and games. They were more than equal to the task. Angelica Chávez and her sisters made paper dolls from pictures found in mailorder catalogs, dressing their dolls in clothes cut from other pages of what many called their "wish book" (chapter 3). Like children everywhere, much of their play involved the rehearsal of future adult roles (especially parenting) and adult relationships (especially marriage).[22]

Displaying a Western propensity for practical jokes, much of childhood play involved mischief of one kind or another. Good-natured adults were often on the receiving end of such practical jokes as children subtly tested the extent of their freedoms and the limits of adult authority. Five-year-old Aubrey Lippincott and his "army brat" companion George Douglass thus raced their burros across the Fort Union parade ground just as the regimental band performed on an otherwise peaceful in northeastern New Mexico (chapter 2). Young Consuelo Baca "accidentally" lit a visiting priest's beard on fire while sitting on his lap and supposedly lighting his cigar. The good-natured Father Kreyer laughed off Consuelo's childish prank.[23] Tomás Brown's teacher was far less forgiving when he placed small lizards under a large bell on her desk. On lifting the bell to ring it, the teacher "screamed louder than the sound of the bell itself" (chapter 10). Youngsters in Dawson routinely went to the home of newlyweds to make as much noise as possible outside the couple's bedroom window. Grooms had to bribe the rabble-rousers with coins or candy in order to get any quiet on their special first night of marriage (chapter 8). During World War II, teenagers at Los Alamos devised several ways to sneak past military policemen stationed at the entrance to their top secret town (chapter 11). To the children's credit, little of their mischief could be considered malicious. To their elders' credit, childhood fun was tolerated when considered innocent, albeit punished when it was not.

Education

Most children faced the problem of a less-than-satisfactory primary or secondary education in New Mexico.[24] Although most parents wanted their children to receive a good education, families needed children to work at home. As a result, many children were unable to attend school during much of each academic year. Although true of both sexes, this was particularly the case for boys. When able to attend school, farm children were often so far behind in their studies that they were academic years behind their peers. Schools were typically located great distances from most rural homes, making it difficult—and sometimes impossible—for pupils to travel back and forth each school day, especially in bad weather. For rural students to attend school, they often had to stay with relatives in town or live in town on their own when old enough. In many cases, mothers lived in town with their school-age children while fathers stayed behind to work on distant farms or ranches.

Primary school classes were often held in the spare rooms of private homes or in poorly supplied one-room buildings used for other activities—from church services to community dances—at other hours of the day or week. Segregated black schools, especially on the state's eastern plains, were consistently inferior, often relying on discarded supplies and equipment from neighboring white schools (chapter 10). For various reasons, including a justifiable fear of Americanization and loss of language, territorial public school bills were regularly defeated at the polls in New Mexico until 1891.[25] According to U.S. census data, New Mexico could claim only five schools per thousand school-aged students in 1890, placing it among the lowest school-to-school-age ratios among states and territories in the country.[26] Writing fifty years later, George I. Sanchez found that in Taos County nearly one-third of the local population had less than a third grade education, while about two-thirds had not completed the sixth grade.[27]

Billy Jones and fellow students at their rural school, Orange, New Mexico, ca. 1924. Bob and Panzy Jones Collection, Neg. No. RG98-020-28. Courtesy of the Rio Grande Historical Collections, New Mexico State University Library, New Mexico State University, Las Cruces, New Mexico.

A student reads "Plan for Today," 1938. Neg. No. 000-289-0046. Courtesy of the Center for Southwest Research, General Library, University of New Mexico, Albuquerque, New Mexico.

Recruiting and retaining good teachers were additional challenges for families with school-age children in New Mexico. Few communities could afford to pay much in teacher salaries, and teachers were among the first to go unpaid or lose their jobs during economic crises when few families could afford to pay school or any other forms of taxes. With little funding and irregular enrollment, schools remained open for only a few months of the year and, in some years, not at all. In 1880 the average New Mexico school remained open only five and a half months.[28]

Even if good teachers were found and paid, they were not always easy to keep. James Hastings recalled that traveling teachers in his mining camp home usually "taught a few of us [only] long enough to get money to move on" (chapter 8). Aubrey Lippincott had five different enlisted men assigned to serve as his teachers at the Fort Union school he attended from 1889 to 1890 (chapter 2). Once hired in public schools, young female teachers might marry and start families of their own shortly after their arrival on the job. Other teachers might be intimidated by adolescent male students who were sometimes older and quite a bit larger than themselves.[29] In 1920 the state superintendent of schools identified teacher retention as the number one problem in New Mexico's educational system. In that year alone, forty percent of all teachers were new in half of the county's in New Mexico; Hidalgo County's new staff equaled seventy-two percent of the teaching faculty.[30] Even the affluent Baca family of Rociada had trouble keeping good tutors for their children in their isolated village home.[31]

There were of course exceptions to these generalizations about New Mexico schools. The Phelps Dodge Corporation spared little expense in educating—some would say Americanizing—the diverse school population at its coal mining operation in Dawson (chapter 8). Students at the elite Los Alamos Ranch School faced rigorous living conditions, including sleeping on open-air porches all winter, but such a regimen was meant to improve their physical health and fitness. With excellent teachers, their academic program was second to none in the region (chapter 10). Founded in 1891 as the Goss Military Institute, the New Mexico Military Institute stressed equally rigorous conditions and a fine academic program to fulfill its mission: *mens sana in corpore sano* (a healthy mind in a healthy body).[32] Parochial schools like the Catholic Loretto girls schools, St. Michael's boys school, and the Presbyterian Menaul School in Albuquerque could also boast superior academic standards for most of their histories (chapter 10).[33] Some upper class students were sent back East to prestigious private schools or had private tutors teach them in their homes.

Americanization at Menaul School: students impersonating (l. to r.) a Union soldier, Abraham Lincoln, a Confederate soldier, Albuquerque, New Mexico, ca. 1918. Accession No. 1995.174. Courtesy of the Menaul Historical Library, Albuquerque, New Mexico.

Girls at Loretto Academy, Las Cruces, New Mexico, ca. 1930s. Henry Berroteran Collection, Neg. No. A74-012. Courtesy of the Rio Grande Historical Collections, New Mexico State University Library, New Mexico State University, Las Cruces, New Mexico.

But these were the exceptions rather than the rule. Few students enjoyed the privilege of corporate wealth or the affluence of parents who could afford the high tuition of private schools or the considerable cost of private tutors. Hispanic Catholics feared the religious views, loss of language, and Americanization of Protestant schools, while Protestants feared the Catholic Church's domination in many public as well as church schools.[33] Most New Mexico children were left to learn rudimentary academic skills from their elders, their siblings, or on their own. As a result, few completed the eighth grade (a major goal, roughly equivalent to completing high school today), illiteracy was high, and, for better or worse, most children pursued the same jobs as their parents. The adage "once a miner, always a miner" (meaning that one generation after another in a family entered the mines for jobs) held equally true for farmers, herders, and laborers of all kinds until at least the mid twentieth century.

Fears

Childhood was a happy stage of life for most youngsters in New Mexico. But, like children everywhere, they harbored their share of real and imagined fears. Many of these fears came from direct experience or from frightening stories or legends told to children by either their peers (including siblings) or adults hoping to teach them valuable lessons or reinforce earlier warnings.

Hispanic mothers often told their children the most famous folk tale of their culture, the legend of *La Llorona* (the Weeping Woman). According to this story, *La Llorona*'s children drowned in a ditch (or river) for several possible reasons (usually related to a failed romance), leaving the distraught mother to walk the banks, constantly mourning her tragic loss. Children were told that the sound of the wind at night was actually *La Llorona*'s weeping. Generations of frightened youngsters heard this tale and were properly warned to avoid ditches (or rivers) and stay close to home at night. Children took these warnings so seriously in Dawson that flashlight sales increased sharply at the coal camp's company store whenever *La Llorona*'s cries (or simply the wind) became particularly loud through the valley (chapter 8).

Despite their love of nature, many other outdoor phenomena could frighten children and haunt their bedtime dreams. Thunder storms plagued Marion Sloan Russell's wagon train as it advanced down the Santa Fe Trail (chapter 1). Although sheltered in a fine home, Consuelo Baca and her two sisters were horrified by the "terrific roll and echo of the thunder, the blinding flashes coming ever nearer, [and] the rush and force of the rain on the roof" in their mountain community. When nature "cut loose" in such a manner, the Baca girls would kneel at a small altar, "praying industriously to the image of the Blessed Virgin. . . until at last God let the storm roll away to other valleys."[35]

Many children had a natural fear of certain insects and animals. Marion Sloan Russell made her "first acquaintance with the big hairy spider called tarantula" as she crossed the plains into New Mexico (chapter 1). New Mexican children were similarly fearful of other intimidating creatures, including fast-moving centipedes and the dreaded *niño de la tierra* (Jerusalem cricket). Among animals, rattlesnakes were feared most consistently. Lindley Stiles recalled several misadventures involving rattlesnakes on the open range. Once, Lindley and his father spent the night in an isolated adobe ranch house only to be awakened as not one, but two large rattlers crawled over them before dropping onto the dirt floor below. Father and son were relieved to exit that snake-infested dwelling soon after sunrise the next morning (chapter 6).

Larger animals caused great fear as well, especially when children traveled or worked whole days outdoors. Ruth Collins disliked howling coyotes so much that when she was sent to her neighbors on an early morning errand, she walked through a herd of cattle, using the herd as "protection from the coyote which I imagined must be nearby" (chapter 5). Tall Woman was equally frightened by bears when she and her sister herded sheep in the mountains each summer. Although they never saw a bear, the girls sensed that one must have been near when their dogs "started barking and howling and carrying on." Hearing of this incident when the girls returned home, their father, Man Who Shouts, confirmed that it might have been a bear, although "he told us that as long as we didn't bother them, and as long as they weren't hungry, [bears] wouldn't attack." He nevertheless cautioned his young daughters never to say the word *shash* (bear, in Navajo) when the girls were angry or at any other time in the mountains "because the bears would hear us and be offended" (chapter 9).

Closer to home, children were vulnerable to contagious diseases. Cholera plagued Marion Sloan Russell's caravan in 1852 (chapter 1) and many other wagon train travelers over the years. Sixteen-year-old José Gurulé, who worked as a laborer on a caravan headed to Missouri in 1867, recalled many cases of cholera among his fellow workers. Their treatment of "water with plenty of whiskey and *chile* in it" did little good, and many died (chapter 1). Small children were most likely to contract infectious diseases, including smallpox, diphtheria, pertussis, influenza, and measles.[36] Cleofas Jaramillo's little brother, Tomasito, died in a diphtheria epidemic that swept through their village of Arroyo Hondo. Although still very young, Cleofas remembered her brother's wake, his small board casket, and "the silent line of carriages forming the funeral procession."[37] Children infected with contagious diseases in crowded towns like Dawson were often quarantined at home or confined to pesthouses on the outskirts of their communities where they could recuperate, but not spread their disease to susceptible siblings and playmates (chapter 8).

But not all communities could afford pesthouses or other means of precaution or prevention against illnesses like pneumonia and smallpox.[38] A doctor was called when two children came down with pneumonia near Weed, New Mexico. One child had already died before the doctor arrived. Neighbors were making a small coffin for this first victim when they learned that the second child had died even after the doctor appeared. Frugally, they broke down the first coffin and rebuilt it double-sized.[39] An important study of the burial records of seven Hispanic villages of the Rio Abajo reveals that *párvulos* (children under thirteen) accounted for over fifty percent of all deaths in the late eighteenth and early nineteenth centuries. Seventy-three percent of those who died in the smallpox epidemic of February and March 1826 were children. Similar outbreaks occurred at regular four- to six- year intervals.[40]

And what was true for Hispanic children was equally true—and often worse—for Indian children, especially those confined to crowded boarding schools. When Dr. Thomas L. Craig was appointed the new government physician on the Navajo Reservation in 1889, he discovered terrible conditions at the Fort Defiance Indian School. He reported that "Medicine prescribed for ill students was not administered by the staff, sick children were permitted to lie in bed unattended, and sanitary conditions in dormitories approached dangerous levels."[41] As a result, germs and contagious diseases spread quickly. In one instance, four pupils at the Fort Defiance school died of whooping cough, and an estimated third of all students suffered from "sore eyes" (trachoma) during the 1891-92 school year.[42] Similar or worse conditions existed in other boarding schools. An Apache boy at the Santa Fe Indian School recalled that everyone in his dorm used the same towel. "I mean, we'd wash and then we'd just pass the towel around and as long as [a part] was still dry, we'd use it. There [were] never enough towels. So we all got trachoma" (chapter 10).

In 1918, the devastating Spanish flu epidemic affected mostly victims in their twenties and thirties, but children often caught the flu and perished as well. Hispanic, Indian, and immigrant households were particularly hard hit by the flu. The Reverend E.J. Waltz reported that in rural Chilili "there was not a single home where there were less than two sick and many times the number reached seven or eight. In one home we found eight children lying on the bare floor. Three of these were dead and the others were so sick they were entirely helpless."[43] So many died of the flu or its complications that church bells announcing their deaths rang day and night. Coffins could not be built fast enough to meet the horrific demand. Tall Woman's father helped bury victims of the flu on the Navajo Reservation when everyone else in a family had died of the disease or, "if there were still some left, they were barely breathing, or they were too weak to stand up."[44]

Children with the body of Fermin Marquez, San Mateo, New Mexico, 1931. Abe Peña Family Collection, Neg. No. RG90-006. Courtesy of the Rio Grande Historical Collections, New Mexico State University Library, New Mexico State University, Las Cruces, New Mexico.

This ravaging epidemic passed by early 1919, but some childhood ailments were ever-present, if only because some were said to have demonic origins. This was clearly the case with the much-feared *ojo* (evil eye) of Hispanic culture. Attractive infants were susceptible to *el ojo* if an adult consciously (or even subconsciously) admired and coveted them too much. A baby's sudden illness was taken as a sure sign that it had recently suffered such excessive attention; some adults insisted that the most beautiful babies could even die from *el ojo*. If a child was stricken, the only course of action was for the baby's parents to find the responsible party (who would also be ill) and have that person spit on his or her thumb and then use the moistened digit to make the sign of the cross on the child's small forehead. If this was done before the next Sunday's sunset, babies were said to recover almost immediately. To prevent such traumatic events, parents could ward off the threat of *el ojo* by having their infants wear *chaquiras* (beaded bracelets). The parents of even homely babies had their children wear *chaquiras* as everyone believed that their babies were beautiful and, hence, they feared *el ojo* and its awful consequences.

For everyday injuries, children were often cared for by loving elders who chanted a familiar little song:

Sana, sana	Heal, heal
Colita de rana.	little frog tails.
Si no sanaras hoy,	If you don't heal today,
Sanaras mañana.	you will heal tomorrow.

But no wearing of charms or chanting of songs could protect children from abusive, often violent adults. References to such treatment were rare among the authors of our chapters either because these children were fortunate enough not to experience abuse or because it was long considered an embarrassing scandal or, in earlier generations, a parent's perverse prerogative.[45] When mentioned at all, it has been in more recent years when abuse has been more candidly reported and confronted. Speaking in the late twentieth century, Menaul School alumni thus spoke of an early school superintendent who was "a very strict disciplinarian in a sort of militaristic [way]. He'd slap somebody every day for little things that did not harm [anyone]" (chapter 10). Jimmy Santiago

Baca suffered extreme physical and emotional abuse not only by members of his family, but also by adults in institutions responsible for his care, including at least one nun at St. Anthony's orphanage (chapter 7).[46]

Children could, of course, be abusive to each other as well, lashing out with violence or ridicule against those who were found to be weak and vulnerable. Wilbur Coe was fortunate indeed to be raised in a loving environment where his siblings and friends were far more supportive than cruel (chapter 6).

Among Hispanic and Anglo youths, the most universally expressed childhood fear of the nineteenth century was of Indian attack. From their earliest years, Hispanic and Anglo children heard stories of Indian massacres along desolate trails, in small camps or villages, and on remote ranches. Agnes Morley was taken to a spot near the Datil Divide to see where Indians had attacked several Mexicans: "there was little to see— just two grave-shaped mounds of loose rock with rough wooden crosses at the heads and beside them a litter of iron junk,. . . those parts of a wagon that would not burn." What Agnes's eye could not see, her mind could imagine: the "sudden clash" of attacking Indians, the "swift, terrible slaughter of the surprised and helpless men. . . ." Having seen and imagined enough, "We mounted our ponies and rode away in silence" (chapter 6). James Hastings had a similar experience when he saw the results of another raid, later described by James as the "saddest sight that I ever saw in a long life." As he recalled, it was a Sunday morning "when two soldiers came down the street to our town,. . . driving. . . a [stage]coach filled with bullet holes and covered with human blood." Apache raiders had "killed every mortal on board" and shed so much blood that even the letters from the coach's mail sack "showed plenty of blood" (chapter 8).

Children feared kidnapping, torture, and death at the hands of warring Indians. Many had heard of the tragic killing of Judge H.C. and Juniata McComas and the kidnapping of their six-year-old son, Charlie, on the road from Silver City to Lordsburg in March 1883. Despite a massive search, Charlie McComas was never heard from again.[47] With such incidents in mind, the mere rumor of Indian attack caused near-panic among children and their protective parents. When news spread that Geronimo and his band of followers were in the Datil area, Agnes Morley's mother took her three children ten miles to a ranch where many terror-stricken families had gathered for mutual defense. Told to sleep on the floor with the other children that night, Agnes could not rest when she heard the men in the next room planning what they would do in case of Indian attack. "I heard old Jim Wheeler delegated to use his next to last cartridge to shoot me in the head in the event the Apaches' ammunition outlasted ours. The last [bullet] was for himself." But the Apaches did not attack that night and "with daylight came news that they were far to the south, heading for the Mexican border, having left a trail of unspeakable carnage behind them." Agnes was nevertheless changed by this harrowing experience, realizing that "life itself loomed as a blessing so great that nothing again. . . ever seemed very important by contrast. I rode back to the site of the new home a quite different person from the one who had passed over that trail a few hours before" (chapter 6).

Despite such fear of Indian raiders, at least some children—and white adults—of the late nineteenth century attempted to understand why the Navajos and Apaches behaved as they did until their final defeat by U.S. troops in the 1860s and 1880s respectively. Young Lewis Garrard realized the resentment that Indians harbored when they were "too much exposed to the seductive language of the unprincipled [white] trader in liquor" and, under the influence of liquor, "soon barter[ed] away all [their] valuables."[48] James Hastings was similarly astute. According to James, while most of the white men of his youth were "as fine as one could ask for," there were some who were "just scum and by their actions caused the Indians to hate the whites and that hatred was often taken out on defenseless people." James gave the tragic example of an Apache who had been arrested for "some misdemeanor" and was being held in the guard house of an Army fort in southern New Mexico. One of the "less desirable" soldiers on duty heated a steel rod and stuck it through the guard house wall, burning the unsuspecting Indian prisoner. "In his pain and fright [the Apache] dashed out the door and was promptly shot and killed by [a] guard, who naturally believed that the prisoner was attempting to escape." On hearing of this incident, the Apache chief Cochice reportedly swore to make "the 'trail run red from Taos to Tucson,' and figuratively speaking he did just that" (chapter 8). Such incidents were part of the tragic cycle of violence—outrage, revenge, outrage, revenge—that had begun hundreds of years before and sadly continued through most of the nineteenth century.

Indian children often feared whites and Hispanics in much the same ways that whites and Hispanic children feared Indian warriors. Tall Woman never saw a *Bilagaana* (white person) during most of her youth on the Navajo reservation, only hearing her father's stories about a few of these strangers who traveled through her homeland on horseback, usually leading pack horses. The first time Tall Woman and her sister encountered such travelers, the girls were so frightened by them and their "big beards" that the children hurried home to tell their parents. No one knew the white men's purpose on the reservation, although some Navajo thought they might be traders, while others "said those white people were spies or something like that" (chapter 9). When Left Handed, another Navajo child, heard of white soldiers riding on the Navajo reservation in search of a suspected killer, the boy's father declared, "They want us to catch the fellow who killed the white men. . . . If we take him in then the troops won't get after us. If we don't they'll be out here killing everyone they see."[49] Undoubtedly remembering the Navajos' disastrous Long Walk of the 1860s in which thousands were rounded up and punished at Bosque Redondo for the actions of a few, many, including Left Handed's family, fled toward a distant mountain.[50]

The Indians' fear of white men moving in their midst mirrored white and Hispanic fears whenever Indians were seen in the wilderness or near their camps or ranches. In either case, the strangers—be they Indians or Hispanics or whites—were far more likely to seek trade and mutually beneficial relations than trouble and violence. When an Indian band approached José Gurulé's wagon train on the Santa Fe Trail, a few members of the caravan panicked and fired at the strangers. When calmer heads prevailed and the Indians came closer, José noticed an Indian woman who was eyeing the sugar cube he held in his hand. José not only gave her his cube, but gave her a second one "from the scanty hoard in his pocket." Grateful, the woman untied a bundle and took out a pat of ground meat to give to José. "He thanked her in his own language," to which "she smiled" (chapter 1). Unfortunately, such scenes of mutual trust and generosity were rare. All too often fear and misunderstanding evoked irrational, prejudicial reactions that few adults—no less children—could move beyond.[51]

Just as white and Hispanic children feared kidnappings by Indian raiders, Indian children feared being kidnapped by Hispanic settlers and, later, by white officials sent from Indian boarding schools. The Hispanic practice of kidnapping Navajo children to make them slaves was so "firmly fixed as a way of life" by the mid-nineteenth century that "most New Mexican communities recognized a band or company of men. . . whose principle occupation was stealing Navajo children to sell them to other towns." By Hispanic tradition, wealthy fathers hired these slave raiders to capture a Navajo boy or girl to serve as an expected bridal gift for their sons' or daughters' new households. Ironically, some of these Hispanic raiders were little more than children themselves, as when sixteen-year-old Manuel Chaves joined fifteen other youths from his village of Cebolleta southeast of the Navajo homeland.[52]

White representatives of Indian boarding schools were kidnappers of another sort: total strangers who took Indian children from their reservation homes, held them as captives for years, robbed them of their Indian culture, and replaced their traditional customs with so-called modern ways. In this process, Indian children were uprooted from their family homes and forced to become Anglo in thought and deed in strict boarding school surroundings. Historian Sally Hyer describes one such heart-renching abduction of a five-year-old San Juan Pueblo girl in 1915. Symbolically, the girls' Indian shawl (a last minute gift from her distressed mother) was replaced by a Santa Fe Indian School uniform and two Anglo-style dresses. Later, she and other students were punished for speaking their native languages instead of English. This was simply the beginning of the transformation of a young victim who suffered the loss of her cultural identity as had happened to thousands of other Indian children who were separated from their families and kept in boarding schools across the nation (chapter 10). While school officials liked to photograph students "before" (when they first arrived in native dress) and "after" (when they wore school uniforms) to demonstrate the overt progress of this cultural change, these pictures can just as readily be interpreted as evidence of a tragic deterioration of culture and personal identify, rather than the acquisition of a new or better lifestyle.[53] Fearing such loss of culture and self-esteem, many Indian parents, including Tall Woman's, "told us to watch for those [white people from the boarding schools] and try to hide ourselves if they [ever] came around where we were."[54] Tall Woman obeyed and was never taken from her family's safe *hogan* (home).

Navajo Tom Toslino (his assigned name) as he appeared when he arrived at the Carlisle Indian School, Carlisle, Pennsylvania, ca. 1882. Photograph by J. N. Choate. Neg. No. 43501. Courtesy of the Museum of New Mexico, Santa Fe, New Mexico.

Navajo Tom Toslino as he appeared after about two years at the Carlisle Indian School, ca. 1884. Photography by J. N. Choate. Neg. No. 43500. Courtesy of the Museum of New Mexico, Santa Fe, New Mexico.

Courage

It often took great courage to endure the hardships and face the dangers of childhood in the nineteenth and twentieth centuries. Over and over, children rose to the occasion and faced crises as well as—and sometimes better than—their elders. When twelve-year-old Agnes Morley met a band of Indians while riding in the wilderness, the Indians "rode slowly around and around." But while Agnes "had heard of this encircling maneuver as something Indians did before they attacked, it still did not occur to me to be frightened. I was as interested in the Indians as they were in me." After a time, "the leader broke the ring and resumed the straight direction in which the group had originally been traveling, followed each in his place by the whole forty of them. I had even taken time to count them" (chapter 6).

Many Indian children showed equal courage in traumatic moments of their own. In 1892 an eight-year-old Navajo boy was punished by being held prisoner without food in the Fort Defiance Indian School belfry. After two days of such harsh treatment, the boy was released, but was made to wear leg shackles in the school yard. Bravely, the boy escaped to his family's nearby home by crawling on his hands and knees until he fell, exhausted, within a short distance of his *hogan*. When his mother finally found her son, she carried his limp body the rest of the way home, his shackles still in place.[55]

In an example of Hispanic courage, sixteen-year-old Manuel Chaves and fifteen other youths battled Navajo scouts in northwestern New Mexico. Their 1834 battle ended in disaster. In addition to suffering multiple wounds of his own, Manuel lost his brother, José, and his friend, Pahe. It took days of agonizing struggle for Manuel to return safely home. In the words of his biographer, Manuel's trip home "remained in his memory afterward only as misty, dreamlike fragments: endless placing of one foot before the other. . . a pain-wracked body. . . drops of his blood spattering on rocks. . . a coyote or a phantom dogging his trail. . . moccasin tracks leading to a tiny pool of fetid water. . . gnawing of more cactus pads. . . visions of home and his mother."[56] Manuel eventually came across sheep herders who carried him the rest of the way home to Cebolleta.

But Manuel's courage did not end with his return home. According to one story, several friendly Navajos were in Cebolleta when Manuel arrived, but a bitter group of local residents, led by Manuel's brother Pedro, "plotted to kill them in their sleep in retaliation for the youths who had lost their lives" in the recent battle. Hearing of this plan, Manuel woke the Navajos, armed them, and confronted Pedro, urging him to leave their guests in peace. The Navajos left Cebolleta the next morning, accompanied by an escort of volunteers eager to guarantee the Indians' safe passage to their home camp.[57]

The list of such individual acts of courage goes on and on, as demonstrated in many of the personal stories in this book. But courage is an admirable quality that often transcends one incident or emergency and requires bravery over long periods of time, including entire childhoods in some cases. Such persistent courage was clearly required in dealing with the sting of racial prejudice (as with Hispanics, blacks, and Indians in white communities) and religious discrimination (as with Protestants in some Catholic communities or Mormons in Protestant or Catholic communities). Prolonged courage was especially needed in facing the loss of one or more parents, a tragedy that often thrust burdensome new responsibilities on young children. It was also needed in coping with lingering, sometimes fatal diseases of their own. John Watts thus dealt with his illness, Wilbur Coe with his case of spinal meningitis, and John Baker with the cancer that ultimately took his life (chapters 4, 6, and 12). Countless children suffered physical and often emotional anguish at Carrie Tingley Hospital, the school for the blind in Alamogordo, the school for the deaf in Santa Fe, and the Los Lunas Hospital and Training School.[58] Despite the extreme challenges they faced, afflicted children usually displayed a defiant "can do" attitude and heightened self-respect, as reflected in Wilbur Coe's assertion that "The tougher the game was, the harder I tried to keep up with the others." With few exceptions, "I could hold my own" (chapter 6).

Similar courage was needed to deal with the prolonged illnesses of loved ones, especially when these illnesses were potentially dangerous to a child's own physical or emotional health. Lori Arviso Alvord greatly admired her Navajo father for his intelligence, his love of the outdoors, his respect for wildlife, and his natural good looks. But Lori grew up in a fragile environment in which her father "hate[d] himself for not being able to fit into the white world and for not fulfilling his dreams" of becoming a medical doctor. To cope, "He flooded his grief with alcohol." Lori was constantly aware of the "darkness of this subjugation over our lives," especially when discrimination touched her life as well. Lori recalled the many nights of uncertainty, filled with angry words, slamming doors, "and cars roaring off into the darkness." But somehow Lori mustered the courage to persevere, first by taking refuge "deep in the pages of books" and later by learning about the historical and social roots of her father's despair and the despair of many other Native Americans. With courage, Lori eventually helped her father control (but never conquer) his disease, and she never let it conquer her. On the contrary, Lori defied the odds and did what her father could not: she went off to college and medical school and later returned to serve as a doctor on the Navajo Reservation (chapter 9). Kenneth T. Meredith displayed similar courage in dealing with his alcoholic white father during the Great Depression. As an adult, Kenneth became a respected pastor in the Church of the Nazarene. Jimmy Santiago Baca faced even greater abuse before reaching adulthood and becoming a famous poet and author (chapter 7). Like many other children, Lori, Kenneth, and Jimmy successfully conquered their fears and hardships as children so they could bravely move forward with high self-esteem and strong inner character as adults.

In Summary

Fortified by family values and cultural traditions, New Mexico children developed strong roots from which they could grow and blossom. Aware of the splendor as well as the potential dangers of nature, children grew to respect their environment and all forms of animal life found in it. Expected to work and resolve problems from an early age, children took great pride in the fruits of their labor, in their pragmatic solutions, and in their contributions to the welfare of their families and larger communities. Making friends (both young and old) and having fun, children expanded their worlds and enjoyed these valued treasures of youth. Despite generally poor schools, children acquired essential skills at home and on-the-job. Finally, children endured their fears and hardships with extraordinary courage, often overcoming danger in the short run and extended ordeals over many months or years. Truly, adversity helped build character in those who lacked it, but revealed character in children who already possessed it.

Forming values, learning traditions, respecting nature, valuing work, solving problems, cultivating friendships, enjoying fun, mastering skills, enduring hardships, and displaying courage: these were the vital elements that nourished most New Mexico children, preparing them to come of age as responsible adults. New Mexico—and the world—was a far better place for how they grew and what they eventually achieved over the long history of the nineteenth and twentieth centuries.

Final Bow

Every generation of New Mexicans has set its historical stage (building structures, altering landscapes, using and abusing natural resources), much like the stage of a theater is set for each new play performed. Only the floorboards (symbolizing the earth) and the backdrop (representing New Mexico's amazing sky and distant horizons) have remained largely the same from performance to performance (generation to generation).

The children of New Mexico spent their earliest years on the stage that their parents' generations created, only to grow up and either leave the region or rearrange the stage themselves when their generations came of age. Those who left could return to visit the New Mexico they once knew, but most of what they remembered, be it of Los Alamos or Dawson or any home community, had changed. Only memories remained, but that was often enough to strengthen and sustain them as adults in good times and in bad. Most New Mexicans could never go home again in the physical world, but they could always go home through their history.

As our cast of children take their curtain call on the stage of New Mexico history, it is clear that their foremost characteristic is diversity. Yet by holding hands in a common bow they display a unity and pride that few observers can deny and all can admire and treasure.

> The faces I love, I see only dimly.
> The voices I love come from afar. . . .
> The inner chamber of my heart is open wide,
> its pearls of memory just inside.

> Marion Sloan Russell
> *Land of Enchantment*

CHAPTER NOTES

Chapter 1: Trail Childhoods
Marion Sloan Russell: Adventure on the Santa Fe Trail, 1852

1   Marian Russell, *Land of Enchantment: Memoirs of Marian Russell Along the Santa Fe Trail* (Albuquerque: University of New Mexico Press, 1981): 12-29. Published with permission. Although Russell's first name has often been spelled Marian, she always spelled it Marion.

2   Based on genealogical research, at least one descendent questions if Eliza's two husbands died before she left for California. Noreen Stringfellow interview by the author, September 27, 2001.

3   See Stella M. Drumm, ed., *Down the Santa Fe Trail and into Mexico: The Diary of Susan Shelby Magoffin, 1846-1847* (Lincoln: University of Nebraska Press, 1982); Marian Meyer, *Mary Donoho: New First Lady of the Santa Fe Trail* (Santa Fe: Ancient City Press, 1991).

4   For Francis X. Aubry's life on the Santa Fe Trail, see Donald Chaput, *Francois X. Aubry: Trader, Trailmaker and Voyageur in the Southwest, 1846-1854* (Glendale, California: Arthur H. Clark, 1975).

José Librado Gurulé: Working on the Santa Fe Trail, 1867

1   Oral history transcription of José Librado Gurulé interview by Lou Sage Batchen, February 16, 1940, WPA New Mexico Federal Writers Project File, Fray Angelico Chavez History Library, Museum of New Mexico, Santa Fe, New Mexico. Another version of this oral history appeared in Marc Simmons, ed., *On the Santa Fe Trail* (Lawrence: University Presses of Kansas, 1986): 120-33.

2   Other youths who traveled on the trail included seventeen-year-old Kit Carson in 1826, seventeen-year-old David Slusher in 1854, and sixteen-year-old George Vanderwalker in 1864.

Traveling from Missouri to New Mexico, none of these Anglo youths worked to pay off family debts as José did.

Chapter 2: Military Childhoods
Douglas MacArthur: The Future General's Youth at Fort Selden, 1884-86

1   Douglas MacArthur, *Reminiscences* (Annapolis: U.S. Naval Institute, 2001): 14-16. Published with permission.

Aubrey Lippincott: The Post Surgeon's Son at Fort Union, 1887-91

1   Oral History Interview, Colonel Aubrey Lippincott by Dale Giese, October 1968, Fort Union National Monument Archives, Fort Union, New Mexico. For family life in the Western army, see Patricia Y. Stallard, *Glittering Misery: Dependents of the Indian-Fighting Army* (Norman: University of Oklahoma Press, 1991): chapter 4.

2   The school had five different privates assigned to teaching duties in a single twenty-two month period, March 1889 to December 1890, while Aubrey attended. Leo E. Oliva, *Fort Union and the Frontier Army in the Southwest* (Santa Fe: National Park Service, 1993): 490.

3   As Fort Union's last surgeon, Dr. Lippincott closed the post hospital in April 1891. *Ibid.*, 636, 666.

Chapter 3: Village Childhoods
Abe Peña: Cibola Memories Filled With Tradition

1   Abe Peña, *Memories of Cíbola: Stories from New Mexico Villages* (Albuquerque: University of New Mexico Press, 1997): 11-13, 20, 51-3, 80-2, 190-1. Published with permission.

Cleofas Martínez Jaramillo: A Life of Harmony and Respect

1   Cleofas M. Jaramillo, *Romance of a Little Village Girl* (Albuquerque: University of New Mexico Press, 2000): 10-6; Cleofas M. Jaramillo, *Shadows of the Past* (Santa Fe: Ancient City Press, 1972): 35-6. Published with permission.

2   Jaramillo, *Romance*, xxi.

Chapter 4: City Childhoods
John Watts: A Healthseeker's Diary, Santa Fe, 1859

1   David Remley, ed., *Adiós Nuevo Mexico: The Santa Fe Journal of John Watts in 1859* (Las Cruces: Yucca Tree Press, 1999): 3-6, 13, 43-4, 51-3, 56-7, 71-3, 84-6, 122, 127-8, 154, 200, 215-16.

Published with permission. All grammar and spellings are as in the original text written by John Watts.

Kenneth C. Balcomb: Going to the Territorial Fair

1   Kenneth C. Balcomb, *A Boy's Albuquerque, 1898-1912*, (Albuquerque: University of New Mexico, 1980): 1-8, 28-32, 71-5. Published with permission.

Chapter 5: Farming Childhoods

Francis Quintana: Becoming a *Péon de la Acequia*

1   Francis Quintana, "The *Acequia* Legacy," *La Herencia del Norte*, 21 (Spring 1999): 24-25. Published with permission. Other important works on *acequias* include Marc Simmons, "Spanish Irrigation Practices in New Mexico," *New Mexico Historical Review*, 47 (April 1972): 135-50; Stanley Crawford, *Mayordomo: Chronicle of an Acequia in Northern New Mexico* (New York: Anchor Books, 1988); José A. Rivera, *Acequia Culture: Water, Land and Community* (Albuquerque: University of New Mexico Press, 1998). The best book on farming and *acequias* from a child's point of view is Oliver La Farge, *The Mother Ditch* (Santa Fe: Sunstone Press, 1983).

Angelica Gurulé Chávez & Marcelina Miranda Chávez: Humble Lives Filled with Joy

1   Oral Histories, Angelica Gurulé Chávez and Marcelina Miranda Chávez, Belen, New Mexico. Tapes and transcripts in the author's possession. Published with permission.

Lula Collins Daudet & Ruth Collins Roberts: Homesteading on the Prairie

1   Lula Collins Daudet & Ruth Collins Roberts, *Pinto Beans and a Silver Spoon* (Ardmore, Pennsylvania: Dorrance & Company, 1980): 5-9, 31-6, 53-7, 95-9, 125-6. Published with permission.

2   *Ibid.*, ix.

Chapter 6: Ranching Childhoods

Fabiola Cabeza de Baca: Waiting for Rain—and Storytelling—on the *Llano*

1   Fabiola Cabeza de Baca, *We Fed Them Cactus* (Albuquerque: University of New Mexico Press, 1954): 9-16. Published with permission.

2   *Ibid.*, 178.

Agnes Morley Cleaveland: Live and Let Live in Cattle Country
1   Agnes Morley Cleaveland, *No Life For a Lady* (Lincoln: University of Nebraska Press, 1977): 30-1, 34-42, 44-5. Published with permission.
2   Norman Cleaveland, *The Morleys* (Albuquerque: Calvin Horn, 1971). Norman Cleaveland was Agnes Morley Cleaveland's son.

Wilbur Franklin Coe: Bravely Defying His Handicap
1   Wilbur Coe, *Ranch on the Ruidoso: The Story of a Pioneer Family in New Mexico, 1871-1968* (New York: Alfred A. Knopf, 1969): 74-88. Published with permission.
2   Both Alexander A. McSween and Billy the Kid were allied with John H. Tunstall's faction in the Lincoln County War.

Ralph Reynolds: Branding Calves and Saving a Cow
1   Ralph Reynolds, *Growing Up Cowboy: Confessions of a Luna Kid* (Golden, Colorado: Fulcrum Publishing, 1991): 14-23. Published with permission.
2   *Ibid.*, 5.
3   *Ibid.*, 39.
4   *Ibid.*, 176.
5   *Ibid.*, 179.

Lindley J. Stiles: The Trouble with Rattlesnakes
1   Lindley J. Stiles, *I Never Rode Alone: My Boyhood on a New Mexico Cattle Ranch* (Las Cruces: New Mexico Farm & Ranch Heritage Museum, 1998): 43-53. Published with permission.
2   *Ibid.*, 9.
3   The best volume on rattlesnake lore in the West remains J. Frank Dobie, *Rattlesnakes* (Austin: University of Texas Press, 1982).

Chapter 7: Troubled Childhoods
Billy the Kid's Teenage Years in Silver City
1   Robert M. Utley, *Billy the Kid: A Short and Violent Life* (Lincoln: University of Nebraska Press, 1989): 1-9. Published with permission.

Jimmy Santiago Baca: Finding a Place to Stand
1   Jimmy Santiago Baca, *A Place to Stand: The Making of a Poet* (New York: Grove Press, 2001): 1-5, 7-8, 12-4, 17-8, 20-1, 23, 27, 151, 171, 173-4. Published with permission.
2   *Ibid.*, 5.
3   *Ibid.*, 238.
4   *Ibid.*, 257.
5   *Ibid.*, 139.
6   *Ibid.*, 149.

Chapter 8: Mining Childhoods
James K. Hastings: Boyhood in a Frontier Silver Mining Camp
1   James K. Hastings, "A Boy's Eye View of the Old Southwest," *New Mexico Historical Review*, 26 (October 1951): 287-301. Published with permission.

Oral Histories: Coal Town Childhood
1   Toby Smith, *Coal Town: The Life and Times of Dawson, New Mexico* (Santa Fe: Ancient City Press, 1993): 29-40. Published with permission. For a largely autobiographical, but fictionalized account of childhood in the coal camps of northeastern New Mexico, see Ricardo L. García, *Coal Camp Days: A Boy's Remembrance* (Albuquerque: University of New Mexico Press, 2001).

2   Quoted in *ibid.*, 127. On the reasons why Dawson closed in 1950, see Richard Melzer, "A Death in Dawson: The Demise of a Southwestern Company Town," *New Mexico Historical Review*, 55 (October 1980): 309-30.

Chapter 9: Native American Childhoods
Tall Woman: Hard Times and Good on the Navajo Reservation
1   Rose Mitchell, *Tall Woman: The Life Story of Rose Mitchell, A Navajo Woman, c.1874-1977* (Albuquerque: University of New Mexico Press, 2001): 27, 29-35, 37-40, 44-7. Published with permission.

2   *Ibid.*, 305.

Lori Arviso Alvord: Full Circle
1   Lori Arviso Alvord, "Full Circle" in Andrew Garrod and Colleen Larimore, eds., *First Person, First Peoples: Native American College Graduates Tell Their Life Stories* (Ithaca, New York: Cornell University Press, 1997): 212-15, 229. Published with permission.

Chapter 10: School Lives
Tomás Wesley Brown: Mischief and Responsibility at a Homesteaders' School
1   Tomás Wesley Brown, *Heritage of the New Mexico Frontier* (New York: Vantage Press, 1995): 63-7. Published with permission.

2   For the Civilian Conservation Corps in New Mexico, see Richard Melzer, *Coming of Age in the Great Depression: The Civilian*

Conservation Corps Experience in New Mexico, 1933-42 (Las Cruces: Yucca Tree Press, 2000).

3   Brown, *Heritage*, 313.

Oral Histories: Pueblo Children at the Santa Fe Indian School

1   Sally Hyer, *One House, One Voice, One Heart: Native American Education at the Santa Fe Indian School* (Santa Fe: Museum of New Mexico Press, 1990): 1-2, 8-9, 10-15, 21-22, 25-27. Published with permission.

2   Few studies have been done on the Albuquerque Indian School. They include Lillie G. McKinney, "A History of the Albuquerque Indian School" (Unpublished M.A. thesis, University of New Mexico, 1943); James Riding In, "The Contracting of Albuquerque Indian School," *The Indian Historian*, 11 (1978): 20-9.

3   Margaret Connell Szasz, *Education and the American Indian: The Road to Self-Determination Since 1928* (Albuquerque: University of New Mexico Press, 1974).

4   Hyer, *One House*, 29-98.

Oral Histories: Hispanic Boys at the Menaul School in Albuquerque

1   Abel Sandoval was interviewed by Mark Banker on February 6, 1984. Julián Dúran was interviewed by Tomás Gonzales (no date recorded). Manuel A. Gallegos was interviewed by Lydia T. Gallegos, on January 6, 1999. These and dozens of other oral histories of former Menaul School students and staff are on file at the Menaul School's Historical Library, Albuquerque, New Mexico. Published with permission. Some excerpts from these interviews appear in Jane Atkins Vasquez and Carolyn Atkins, eds., *Remembering Presbyterian Missions in the Southwest: 25th Anniversary of the Menaul Historical Library* (Albuquerque: Menaul Historical Library, 1988): 68-71.

2   Quoted in Howard Morrison, *American Encounters* (Washington, D.C.: Smithsonian Institution, 1992): 39.

3   While the vast majority of students at Menaul were Presbyterian, there were some Catholic boys as well. The school became coeducational in 1932.

4   On the conversion process in southern Colorado and New Mexico, see Randi Jones Walker, *Protestantism in the Sangre de Cristos* (Albuquerque: University of New Mexico Press, 1991).

5   John C. Ross served as the Menaul School's superintendent from 1897 to 1916. His controversial article, entitled "What Menaul Is Doing for Mexican Boys," appeared in the *Home Mission Monthly*,

29 (1914-15): 14-5. Also see John C. Ross, "Industrial Education for the Spanish-Speaking People," *New Mexico Journal of Education*, 7 (February 1911): 20-1. It is an exaggeration to state that all teachers left with Ross in 1916, although nine of the staff of fourteen did not return for the 1916-17 school year. The highly respected Harper C. Donaldson served as Ross's successor from 1916 to 1953.

Charles S. Pearce: Roughing It at the Elite Los Alamos Boys Ranch School

1   Charles S. Pearce, *Los Alamos Before the Bomb* (New York: Vantage Press, 1990): 1-19, 54-8, 101-2. Published with permission.

2   The Ranch School's founding principles were outlined in the *Santa Fe New Mexican*, November 14, 1920.

3   This may well have been Arthur J. Connell, whom Pond had hired to run the Ranch School.

Haroldie Kent Spriggs & Sammie J. Kent: Integrating a White High School in the 1950s

1   Oral history interviews of Haroldie Kent Spriggs and Sammie J. Kent conducted by the author, Albuquerque, New Mexico, July 13 & 19, 2001. Tapes and transcripts in the author's possession. Published with permission.

2   For young people involved in the civil rights movement in the country as a whole, see David Halberstam, *The Children* (New York: Random House, 1998).

3   Without mentioning names (because all involved were juveniles), this incident was reported in the *Tucumcari News*, May 20, 1958.

4   Slaves as far west as Texas learned of their freedom from slavery on June 19, 1865. Juneteenth is the holiday that celebrates this important event.

5   The Tucumcari Board of Education officially segregated it public schools by a motion passed on July 30, 1937. The motion called for "all necessary arrangements for the establishment of a school for colored children, thirteen of school age having been reported as living within this district." Quoted in Haroldie Kent Spriggs, "Minority Group Education in New Mexico Prior to 1954" (Unpublished M.A. thesis, Howard University, 1966): 48. Also see Ellis O. Knox, "Racial Integration in the Public Schools of Arizona, Kansas, and New Mexico," *Journal of Negro Education*, 23 (Summer 1954): 290-5.

6   The integration of Tucumcari schools thus took place two years before the U.S. Supreme Court's landmark decision, *Brown v. Topeka Board of Education*, which led to integration of public education nationwide.

Chapter 11: Wartime Childhoods
Marge Armijo: World War II in Albuquerque
1   Sharon Niederman, *A Quilt of Words: Women's Diaries, Letters, and Original Accounts of Life in the Southwest, 1860-1960* (Boulder, Colorado: Johnson Books, 1988): 214-20. Published with permission.

Oral Histories: Teenage Years at Los Alamos, the Most Secretive Town of World War II
1   Katrina R. Mason, *Children of Los Alamos* (New York: Twayne Publishers, 1995): 63-4, 66-71. Published with permission.

2   On the issues of security, or the lack of it, at Los Alamos, see Richard Melzer, *Breakdown: How the Secret of the Atomic Bomb was Stolen During World War II* (Santa Fe: Sunstone Press, 2000).

3   For the history of wartime housing construction at Los Alamos, see Craig Martin, *Quads, Shoeboxes, and Sunken Living Rooms: A History of Los Alamos Housing* (Los Alamos: Los Alamos Historical Society, 2000): 1-20.

4   Mary Palevsky, one of the children who lived in Los Alamos during the war, described her feelings about the bomb and the moral dilemmas it created in her life in her *Atomic Fragments: A Daughter's Questions* (Berkeley: University of California Press, 2000).

Chapter 12: Athletic Childhoods
Roy A. Stamm: Sports—From Football to Bicycling—in the 1890s
1   James S. and Ann L. Carson, eds., *For Me, The Sun: The Autobiography of Roy A. Stamm* (Albuquerque: Albuquerque Museum, 1999): 37-44. Published with permission.

2   Abe Peña described rooster pulls in his chapter, "Cibola Memories Filled With Tradition."

3   Carson and Carson, *For Me, The Sun*, 5.

John Baker: A Track Star in Albuquerque, 1960s
1   William J. Buchanan, *A Shining Season: The True Story of John Baker* (Albuquerque: University of New Mexico Press, 1987): 31-42. Published with permission.

2   Quoted in the *Albuquerque Tribune*, October 27, 1978.

3   Buchanan, *Shining Season*, 209.

Conclusion

1   Few authors have attempted to relate childhood experiences to what it means to be a New Mexican. An admirable example is Fray Angélico Chávez, *My Penitente Land: Reflections on Spanish New Mexico* (Albuquerque: University of New Mexico Press, 1974).

2   Reportedly, Billy and his step-father, William Henry Harrison Antrim, were never close. According to one historian, Antrim "was a mild-mannered, indifferent man. He understood how to do a day's work but not how to raise someone else's children.... His desultory care was largely responsible for the trouble [Billy and his brother Joe got] into [in Silver City]." Jerry Weddle, *Antrim is My Stepfather's Name: The Boyhood of Billy the Kid* (Phoenix: Arizona Historical Society, 1993): 18.

3   It is, of course, impossible to describe all the many customs of New Mexico cultures. For Hispanic culture, see Mary Montaño, *Tradiciones Nuevomexicanos: Hispano Arts and Culture of New Mexico* (Albuquerque: University of New Mexico Press, 2001); Arthur L. Campa, *Hispanic Culture in the Southwest* (Norman: University of Oklahoma Press, 1979); Marta Weigle and Peter White, *The Lore of New Mexico* (Albuquerque: University of New Mexico Press, 1988); Angel Vigil, *Una Linda Raza: Cultural and Artistic Traditions of the Hispanic Southwest* (Golden, Colorado: Fulcrum Publishing, 1998); Cleofas M. Jaramillo, *Shadows of the Past* (Santa Fe: Ancient City Press, 1972); Fabiola Cabeza de Baca Gilbert, *The Good Life: New Mexico Traditions and Foods* (Santa Fe: Museum of New Mexico Press, 1986); Lorin W. Brown, *Hispanco Folklore of New Mexico* (Albuquerque: University of New Mexico Press, 1978). For Indian customs, see such classic studies as Ruth Underhill, *Life in the Pueblos* (Santa Fe: Ancient City Press, 1991); Clyde Kluckhohn and Dorothea Leighton, *The Navajo* (Cambridge: Harvard University Press, 1974); H. Henrietta Stockel, *Chiricahua Apache Women and Children: Safekeepers of the Heritage* (College Station: Texas A&M Press, 2000).

4   Charles F. Lummis, *Pueblo Indian Folk-Stories* (Lincoln: University of Nebraska Press, 1992): 6-11. Also see Franc Johnson Newcomb, *Navajo Folk Tales* (Albuquerque: University

of New Mexico Press, 1990); Stockel, *Chiricahua Apache Women and Children*, 23-24.

5   For these and other folk dramas in Hispanic culture, see Montaño, *Tradiciones*, 168-72.

6   Because San Jaun Bautista baptized Christ in a running river, many Catholics believed that running water had special powers on San Juan's day. Jim Griffith, *Saints of the Southwest* (Tucson: Rio Nuevo Publishers, 2000): 39. Also see Marc Simmons, "Saint John's Day, Remnant of an Ancient Festival" in his *Spanish Pathways: Readings in the History of Hispanic New Mexico* (Albuquerque: University of New Mexico Press, 2001): 137-56.

7   Vigil, *Linda Raza*, 23-4; Mary D. Lankford, *Quinceañera: A Latina's Journey to Womanhood* (Brookfield, Connecticut: Millbrook Press, 1994).

8   For Navajo female pubity rites, see Mitchell, *Tall Woman*, 63-5; Charlotte J. Frisbie, *Kinaaldá: A Study of the Navaho Girl's Puberty Ceremony* (Salt Lake City: University of Utah Press, 1993). For Chiricahua Apache rites, see Stockel, *Chiricahua Apache Women and Children*, 33-40. And for pueblo Indian rites, see Ruth Underhill, *Life in the Pueblos* (Santa Fe: Ancient City Press, 1991): 140-42.

9   Janaloo Hill, *The Hill Family of Shakespeare* (n.p.: Privately published, 2001): 140-43.

10   Elliott West, *Growing Up With the Country: Childhood on the Far Western Frontier* (Albuquerque: University of New Mexico Press, 1989): 105-6. *Growing Up With the Country* remains the best book on childhood in the West. For an insightful analysis of West's pivotal work, see Annette Atkins, "The Child's West: A Review Essay," *New Mexico Historical Review*, 65 (October 1990): 477-90. One of Atkins's main observations was that West focused on white, native-born children in subject and point of view. Regions of the West, particularly the Southwest, require far broader perspectives if their childhood experiences are to be appreciated and better understood.

11   Linda Peavy and Ursula Smith, *Frontier Children* (Norman: University of Oklahoma Press, 1999): 56-8.

12   West, *Growing Up*, 74. Also see Peavy and Smith, *Frontier Children*, 102-13.

13   West, *Growing Up*, 137.

14   Tibo J. Chávez, *New Mexican Folklore of the Rio Abajo* (Santa Fe: William Gannon, 1987): 1-40; Michael Moore, *Los Remedios:*

Traditional Herbal Remedies of the Southwest (Santa Fe: Red Crane Press, 1990).

15   Stephen E. Ambrose, *Comrades: Brothers, Fathers, Heroes, Sons, Pals* (New York: Simon & Shuster, 1999): introduction to audio-book edition.

16   Cleofas's wedding was not as traditional as her cousin Biatriz's, which Cleofas witnessed when she was eight years old and described in her *Shadows of the Past*, 31-4. Other traditional Hispanic weddings are described in Oliver La Farge, *Behind the Mountains*, (Santa Fe: William Gannon, 1974): 5-14; de Baca, *Good Life*, 31-5.

17   Campa, *Hispanic Culture*, 50-1; Weigle and White, *Lore*, 404-5.

18   Weigle and White, *Lore*, 405.

19   Richard Melzer, "Chautauquas: Caravans of Culture," *New Mexico Magazine*, 72 (September 1994): 56-63.

20   Tom Mix was a famous cowboy movie star. The Little Rascals were child movie stars well known for their on-screen misadventures.

21   West, *Growing Up*, 168.

22   *Ibid.*, 112-13.

23   La Farge, *Behind the Mountains*, 47.

24   Despite its singular focus, the best book on New Mexico education in the late nineteenth and early twentieth centuries is Lynne Marie Getz, *Schools of Their Own: The Education of Hispanos in New Mexico, 1850-1940* (Albuquerque: University of New Mexico Press, 1997).

25   West, *Growing Up*, 188-89; Dianna Everett, "The Public School Debate in New Mexico, 1850-1891," *Arizona and the West*, 26 (Summer 1984): 107-34. Of course, the debate over language continued long after 1891. See Erlinda Gonzales-Berry, "Which Language Will Our Children Speak?: The Spanish Language and Public Education in New Mexico, 1890-1930" in Erlinda Gonzales-Berry and David R. Maciel, eds., *The Contested Homeland: A Chicano History of New Mexico* (Albuquerque: University of New Mexico Press, 2000): 169-89.

26   West, *Growing Up*, Table 2, 190.

27   George I. Sanchez, *Forgotten People: A Study of New Mexicans* (Albuquerque: Calvin Horn, 1967): 79. Sanchez's study was first published in 1940.

28   West, *Growing Up*, Table 3, 191.

29   Rita Hill was an exception. Rather than be intimidated by a
        "bullyboy" at the school where she taught in the 1930s, Rita
        fought the large student until he "turned loose quite suddenly
        and ran out the front door." Hill, *Hill Family*, 111-13.

30   *Santa Fe New Mexican*, November 23, 1920.

31   La Farge, *Behind the Mountains*, 101-19; John Pen La Farge,
        *Turn Left at the Sleeping Dog: Scripting the Santa Fe Legend,
        1920-1955* (Albuquerque: University of New Mexico Press, 2001):
        129. Although New Mexico is never mentioned directly, much of
        what Polly Welts Kaufman has written about Western teachers
        in general applied to conditions in New Mexico as well. Polly
        Welts Kaufman, *Women Teachers on the Frontier* (New Haven:
        Yale University Press, 1984). Also see Peavy and Smith, *Frontier
        Children*, 115-35; Elizabeth Hampsten, *Settlers' Children*
        (Norman: University of Oklahoma Press, 1991): 35-62.

32   William E. Gibbs and Eugene T. Jackman, *New Mexico Military
        Institute: A Centennial History* (Roswell: New Mexico Military
        Institute Centennial Commission, 1991): 20.

33   Getz, *Schools of Their Own*, 15-6. On Protestant missionary
        schools, see Sarah Deutsch, *No Separate Refuge: Culture, Class,
        and Gender on the Anglo-Hispanic Frontier in the American
        Southwest, 1880-1940* (New York: Oxford University Press, 1987):
        63-86; Mark T. Banker, *Presbyterian Missions and Cultural
        Interaction in the Far Southwest, 1850-1950* (Urbana: University
        of Illinois Press, 1993); Randi Jones Walker, *Protestantism in the
        Sangre de Cristos, 1850-1920* (Albuquerque: University of New
        Mexico Press, 1991). The most unusual school of this era was
        established by John Ballou Newbrough in the Shalam colony for
        orphan children in Doña Ana County. Based on Newbrough's
        new religion, called Oahspe, the colony existed from 1884 to 1907.
        Lee Priestley, *Shalam: Utopia on the Rio Grande* (El Paso: Texas
        Western Press, 1988).

34   Protestant missionaries in particular complained that public
        schools were often dominated by the Catholic Church, with
        priests and nuns sometimes serving as teachers and
        administrators. As a result, Emily J. Harwood, a Methodist
        missionary, wrote that "little is taught in these schools except
        prayers, and the superstition of the Romish Church." Harwood
        and her husband Thomas hoped to reduce this Catholic influence
        in education by opening Methodist schools (like their Harwood
        School) to Americanize New Mexicans. According to Emily

Harwood, "The natives here are *foreign* in respect to language, customs, and everything which pertains to American civilization." Quoted, with emphasis in the original, in Thomas Harwood, *History of the New Mexico Spanish and English Missions of the Methodist Episcopal Church from 1850 to 1910* (Albuquerque: El Abogado Press, 1908): 253-55. Protestants successfully challenged this infringement of the principle of the separation of church and state in the 1953 New Mexico Supreme Court decision (No. 5622) *Zellers v. Huff*, involving public schools in Dixon, New Mexico.

35 La Farge, *Behind the Mountains*, 44-5.

36 On the wide variety of childhood diseases in the West, including New Mexico, see West, *Growing Up*, 229-35.

37 Jaramillo, *Shadows of the Past*, 35-6.

38 On early attempts at disease prevention New Mexico, see Marc Simmons, "Hygiene, Sanitation, and Public Health in Hispanic New Mexico," *New Mexico Historical Review*, 67 (July 1992): 205-25.

39 West, *Growing Up*, 230-31.

40 Oswald G. Baca, "Analysis of Deaths in New Mexico's Rio Abajo During the Late Spanish Colonial and Mexican Periods, 1793-1846," *New Mexico Historical Review*, 70 (July 1995): 245-46.

41 Robert A. Trennert, *White Man's Medicine: Government Doctors and the Navajo, 1863-1955* (Albuquerque: University of New Mexico Press, 1998): 82.

42 *Ibid.*

43 Quoted in Richard Melzer, "A Dark and Terrible Moment: The Spanish Flu Epidemic of 1918 in New Mexico," *New Mexico Historical Review*, 57 (July 1982): 223-24.

44 Mitchell, *Tall Woman*, 132.

45 What Elliott West has said about the West as a whole is also true of New Mexico: "Violence and child abuse usually remained behind closed doors." West, *Growing Up*, 152. With few exceptions, childhood references to outlaw violence in their communities were equally rare, suggesting that, despite certain periods of extreme violence like the Lincoln County War, day-to-day life was peaceful enough for most children. For an exception to this generalization, see Lily Klasner, *My Childhood Among Outlaws*, Eve Ball, ed. (Tucson: University of Arizona Press, 1972). For a discussion of child abuse in various cultures and

periods of history, see Lloyd deMause, "The History of Child Abuse," *Journal of Psychohistory*, 25 (Winter 1998): 216-36.

46   In perhaps the most famous case of child abuse in New Mexico history, Charles Kennedy reportedly killed (or threatened to kill) his young son in a fit of rage in 1870. Frightened, Kennedy's wife turned her husband in for the alleged murder of several travelers who had stayed at the Kennedy's primitive inn on the road to Elizabethtown. Kennedy was arrested and tried for the murder of at least nine and as many as twenty-one men. When his trial ended with a hung jury, local vigilantes administered their own form of justice by lynching Charles Kennedy on October 7, 1870. Howard Bryan, *Robbers, Rogues, and Ruffians* (Santa Fe: Clear Light Press, 1991): 1-8.

47   Marc Simmons, *Massacre on the Lordsburg Road: A Tragedy of the Apache Wars* (College Station: Texas A&M Press, 1997).

48   Lewis H. Garrard, *Wah-to-yah and the Taos Trail* (Norman: University of Oklahoma Press, 1955): 10.

49   Left Handed, *Left Handed, Son of Old Man Hat: A Navajo Autobiography* (Lincoln: University of Nebraska Press, 1995): 180.

50   For a history of the Long Walk and the Navajo internment at Fort Sumner, see Lynn R. Bailey, *Bosque Redondo: The Navajo Internment at Fort Sumner, New Mexico, 1863-68* (Tucson: Westernlore Press, 1998). A fine fictionalized account for children is Ann Turner, *The Girl Who Chased Away Sorrow: The Diary of Sarah Nita, a Navajo Girl* (New York: Scholastic, 1999).

51   West, *Growing Up*, 214 & 241.

52   Marc Simmons, *The Little Lion of the Southwest: A Life of Manuel Antonio Chaves* (Chicago: Swallow Press, 1973): 35-8.

53   Margaret L. Archuleta, Brenda J. Child, and K. Tsianina Lomawaima, eds., *Away from Home: American Indian Boarding School Experiences, 1879-2000* (Phoenix: Heard Museum, 2000); Sally Hyer, *One House, One Voice, One Heart: Native American Education at the Santa Fe Indian School* (Santa Fe: Museum of New Mexico Press, 1990): 4. For the Chiricahua Apaches' loss of culture at the Carlisle Indian School in Pennsylvania, see Stockel, *Chiricahua Apache Women and Children*, 29-32. Hispanics were also routinely punished for speaking Spanish, even on the playgrounds of their public and parochial schools.

54   Mitchell, *Tall Woman*, 62. In isolated cases, some children were rescued from Indian boarding schools. Charles Lummis, who

described the importance of sharing customs in Isleta, helped secure the release of thirty-six Isleta children who were prevented from returning home from the Albuquerque Indian School. Lummis compared forcing white values on pueblo children to the situation if a so-called "superior race...were to come from Mars, overrun the land, and force [whites] to send our children away from home to be rid of our silly superstitions, religion, and customs, and instructed in the better ways of the people of Mars." In contrast, Superintendent of Indian Schools Daniel Dorchester declared in 1889 that white "civilization...is the best the Indians can get. They cannot escape it, and must either conform to it or be crushed by it." According to Dorchester, "Dynamite would perform a benevolent work if applied under these old pueblos" of New Mexico. Quoted in Mark Thompson, *American Character: The Curious Life of Charles Fletcher Lummis and the Rediscovery of the Southwest* (New York: Arcade Publishing, 2001): 155, 157, 161.

55   Trennert, *White Man's Medicine*, 83.
56   Simmons, *Little Lion*, 41.
57   *Ibid.*, 42-3.
58   See Rudolfo A. Anaya's moving novel about the children at Carrie Tingley Hospital, *Tortuga* (Berkeley: Editorial Justa Publications, 1979).

SUGGESTED READINGS

General Books on Childhood

Aries, Philipe. *Centuries of Childhood*. Trans. by Robert Baldick. New York: Alfred A. Knopf, 1962.

Bremner, Robert H., et al, editors. *Children and Youth in America: A Documentary History*. Cambridge: Harvard University Press, 1974.

de Mause, Lloyd, editor. *The History of Childhood*. New York: Psychohistory Press, 1974.

Halberstam, David. *The Children*. New York: Random House, 1998.

Hampsten, Elizabeth. *Settlers' Children: Growing Up on the Great Plains*. Norman: University of Oklahoma Press, 1991.

Handlin, Oscar, and Mary F. Handlin. *Facing Life: Youth and the Family in American History*. Boston: Little, Brown & Company, 1971.

Hiner, N. Ray, and Joseph M. Hawes, editors. *Childhood in America: A Research Guide and Historical Handbook*. Westport, Connecticut: Greenwood Press, 1985.

_____. *Growing Up in America: Children in Historical Perspective*. Urbana: University of Illinois Press, 1985.

Hoose, Phillip. *We Were There Too!: Young People in U.S. History*. New York: Farrar Straus Giroux, 2001.

Illick, Joseph E. *American Childhoods*. Philadelphia: University ofPennsylvania Press, 2002.

McCullough, David Willis, editor. *American Childhoods: An Anthology*. Boston: Little, Brown & Company, 1987.

Peavy, Linda, and Ursula Smith. *Frontier Children*. Norman: University of Oklahoma Press, 1999.

Robb, Theodore, and R.I. Rotberg. *The Family in History*. New York: Harper and Row, 1971.

_____. *Rites of Passage: Adolescence in America*. New York: Basic Books, 1977.

Thompson, Kathleen, and Hilary MacAustin, editors. *Children of the Great Depression*. Bloomington: Indiana University of Indiana Press, 2001.

West, Elliott. *Growing Up with the Country: Childhood on the Far Western Frontier*. Albuquerque: University of New Mexico Press, 1989.

West, Elliott, and Paula Petrik, editors. *Small Worlds: Children and Adolescents in America, 1850-1950*. Urbana: University of Illinois Press, 1992.

Wormser, Richard. *American Childhoods*. New York: Walker & Co., 1996.

Southwestern Childhood Memoirs, Biograhphies, & Autobiographies

Adams, David Wallace. *Education for Extinction: American Indians and the Boarding School Experience, 1875-1928*. Lawrence: University Press of Kansas, 1995.

Archuleta, Margaret L., Brenda J. Child, and K. Tsianina Lomawaima, editors. *Away from Home: American Indian Boarding School Experiences, 1879-2000*. Phoenix: Heard Museum, 2000.

Armijo, Rosemary Gallegos. *La Hija de Juan Gallegos*. Albuquerque: West End Press, 2000.

Burroughs, Jean M. *Children of Destiny: True Adventures of Three Cultures*. Santa Fe: Sunstone Press, 2001.

Chávez, Fray Angelico. *My Penitente Land: Reflections on Spanish New Mexico*. Albuquerque: University of New Mexico Press, 1974.

Eidenbach, Peter L. & Beth Morgan, editors. *Homes on the Range: Oral Recollections of Early Ranch Life on the U.S. Army White Sands Missile Range, New Mexico.* White Sands Missile Range: U.S. Department of Defense, 1994.

Garrard, Lewis H. *Wah-to-yah and the Taos Trail.* Norman: University of Oklahoma Press, 1955.

Hungry Wolf, Adof and Beverly. *Children of the Sun: Stories By and About Indian Kids.* New York: William Morrow, 1987.

Jaramillo, Cleofas M. *Shadows of the Past.* Santa Fe: Ancient City Press, 1972.

Klasner, Lily. *My Girlhood Among Outlaws.* Tucson: University of Arizona Press, 1972.

La Farge, Oliver. *Behind the Mountains.* Santa Fe: William Gannon, 1974.

Left Handed. *Left Handed, Son of Old Man Hat: A Navajo Autobiography.* Lincoln: University of Nebraska Press, 1995.

Miller, Michael, editor. *A New Mexico Scrapbook: Twenty-Three New Mexicans Remember Growing Up.* Huntsville, Alabama: Honeysuckle Imprint, 1991.

Mullin, Robert N. *The Boyhood of Billy the Kid.* El Paso: Texas Western Press, 1967.

Ramsey-Palmer, Paige. *Young Troopers: Stories of Army Children on the Frontier.* Tucson: Southwest Parks & Monuments Association, 1997.

Stallard, Patricia Y. *Glittering Misery: Dependents of the Indian-Fighting Army.* Norman: University of Oklahoma Press, 1992.

Stockel, H. Henrietta. *Chiricahua Apache Women and Children: Safekeepers of the Heritage.* College Station: Texas A&M Press, 2000.

Fictional Literature on Childhood in the Southwest

Abbey, Edward. *Fire on the Mountain.* Albuquerque: University of New Mexico Press, 1978.

Anaya, Rudolfo A. *Bless Me, Ultima*. Berkeley: Tonatiuh-Quinto Sol International, 1972.

_____. *Tortuga*. Berkeley: Editorial Justa Publications, 1979.

Austin, Mary. *Starry Adventure*. Boston: Houghton Mifflin, 1931. (Books 1-5)

Bradford, Richard. *Red Sky at Morning*. New York: Harper Perennial, 1999.

Bright, Robert. *The Life and Death of Little Jo*. Albuquerque: University of New Mexico Press, 1978.

Clark, Ann Nolan. *Little Boy With Three Names: Stories of Taos Pueblo*. Santa Fe: Ancient City Press, 1990.

_____. *Little Herder in Autumn*. Santa Fe: Ancient City Press, 1988.

_____. *Sun Journey: A Story of Zuni Pueblo*. Santa Fe: Ancient City Press, 1988.

García, Ricardo L. *Coal Camp Days: A Boy's Remembrance*. Albuquerque: University of New Mexico Press, 2001.

Goodson, Felix E. *O'Cimarron*. Los Angeles: Red Hen Press, 2001.

Laughlin, Ruth. *The Wind Leaves No Shadow*. New York: McGraw-Hill, 1948. (Chapters 1-6)

Lucero, Evelina Zuni. *Night Sky, Morning Star*. Tucson: University of Arizona Press, 2000.

Turner, Ann. *The Girl Who Chased Away Sorrow: The Diary of Sarah Nita, A Navajo Girl, New Mexico 1864*. New York: Scholastic, 2000.

Ulibarrí Sabine R. *Tierra Amarilla: Stories of New Mexico*. Albuquerque: University of New Mexico Press, 1993.

Zollinger, Norman. *Riders to Cibola*. Santa Fe: Museum of New Mexico Press, 1977. (Chapters 1-11)

INDEX

Carson, P.K., 178
Cena, Jesus, 53
Chaves, José, 316
Chaves, Manuel, 314, 316-17
Chaves, Pedro, 317
Chávez, Angelica, 73-101, 274, 289, 300
Chávez, Eduardo, 84, 101
Chávez, Jacobo, 101
Chávez, Marelina, 73-101, 274, 275, 282, 290, 299
Chávez, Mateo, 74
Chávez, Ramona, 77, 78, 84, 87, 91, 94, 95, 97
Chávez, Roy, 284
Cleaveland, Agnes Morley, 120-28, 275, 284, 292, 293, 311-12, 316
Clemens, "Big Train", 241
Cochise, 174, 312
Coe, Agnes, 129
Coe, Frank, 129, 132, 133, 138
Coe, Wilbur Franklin, 129-38, 291-92, 311, 317
Collier, John, 205
Collins, Effie Blanche, 102, 103, 105, 108
Collins, James S., 102, 103, 106-10
Collins, Jim, 104, 110
Collins, Laura, 110
Collins, Louise, 103
Conclin, Charley, 53
Connell, Arthur J., 325n
Crosby, John, 217
Covert, Mary Lou, 180
Craig, Thomas L., 308

Dale, Bill, 180
Dale, George, 180
Daudet, Lula Collins, 102-12, 199, 288, 289
Davenport, Henry, 121
Davis, Bette, 253
Davis, Jefferson, 30

Dennis, Loyd, 197
DiLorenzo, Alice, 180
DiLorenzo, Domenic, 180
Donaldson, Harper Collins, 214-16, 325n
Donoho, Mary, 13
Dorchester, Daniel, 331n
Douglass, George   , 32-5, 300
Douglass, Henry, 32, 34
Dúran, Julián, 207, 208, 210-12, 214, 216
Dúran, Leonides, 207-9

Edgar, Jimmie, 59
Edwards, Riley, 66
Ellison, Samuel, 53

Farmer, Jim, 153-54
Fenlon, George, 177-78
Forte, Lena Colaizzi, 180
Fox, Bill, 250-52

Gallegos, Lily Ortega, 208
Gallegos, Manuel, 208, 210-13, 216
Gallegos, Manuel A., 208
García, Amelia Lopez, 182-83
García, Cosme, 209-10
García, Desiderio, 40-1
Garrard, Lewis, 312
Garrett, Pat, 159
Geronimo, 125, 169
Giese, Dale, 32
Goff, Lloyd, 268-69
Gonzales, José, 71
Gonzales, Nesario, 20-22, 24, 26
Gonzales, Nick, 184
Gordon, Helen, 237
Gordon, Thomas, 237
Gorman, Samuel, 52
Green, Bill, 171
Gurulé, Jacobo, 74, 79, 86, 89, 91, 95
Gurulé, José Librado, 20-7, 308, 313, 321n

Printed in the United States
1111500001B/481-501